Sanctuary

Sanctuary

THE STORY OF NATURALIST
MARY MAJKA

DEBORAH CARR

GOOSE LANE

Edited by Paula Sarson.
Cover photos: large colour photo by Deborah Carr, small inset photos (left to right): courtesy of Mary Majka, courtesy of Jack Christie, courtesy of David Christie.

Photos courtesy of Mary Majka unless otherwise noted.
Cover and page design by Jaye Haworth.
Art direction by Julie Scriver.
Printed in Canada.
10 9 8 7 6 5 4 3 2

Library and Archives Canada Cataloguing in Publication

Carr, Deborah, 1960-
Sanctuary: the story of naturalist Mary Majka / Deborah Carr.

Includes index.
ISBN 978-0-86492-624-1

1. Majka, Mary. 2. Naturalists — Canada — Biography.
3. Environmentalists — Canada — Biography. I. Title.

QH31.M33C37 2010   508.092   C2010-902423-0

Also available in electronic form under ISBN 978-0-86492-710-1.

Goose Lane Editions acknowledges the financial support of the Canada Council for the Arts, the Government of Canada through the Canada Book Fund (CBF), and the government of New Brunswick through the Department of Wellness, Culture, and Sport.

Visit www.deborahcarr.ca for information on the author.

Goose Lane Editions
Suite 330, 500 Beaverbrook Court
Fredericton, New Brunswick CANADA E3B 5X4

Visit www.gooselane.com for a book club guide and more information on the book.

Mixed Sources
Product group from well-managed forests,
controlled sources and recycled wood or fiber
www.fsc.org Cert no. SW-COC-000952
© 1996 Forest Stewardship Council
FSC

For Pat

Throughout my life, I was very much aware that it is not what you have, or what you do, or what you achieve that makes happiness. It is your personal dream, your personal aims that will bring you happiness.

Mary Majka
August 23, 2005

(Artwork by Brenda Berry)

Contents

Preface

When it was quiet, you had the feeling you were alone, you were the crown of the mountain. They called me Mountain Mary or Queen of the Mountain. And I was. The Queen of My Territory.

Mary Majka

It is not an easy thing to excavate a life, to dig into depths long buried and bring air and light to darkness.

My decision to write a biography of Mary Majka stemmed at first from hoping to document the life and accomplishments of this extraordinary woman. I will never forget our regular Thursday afternoon interviews, drinking African tea in the sunroom of her present home at Mary's Point, listening to memories and anecdotes and tales that shifted from Poland to Austria to Ontario and, finally, to New Brunswick. She was — is — a remarkable interview subject.

Our interviews for the most part were full of intensity and humour. As with all relationships, we had moments of miscommunication and frustration. Some of these moments arose because of our differing backgrounds: me, a self-taught writer from rural New Brunswick; she, a Polish girl born and raised in wartime Europe, forced to endure imprisonment, starvation, displacement, and emigration.

Yet over the months and years of our time together, I came to feel that Mary's biography embodied something larger than a simple recording of events, dramatic though they were.

Mary often referred to her character as a kaleidoscope — and I tended to agree — it shifted and changed and rearranged itself each time I tried to focus.

"What is it that makes me the way I am?" she asked herself as a teenager. She finally decided it just happens. "When you pick a bouquet of flowers, they are all uniform, but there will be one a little taller, or a different colour, or some small difference. Perhaps this is who I am."

She lives at the sharp edge of emotion, in all its extremes. Truthfully, I sometimes despaired that I would never really know her. In the beginning, she told me that she was a composition of all who had lived before her, tempered by those who touched her each day of her life.

It is a chilly day in April 2007 when Mary Majka, David Christie, and I drive the rubbled road up Caledonia Mountain in southeastern New Brunswick to visit their former homestead. Flurries swirl beneath an overcast sky. The view across the valley is muted, like a faded photograph. I notice the gentle shape of the land, the hills and valleys as softly contoured as a face in repose. Farther down the valley, most of the snow has melted, but at this higher elevation, crusty patches remain in shadowed spaces. Spring always comes last to Caledonia Mountain. This is a harsh and wild place. In this way, Caledonia Mountain has changed little in the forty years since "Mountain Mary" and her family were its only permanent residents.

But now, as ATVers and snowmobilers gather in noisy groups to cruise the woods roads and paths dissecting the landscape, and hunting camps line the roadway, it is gradually becoming more appreciated as a location for year-round homes with a view.

It was partly the increase in motorized vehicles that eventually drove the Majkas to seek the quieter refuge of nearby Mary's Point on the Bay of Fundy. Mary's Point, the place so closely associated with Mary Majka that many assume it took her name. Mary's Point, scene of her greatest triumph and some of her deepest sorrows.

Reaching our destination, David parks on the frozen ground by a dirt driveway. Mary announces she will stay in the car. She had no reason to join David and me today and could have remained at home where it was warm. But like pepper and salt, Mary and David, often mistaken for the Majkas' adopted son, are rarely seen apart. For years she danced with grace through meadows of hawkweed and daisies. Now she lists like a wave-rocked ship, relying on the wheeled walker that also accompanies her everywhere. She has brought a book to read while she waits. Idleness is not a characteristic she embraces. At age eighty-four, she says, she is tired but still has much to accomplish. Thoughts of unfinished business frequently trouble her mind.

On this cold spring day on Caledonia Mountain, Mary is petulant and impatient, perhaps feeling the frustration of a young soul trapped in an aging body. She can no longer manoeuvre the rough terrain she once knew as intimately as her own skin. The paths and trails she once prowled as effortlessly as a coyote are grown over. She must find contentment in sunshine and memories. Yet she insists she doesn't miss the freedom of her young body. She has lived and accepted each season of her life. This is her winter.

David leaves the engine running so she will be warm. "I won't be long," he promises, closing the car door.

A wet wind blows past and he shivers. Dwarfed by a bulky parka, he slides on oversized black gloves. Grey wisps of hair escape a knitted toque, and pilled pants bunch above the rim of loose rubber boots. An expensive digital camera swings from his narrow shoulder and Bausch & Lomb binoculars thump against his thin chest.

We walk past a three-storey weekend home built by the current owner of the property and down a lane lined with mature birch, spruce, and fir that shield us from the wind. Our footsteps crunch as we step around piles of rotting snow. Discarded machinery, sheet metal, and several decrepit vehicles lie beside or against the trees.

"These trees were just small when I first came here," says David, sweeping his arm outward, ignoring the rusted heaps. "This field had masses of blueberries and in some places wild strawberries. We'd fill the freezer, and then the dogs would eat what was left off the bushes. And mushrooms...we gathered all kinds of different mushrooms. Our favourite patch was across the road." He grins. "I'd never gathered mushrooms before coming to live here."

About forty-five metres ahead, the lane opens to a field, and there it is: Aquila, the deserted Caledonia Mountain home of the Majka family. Over the years, naturalists, birdwatchers, scientists, reporters, and politicians found themselves drawn or summoned here. To many, Aquila represented a centre of — and catalyst for — change.

Now, the windows look hollow, the house turned in on itself. Cedar shingles on the walls sprout moss, and the roof appears shrunken. The fieldstone chimney crumbles beneath a tangle of Virginia creeper. Raspberry canes beside the house snatch at my mittens when I brush by. More abandoned machinery and vehicles litter the grounds. Not a sign remains of Mary's once-thriving flower gardens.

Despite the overcast sky, I can see northward across the valley to the city of Moncton, a half-hour's drive away. I comment on the view. David aims his binoculars to the east. "On a clear day, we could see Northumberland Strait and sometimes Prince Edward Island."

Behind the cottage is a stand of maples, ravaged by an ice storm more than a

Aquila, Caledonia Mountain, as it looked in April 2007. (Courtesy of Deborah Carr)

decade ago. David touches a twisted trunk. "This was a magnificent maple," he says, his eyes tracing furrows in the bark. "It shaded our picnic table. We often ate outside." He steps around alder branches to peer through a cloudy, cracked window. "In winter, the wind blew over the top of the house and snow drifted to the eaves, covering this window. We'd walk up the snowbank onto the roof for the view up there."

David stands quietly for a moment.

His language becomes spare and thin, like him. He turns around. "The outhouse was there in the maple grove. Birdfeeders over there."

The door to the house is unlocked so we enter together. The ceiling is caving and the floor strains upward. The walls bow in like a child sucking his cheeks. Wallpaper hangs in shreds, a mattress belches stuffing, and mildew etchings creep high up the walls. Books lie helter-skelter on the floor amid a scattering of stained pages.

David picks up a book and leafs through the pages. It is a medical text, the title print worn to a gold glint. "This must have been Mike's." He gently places it on a sagging table.

At the top of narrow stairs, David points out the alcove where he slept, his bed squeezed between the knee wall and stair rail. He indicates the single room shared by Chris and Marc, the two Majka sons. Faded Charlie Brown and Snoopy stickers still adhere to the panelled walls.

Piles of animal excrement and the stench of urine confirm that a family of raccoons has set up housekeeping here. The smell seems not to bother David, but I find it hard to breathe and escape down the rickety stairs to the living room. David follows shortly. There, he stands for a moment and stares at the fireplace, now a pile of moss-covered river rock and chunked mortar. "At night, we'd gather together in the living room, fire crackling, and drink tea with honey and lemon."

With a shrug, he turns away. We leave the house and I close the door.

൭

Prelude

*I find a shift in myself now. It has to do with age. I seem to reach
back a lot and remember things that were always with me, but I
think about them more often than before. I seem to reflect on the
connections.*

Mary and Mike Majka (My-kah) left Poland after World War II, immigrating to
Canada in 1951 together with many other displaced persons (DPs). They lived
first in Ontario before moving to New Brunswick in 1961, choosing to raise their
family in the wildness of Caledonia Mountain. Within a decade of arriving in the
province, Mary emerged as a visionary and a pioneer of New Brunswick's fledgling
environmental movement. She became a spokesperson for nature, advocating for
rare orchids and gray treefrogs. She initiated projects that led to the protection of
ecologically sensitive natural habitats. She hosted a children's television show called
Have You Seen?, taught outdoor education, and started the first nature centre for
children in a Canadian national park. She was featured in national newspaper and
magazine articles, books, and documentaries that heralded her heritage restoration
and wildlife rehabilitation activities.

Over the course of three decades, her awards gathered like birds on a branch:
the Heaslip Award for Environmental Stewardship, the National Heritage Award,
the Canadian Healthy Environment Award for Lifetime Achievement, the Gulf of
Maine Visionary Award, a Doctor of Science honorary degree from the University of
New Brunswick, the Queen's Golden Jubilee Medal, the Order of New Brunswick,
and the Tourism Industry of Canada VIA Rail Volunteer of the Year Award. Finally,

Mary Majka and Her Excellency, the Right Honourable
Michaëlle Jean, at the investiture ceremony, Order of Canada,
May 4, 2007.
© Office of the Secretary to the Governor General of Canada 2007
GG2007-0099-012: Sgt. Eric Jolin, Rideau Hall. Reproduced with
the permission of the Office of the Secretary to the Governor General.

in 2007 — fifty-six years after arriving in Canada speaking not a word of English
— she travelled to Ottawa to receive the Order of Canada from Governor General
Michaëlle Jean.

The award honoured her lifetime involvement in projects associated with nature
conservation, environmental advocacy, and heritage protection. Best known among
these was the Mary's Point Ramsar site, which became Canada's first designated
Western Hemisphere Shorebird Reserve. But her legacy extends beyond natural
and cultural heritage preservation.

Mary feels ambivalent about her Order of Canada. She wrote to a long-time
friend about the ceremony:

> Most of what I did came from my own initiative or imagination,
> often dreamed up at night. It is tremendously exciting to see your
> dreams become reality, and it is this, not the accolades of others,
> that is the greatest reward. Of course, I like what I have done, but
> not for the reason you might think.... More than thirty youngsters
> shared in our family life for long or short durations. Today, when one
> of these [people] comes to me to say "you were my guiding light,"
> who needs an Order?

While she proudly wears her Order of Canada pin on her lapel wherever she
goes, to be honest, she confides, receiving the Order of New Brunswick in 2005
perhaps meant more because it came from her own province. In recent years, she
has received much recognition for her life's work of helping people connect with
their surroundings in a meaningful way. She is respected as a naturalist, a protector,
and a teacher. This is her public face.

Behind that face is another. One that belongs to the child of a Polish educator

Mary Majka, 2004. (Courtesy of Donald Aguon)

and an Austrian countess; a child for whom nannies, spa vacations, and summers on the Baltic Sea were the norm; a child who swung on the pendulum from affluence to poverty and back; a child who faced grief and war alone, finding resilience in the strength of her ancestors and by focusing on the needs of others. This is the face few chance to see, but even this does not account for all of Mary.

During our many visits, I often found myself studying Mary's face. Her skin hangs loosely about the creases, etched by years in the sun. She is comfortable in that skin and has never bothered to adorn it. One who mattered in her life called her his "little Polish witch" and, later, his "Canadian Indian." I understand this. Her high cheekbones and prominent nose lend themselves to such description. Fine, pure white hair falls long below her shoulders, although you would not know this unless you glimpsed her rearranging it into the sparse, loose coil she always wears. Thin lips frame her mouth, and when she smiles, her face lights up. Eyebrows, scarce as her hair, have all but disappeared; however, the muscles holding their place still rise archly with a question or excitement or laughter.

When she laughs, her hands laugh with her, flying upward like startled sparrows. Often, reclining in her easy chair and immersed in the richness of a story, she unconsciously clicks the edges of her feet together in glee.

Her eyes. Tucked in a web of folds, their blue depths are faded and watery but retain the power to pierce. They reveal little and miss nothing, yet sometimes she finds it difficult to see herself. Her eyes are slow to tear and quick to crinkle in laughter and mischievousness. When they close, images from the past emerge as if on a movie screen, sometimes unbidden, unwanted. Those images evoke burdens, and sometimes pain.

This is the story of how a young Polish girl named Marysia faced sorrow and then war alone and through this discovered a healing connection to nature. It is the story of how she evolved into the award-winning woman known as Mary Majka, who played a key role in preserving the natural and cultural heritage of New Brunswick and encouraged others to pursue their passion and make their own mark on the world. But beneath all this, it is the story of finding sanctuary — of achieving that sacred place of acceptance and refuge, both in the world and within the soul.

႙

The tide is on its ebb flow. At water's edge, a woman lies on her back, arms outstretched, palms skyward, feet pointed to the sea. Mud pillows her head and shoulders as the water swirls around her, lifting strands of her hair, tickling the shadowed crannies of her ears. Sunlight warms her tanned and lined face, gravity smoothing its creases. Her body wavers with the rhythm of the tide, arms and legs briefly buoyant. Suspended between the elements, she is a creature of both, carrying the solidity of land and the fluidity of sea.

She is in and of the world, in communion with the bay, imagining cones of light penetrating her skin, reflecting as rays filter through water. She feels the familiar cadence of the tide as if it had been there all along, rocking in her soul. From birth, she'd always found comfort in water.

"You came out of me like a fish..."

She has been shaped by many places, but she belongs here at Mary's Point. There are those who assume the point was named after her, and this pleases her, but the scythe-shaped hook of land jutting into the Bay of Fundy was named for a different Mary: an Acadian Mi'kmaq outcast who bridged cultures and danced to her own music. A woman who, long ago, found sanctuary at Mary's Point and then death on the Fundy tides.

As the tide pulls back from the shore, the woman is left behind, like a piece of driftwood. The breeze cools her skin, drying the warm, briny water to a fine residue. She lies motionless, eyes closed, giving herself to sensation and sound.

Presently, her hearing sharpens, perceiving murmurs of life. Exposed mud crackles as millions of minute mud shrimp the size of a fingernail clipping emerge from flooded burrows to feed on algae left behind by the retreating tide. She feels the subtle movement of their activity beneath her resting fingertips.

She lies quiet...waiting, anticipating. Within moments, sound rolls over her like a wave and she is surrounded. Tens of thousands of migratory sandpipers and plovers flood the glistening flats, long beaks bobbing up and down, collecting the tiny shrimp. The birds had been resting on the sand and pebbled beach throughout high tide, waiting. Their gentle peeps and the patter of so many tri-pronged feet slapping the silt swells to a crescendo. She slowly turns her face sideways, opening her eyes to watch.

Everything in the world funnels down into the perfection and intensity of this moment. There is only the woman, the mud, the tide; the tiny shrimp beneath her fingertips, the sandpipers close enough to touch. Tears form at the outer corners of her eyes and overflow, rolling past her ears, down the curve of her neck, to drop onto the mud, mingling with the salty puddles left behind by the tide.

ᘏ

CHAPTER ONE

Origins

*I remember being born. I remember things about the very beginning
of my life. I can remember sucking on my mother's breast; today, I can
still recall the scent of her.*

Mary Majka and I are sitting in the "Bridge," the split log and pine-panelled
sunroom of her Mary's Point home. Like a ship's bridge, wide windows dominate
the room, facing southward across the Bay of Fundy, which glimmers in the low
winter sunlight like rumpled glass. Just beyond the windows are bare bushes, their
fruit long since picked by birds that visit the feeders.

The room is filled with light and fragrance, flowering begonias, orchids, and
memorabilia. One wall features a hornet nest, a Lars Larsen painting, and a chickadee
quilt stitched by a friend. A forty-year-old Norfolk pine fills an entire corner while
the leggy branches of a rubber plant cross the full width of the ceiling, suspended
on hooks. A telescope stands by the window. Binoculars rest on the windowsill.

Mary is solicitous. She shows me where to sit and ensures that I am comfortable
with my laptop. A serpentine-patterned wicker hamper rests at her feet, a mug of
cold African tea at her elbow. "I call this my memory box," she says. "It is filled
with treasures." She has been sorting papers and photographs to prepare for this
day. She must do it in small measures; her memories weigh heavy.

Today, she has unearthed draft copies of letters and reports printed on the reverse
side of emails, notes written on envelopes, and drawings on cardboard. She wastes

little. As if looking for a place to start, she shuffles through documents that record some of her achievements. Finally, she begins.

"I am thinking about those people who believe I do things to blow my own horn," she says. "There is no need for me to make myself bigger and better. My background is such that I always knew I was somebody. I never had the feeling that I had to prove myself."

She passes her hand slowly over a photograph of her mother and then continues.

"But to understand my ancestry and aristocratic roots, one has to understand something of the history and culture of Europe — it is not so straightforward. I will start with my mother. Her name was Maria Chorinska."[1]

ɔଃ

Maria Brigitta Chorinska was born on November 9, 1893,[2] the middle child of Count Ignaz Chorinsky and Fanny Werner. Count Ignaz (Mary's maternal grandfather) was descended from a prominent Polish family who joined King Jan Sobieski of Poland in helping Austria to turn back the Turkish armies of the Ottoman Empire during the 1683 Battle of Vienna. After the war, the Austrian emperor gave the Chorinsky brothers the title of count and a tract of land in Skalitz, Austria. Over the next two centuries, the Chorinsky descendants established a small village on the estate lands and remained closely associated with the Austrian court. The women commonly served as ladies-in-waiting to Austrian regents, and the men received their schooling in Vienna's educational institutes reserved for aristocrats.

By the late 1800s, three Chorinsky brothers remained attached to the family estate. The eldest, an adventurer and traveller who enjoyed big-game hunting in Africa, finally returned home when his money ran out, while the youngest was killed in active duty in Bosnia in 1878. The other remaining brother, Ignaz, captained a boat along the Danube River between Vienna and the Black Sea. When his older brother's spendthrift habits gradually destroyed the family inheritance, Ignaz returned to the Chorinsky estate in Skalitz hoping to prevent the inevitable financial ruin. He married Fanny Werner, the daughter of a wealthy merchant, in 1886. Their first daughter, Frieda, arrived in 1887, followed by Mary's mother, Maria, and then a son, Leopold. After Ignaz's efforts to revitalize the family fortunes failed, the brothers sold the estate and parted ways. The young couple settled nearby in Olmütz and Ignaz took work with the railway company there.[3]

Fanny was an elegant, gentle woman who easily assumed the new title of countess, although such distinctions meant little to her. Nonetheless, she exhibited a quiet strength accompanied by a dignified bearing and strong sense of social responsibility, traits she passed on to her daughter Maria as she grew.

Although Maria was an intelligent girl and wanted to attend university, her parents felt that being a girl, she would be better served to learn the social graces. Thus, she educated herself by reading voraciously.

One evening in 1916, Fanny and her two daughters, young women by then, attended a lavish party at the home of the archbishop of Olmütz. It was here that Maria met the archbishop's archivist and researcher, a handsome young educator named Henryk Adler, who would become the father of Mary Majka.

Henryk Adler was born May 15, 1881, the son of Franz Adler (Mary's paternal grandfather), an Austrian engineer, and Maria Krynska (Mary's paternal grandmother), a Pole whose family had moved to Russia in 1762 as part of the agricultural reforms instigated by Catherine the Great. By the time Franz and Maria married, the Krynsky family had come to own prosperous plantations near Kiev in southern Russia.[4] Franz and Maria Adler lived the vibrant, comfortable life of the Russian upper class. As with many non-Russians in their social position, they spoke Russian to their servants and their own language (in this case, Polish) among themselves, ensuring the continuity of their culture. Maria is remembered as a woman who cared for orphaned mice and other small creatures that others might overlook, and who might halt the carriage to gather wildflowers at the roadside, despite an abundance of blooms in her own garden.

Henryk and his sisters, Stanisława and Kazimiera, were taught by tutors at home before heading to Kiev for further schooling. Kazimiera became a doctor, while Stanisława, who was prone to depression, became a nun. Their father, Franz, died of pneumonia when Henryk was in high school, and his Austrian grandfather, Christian Adler, an historian, brought him to Vienna to complete his schooling. Exploring varied interests in history, geography, and astronomy, Henryk furthered his education in Galicia, Odessa, and Berlin. He then found employment in Odessa as a university lecturer and as a high school history and geography teacher. While preparing for his professorship exams, he also tutored the sons of an aristocratic Russian family.

In July 1914, Henryk and his employer's sons boarded a train to visit the boys' relatives in Paris. At the border of Austria-Hungary, all three were arrested because their papers identified them as Russian. Austria-Hungary had just declared war on Serbia and Russia. Henryk managed to send a message to the boys' uncle, the archbishop of Olmütz. Within two days, an opulent carriage arrived at the prison gates to pick up the three detainees. The boys went on to Paris, but the authorities

Henryk and Maria Adler the year they married.

released Henryk only after the boys' uncle promised to keep him under house arrest. The archbishop promptly put the young man to work organizing his archives.

Hence, Henryk found himself working as a "captive" archivist and researcher during the whole of World War I. The archbishop used his guest's presence as an excuse to host entertainment nights. One of these soirées was the party attended by Fanny Chorinska and her daughters.

Henryk and Maria became engaged in October 1917 and married in August 1919. A year earlier, the Russian Revolution had forced Henryk's mother and sisters to flee to Poland in a farmer's hay wagon. They left most of their possessions behind, taking only what they could carry. Their departure effectively severed Henryk's ties with Russia. However, far from missing his Russian connection, Henryk valued his Polish roots and considered himself a patriot. In the aftermath of World War I, Poland was finally free from occupation after a century of subservience, and he wanted to be part of the efforts to help rebuild the country. The archbishop secured Polish citizenship papers for him and a position in Poland as a tutor. In 1920,

Henryk became principal of a prestigious boys' school and moved with his wife, Maria, to the pastoral city of Częstochowa in southwestern Poland. Only then, feeling financially secure, did they decide to start a family.

Maria's first pregnancy ended in miscarriage. She spent much of the final trimester of her second pregnancy in bed, reflecting on the tiny life growing inside her. She prayed to the Madonna that her child would be born healthy and without incident. She promised that, if the baby were a girl, she would christen her Maria — not after herself but to express respect and thankfulness to the Virgin Mother. Meanwhile, she relieved the boredom of her confinement by sewing, embroidering, and singing melodies from her childhood. Maria hoped and expected that this peaceful, prayerful time would result in a quiet and demure child. Instead, she gave birth to a girl who, almost from the beginning, was anything but quiet and demure.

Mary Majka — named Emilia Maria Adler and called Marysia or Mi by her family — was born on March 9, 1923.

> I remember my birth very clearly. I think of that day as a happy event, but I never considered it as the beginning of my life. I was "born" much earlier than that and have many feelings that started much earlier. I remember, as a child of two or three, trying to imitate that state again by lying in my bed with my head hanging down from the edge.
>
> I was delivered at home, which was very normal at that time. My grandmother came to help and it was her voice and her hands that I remember most. I am pretty sure she was the one who held me first in her arms. My bond to her was always much stronger than to my mother, although my mother was a wonderful person and a good parent. Besides my grandmother, there was also a midwife present, and a doctor. I remember the face of that midwife and the touch of her much stronger hands, as opposed to my grandmother. She was the one who actually delivered me and it was a very easy delivery.
>
> "You just slipped out of me like a fish," my mother told me. I had a very small head and very long legs. My father only came into the room after I was cleaned and washed — O, that heavenly feeling of warmth and space in that bathtub! — as opposed to the cramped quarters I just came from. I remember the smell of my father's suit; he only held me a brief moment, but I was told I followed him with my eyes wherever he walked. I was very close to him all my life.
>
> I also remember my mother's smell. That smell, which I did not particularly like, is still very strong in my memory, but it probably has

to do with my long nursing time — twelve months. Her milk had some of that smell too. It was sweet and I can still taste it. Besides the sound of voices, I could hear some other continuous sound. Perhaps it was raining because it was March and the rainy time in Poland. Or was it the wind? The room I was born in faced the garden with tall trees.

I was put into a basket and for about a month or so, this was my home. I remember that basket very well and can see it clearly — where it stood and how it looked inside. At the age of perhaps five, I asked my mother where that basket went, since my brother, who was born four years later, had not been put in the basket. My mother was astonished that I should remember it and asked me where I thought it stood. I showed her the place. Still, it took me quite a few years longer before I realized that not everybody could remember their birth or first years of life. I assumed that it was quite normal.[5]

The city of Częstochowa embraces a thirteenth-century monastery named Jasna Góra. The city's main boulevard flows like an artery from the monastery walls through the city. Jasna Góra is the most hallowed shrine in Poland, and throughout the centuries it has remained a touchstone for national identity, symbolizing Polish strength, liberty, and freedom. Roman Catholic Poles consider Częstochowa to be the holiest place in Poland and even today make regular pilgrimages there.[6]

In the 1920s, Henryk's role as schoolmaster gave him a position of prominence and respect in the city. The abbot of Jasna Góra was an occasional dinner guest in the Adler home and a fond friend; he insisted on christening Marysia at the monastery's chapel, a rare honour.

On the day of the christening, the Adlers' horse-drawn carriage clattered down the cobblestones of the chestnut-lined palisade leading to Jasna Góra. In the back of the carriage bobbed a large potted tree, a gift to the Virgin Mary from Maria, in thankfulness for a healthy child. She had nurtured the tree for several years. The child's christening took place in the ornate inner sanctuary of Jasna Góra, beneath the famous painting of Our Lady of Częstochowa, a Byzantine relic held in highest reverence by the Polish people. Tradition stated that St. Luke the Evangelist painted this image of the Virgin Mary and Jesus on a wooden tabletop that had come from the house of the Holy Family in Nazareth. Also called the Black Madonna for the shade of the Virgin's facial features, devout Poles believed it harboured spiritual powers of protection.[7]

Whether due to the special circumstances of her christening or simply to her inherent nature, Emilia Maria Adler would grow up to follow her own spiritual

Marysia, age one, 1924.

pilgrimages throughout her long life. Her very name conveys a self-fulfilling destiny: Emilia means industrious; Maria means bitter. Even the name Adler, which means eagle, seems significant. The eagle is the national symbol of Poland and a universal emblem of courage and vision. There would come many times in Marysia's life when it appeared both forces of divine protection and destiny just might be at play.

The Adlers' upper middle-class apartment was part of a long row of three-storey residences on one of the city's main boulevards. Placement of a family's apartment denoted social status; those on the ground floor were the wealthiest, those on the second floor had the next enviable spot, while the lower classes had to trudge flights of stairs to the top. The dank, cold basements were reserved for the poorest.

An arched entryway between two stone and stucco buildings led to a rectangular courtyard. The Adlers' apartment lay above that of the building's owner. Their windows and balcony overlooked the courtyard and an enclosed garden. A large lilac grew beside the balcony, and as a baby, Marysia lay for hours in her bassinet inhaling the fragrance of its blossoms, watching the play of light on leaves, listening to birdsong, and entertaining herself with the movement of her hands.

As soon as Marysia was old enough, her nanny took her to the garden. Hand in hand they would walk through the courtyard to the entrance gate. They discovered fossilized designs etched upon the garden's stone walls that her nanny explained were ancient sea snails called ammonites. They also found land snails among the stone pathways, flowers, and large shrubs.

> I remember they were very beautiful with a lovely pattern on their shells. I would admire them and my nanny would pick them up and show me how they hide their feelers. I learned to look at and appreciate beauty, but not to disturb or harm it. I was taught we lived in harmony with nature and you didn't kill everything that moved. Perhaps this is where my initial understanding of our relationship with nature started.

Beyond the garden was the central courtyard: a noisy, active place where chickens and pigs clucked and squealed in wooden stalls. Marysia could watch the courtyard activity from her apartment window. "I was never allowed in the courtyard alone," she explains, "because this is where the poor children played." Itinerant vendors peddled their wares, enticing customers with rapid staccato rhetoric. The community pump provided water for those without indoor taps and served as a public gathering place. Neighbours filled the benches surrounding the pump, sitting for hours to chat and share news. Occasionally a *Leiermann*, or travelling minstrel, arrived with a street organ and a monkey or parrot.

In summer, peasants from across Poland journeyed to Częstochowa for the religious celebrations at Jasna Góra. The apartment owner rented space in the courtyard to the pilgrims and their necessary livestock. Marysia particularly loved these times, staring from her dining room window at those who had come from afar to sing, pray, and show devotion to the Black Madonna.

Marysia's schooling began at age three when she joined several other children for kindergarten. Classes took place in a different apartment each week, and a private

Marysia and her mother, Maria, 1925.

Marysia (age five) with her brother, Heniek (age one), 1928.

teacher instructed them in physical exercises, crafts, and theatre. After two years of kindergarten, her schooling continued at home, where her mother taught her to read and write and calculate sums.

Marysia was four when her brother, Henryk, was born at home on October 27, 1927. Fanny travelled to Częstochowa to keep Marysia occupied. The two of them spent much of the day walking in the park, collecting chestnuts, and playing games. As evening approached, they sat in the guest room before glowing coals in the stove as her *Grossmutter* read a story out loud in German. Fanny, whose mother tongue was German, believed that learning languages was integral to a European education. She wanted Marysia to speak and read German as well as Polish.

Following the delivery, Fanny took her granddaughter in to see her new baby brother. They bonded immediately. While Marysia became particularly fond of Henryk, whom they called Heniek, she admitted to feeling some envy over his eyes, which were deep violet with long lashes.

My nanny would take us out for walks and everyone would admire
this baby, making me jealous because of all the people admiring him
and his eyes, and never looking at me. Nobody paid attention to me
because I was not as pretty.

The children had a succession of nannies and servants, but one in particular —
Hela — was especially important to Marysia. Hela came to the Adlers when she was
eighteen and, through the years, became a trusted friend. A devout Roman Catholic,
Hela considered a religious upbringing to be of utmost importance. She ensured that
Marysia knelt to pray each night before sleep and often took the children to church.
Marysia, it must be admitted, was more interested in the entertaining ceremony
and intricate architecture than in the spiritual meaning of the service.

The Adler household was efficiently run under Maria's direction. In addition to
the nanny, the family employed a cook and a woman who came once a week to wash
laundry. Maria held firm views on how the children should conduct themselves.
She raised them to be courteous and helpful to their elders and the servants, whom
she always treated with respect. Maria loved her children, directing their care and
participating in their ongoing education, but left the nanny to meet their emotional
and disciplinary needs. She never raised her voice. With adults too, Maria displayed
neither great anger nor joy, conveying instead a polite reticence that discouraged
intimacy.

Despite her reserved exterior, Maria exhibited genuine compassion and sensitivity
for less fortunate souls. During the annual religious pilgrimages to the monastery,
she directed her servants to take soup or stew to the hungry travellers camped in the
courtyard. One homeless boy in particular regularly arrived at the Adler doorstep.
On each occasion, he was invited into the kitchen for a bowl of food, which he
would eat quickly. He would then leave without a word.

When Marysia was five, her mother brought home a doll as a Christmas gift
for a little girl across the courtyard who had none of her own. She suggested they
sew some clothes for it.

"You do things with your hands because that is what counts," she said to Marysia.
"Buying things from a store is easy, but when you put your love and attention and
time into doing something yourself, then that is more important."

Mother and daughter worked together cutting and sewing the underpants,
pinafores, and tiny dresses. Marysia found the work tedious, but when it was
completed she felt proud. With Marysia clutching the doll, Maria led her by the
hand across the courtyard to a cellar apartment. There, Marysia handed over the

Marysia and her father, Henryk, circa 1928.

doll and clothes to a girl her own age, one whom she had often seen from her apartment window.

In contrast to his wife, Henryk seemed to extract great enjoyment from life. He was free-spirited and passionate, loving the richness of travel and varied experiences. He took Marysia on adventures — just the two of them together — outings she particularly enjoyed. When she was about five, they visited the Jasna Góra monastery. Females were not permitted in the inner sanctum, so she waited in a large library.

> I remember my father came back and took me into a room where monks were writing large volumes by hand, probably Bibles. These books had painted illustrations. I could see the beginning of a chapter and it had a big picture of the first letter. I was absolutely thrilled to see this beautiful writing.

Books and stories were an important part of the family routine. Each evening after supper, they gathered in the sitting room. While Maria sewed or embroidered,

Heniek played with toys and Henryk sat with a book. Marysia curled at his feet to listen as he read aloud.

While her mother read the Brothers Grimm or Hans Christian Andersen to her children, Henryk preferred Polish classics and history. Marysia's favourite was *W pustyni i w puszczy* (*In Desert and Wilderness*), the story of two Polish children lost in Africa, written by the Nobel Prize-winning novelist Henryk Sienkiewicz, acclaimed for his tales of past defeats overcome by the strength of Poland's patriotic noble spirit. Henryk also read of adventures in far-off places. When he read aloud from Rudyard Kipling's *The Jungle Book*, Marysia imagined wild creatures prowling beneath the tabletop. When he read Jules Verne's *From the Earth to the Moon*, she asked him, "Is it really possible to travel to the moon?" "Oh no, my dear," he answered. "That will never be possible. The moon is much too far from the Earth."

But on another warm summer evening, Henryk took his daughter out onto the balcony and lifted her high in his arms to see a wondrous thing passing low over the city. It was a great floating airship, a Zeppelin.

As time went on and he continued to fill her mind with stories, she came to believe that the world was filled with things once imagined and people who made their dreams become real.

Marysia was six when her father assumed a new position as the principal of a state-run boys' school in Grodno, northeastern Poland. At the time, Grodno (currently called Hrodna and in the country of Belarus) was an ancient, bucolic town of some forty thousand people surrounded by hills, forests, and waterways.

Henryk moved to Grodno at the beginning of the school year. Maria remained with the children in Częstochowa for six months while he established their apartment, which was in a building adjoining his school and reserved for people associated with the institution. Although he returned for short visits, Marysia found the separation painful. "While he was gone, I was lonesome for him very much. I used to go and put my head on the part of the bed where he slept, smell the scent that was his, and kiss the quilt because I missed him so much."

During the five years the family spent in Grodno, Marysia enjoyed increasing freedom as she grew older. It became a period of tremendous character development for the little girl — but also one that ended in irrevocable loss.

Maria tutored her daughter at home during their first year in Grodno, and then in the fall of 1930, Marysia was sent to a nearby school that was an adjunct to a teaching academy. Teachers-in-training often sat at the back of the room, taking notes and observing students in a classroom setting. The small size of the classes allowed for close relationships between teacher and student.

Marysia's teacher was Kazimiera Krzywcowna. Kazimiera had suffered an injury in her youth that over time had twisted her spine and affected her leg. Hobbled, yet kind and wise, she paid close attention to her pupils, displaying great affection toward them and making time to listen to their troubles or triumphs. She kept an altar to the Virgin Mary in her classroom and encouraged her students to bring flowers to show respect. Above all, she taught them through her own example that a physical disability did not lessen a person's value. This left an indelible mark on Marysia, who considered her teacher an understanding friend with whom she could express herself openly.

When Marysia was asked to give a speech and present Kazimiera with a bouquet of flowers for her birthday, she worked hard to memorize the words but once on stage forgot her lines. When she burst into tears with embarrassment, Kazimiera rushed to comfort her with a hug and a kiss. "You did well," she whispered.

The little girl fully redeemed herself later by writing and directing a play about her teacher's influence on generations of students as a way to honour her retirement. The performance achieved great success and, at the close, Marysia saw Kazimiera dab tears from her eyes.

Marysia and other children who lived in her building occasionally played in the cellar of her father's school, a dark maze of furnaces, coal piles, and bats. Whispering and giggling, they scampered along, peering up in search of hanging bats. They found it amusing to watch the tiny mouths open in response to eyedroppers filled with sugar and water. Such experiences contributed to her comfort with and appreciation of creatures others might fear.

One of these friends was the janitor's daughter, Regina. Although they attended different schools, the girls played together every day and often visited each other's apartments. One day, after returning from an afternoon with her friend, Marysia sought out her father in his study.

"Tatusiu, why does Regina's family eat so many potatoes? Always potato dumplings, potato pancakes, potato soup?"

"Poor people eat potatoes because potatoes are plentiful and don't cost much," her father explained. "Regina's father works as a custodian, so they don't have very much money."

Marysia frowned, considering the differences she'd observed between their apartments, clothing, gifts, and possessions.

"Well, why is it like that? Why are some people poor and other people rich? I think we should all have the same amount of money. Then it would be fair."

Marysia with Heniek, her favourite nanny, Hela, and her grandmother, Fanny,
summer 1930, just before the family moved to Grodno.

"Oh my, here we have a little communist!" Her father laughed, then looked at
her face, serious now. "That is the way it was supposed to be in Russia, but alas, it
doesn't work. You see, Mi, each of us is born with certain strengths and weaknesses,
and some just possess more strengths than others. These people, the ones who
recognize their talents and wish to do something with them, are the ones who will
accomplish great things. Others are born without and don't have a chance to make
something of themselves. If we have these talents and the ambition to use them,
we can achieve anything we set our minds to achieve."

Marysia wasn't sure she understood her father's explanation, but she remembered
his words. The concept of those with and those without — whether talent or

money — did not seem fair. She decided that if she were in charge, everyone would have an equal share of money, talent, and opportunity.

She was also sensitive enough to observe the differences between her parents. Their relationship taught her to regard marriage as a partnership based on mutual respect but with little outward display of affection or sentiment. When they argued, which was rarely, they spoke German so the children could not understand.

"Don't fight," Marysia would plead. "We are not fighting, we are discussing," her father would respond. "Now go and play."

The large public school in which Henryk was principal adjoined an expansive park where the family often walked. The park had a zoological and a botanical garden. Marysia spent hours in the greenhouses and gardens watching the workers and animals, and asking questions. The school courtyard also had space for a garden plot and gooseberry patch for the principal. Maria had little interest in gardening, but Marysia relished the thought of growing her own vegetables. She was only eight when she solicited the help of other children in the school apartments, organizing them into the *Towarzystwo Ochrony Ogródka* (Caretakers of the Garden Society). They staged a talent show, collected admission fees, and picked gooseberries to sell. With the proceeds, they bought seeds, plants, and manure, carting the latter home in wheelbarrows. The children transplanted tomato and cucumber plants and sowed lettuce and radish seeds in neat rows. They also bought two rabbits and kept them in a hutch. Daily, Marysia clambered over the fence to the park to collect dandelion leaves or grass for them. When the rabbits began multiplying, they sold the young kits to generate money for the following year.

Her proclivity for outdoor projects continued when, the next year, she volunteered to help with her school's new vegetable garden. One afternoon, Marysia had ventured off to find manure. Meanwhile, Maria and a friend were returning from a leisurely afternoon at the café. The two women, impeccable in their formal attire for mid-day socializing, strolled down the avenue, commenting on window displays, nodding to acquaintances, and discussing social plans for the following week.

Suddenly, Marysia, looking like a dirty peasant girl with bare feet and tangled hair, wove into Maria's view on the other side of the avenue, pushing a wheelbarrow of manure. She hoped her elegant friend would not notice. But a voice rang out.

"Mamusiu!"

Marysia barrelled across the street, pushing her wheelbarrow over the pebbled surface. Clods of manure fell off and bounced along the cobblestones. She stopped, dropped the wheelbarrow, and rescued the precious fertilizer. She arrived by her mother's side out of breath, cheeks flushed. Maria cleared her throat and, with a glance at her friend, raised her chin slightly. "Mi, what are you doing? Look at you!"

"Mamusiu! I'm building a new garden for the school. They asked me to help and gave me money to buy some manure! Look how good this is, so rich, so many worms!" Marysia dug in the soil to produce a sample for inspection. "It will grow very healthy vegetables, don't you think?" A worm wriggled out and fell writhing to the ground.

Maria, hiding her embarrassment, remained composed. "Mi, it's wonderful that you are doing something nice for the school, but I think you need to run home and tidy yourself for supper. It's not proper to parade about the streets barefoot in a dirty dress."

Marysia's keen interest in nature was beginning to extend well beyond gardening. By the time she was ten, she would often awake before dawn in the summer, fully rested. Sometimes she dressed and quietly left the house. She began to appreciate the solitude of early mornings. As she walked through the mauve mist in the park, she slowly learned the language of nature. She passed through lingering pockets of scent and, nose in the air, tried to guess the source...maybe clover or perhaps wild carrot. She observed ducks sleeping on the river, bills tucked under their wings, and earthworms entwined in a mating ritual. She knelt beside intricate webs traced with dew, like filaments of spun glass, touching them to awaken the spider. Her eyes grew accustomed to observing details of the world around her and her mind absorbed the patterns she saw there.

She found great contentment in her own company. Eventually, she found herself choosing solitude over play with others and began to wonder, 'Why do others play together, yet I just want to be alone?' During these times, she imagined a life without limitations, one in which she assumed a leadership role. This imaginary world would become so real and imperative that no matter what she undertook, Marysia never considered that she might fail.

Sometimes in the summer, the family travelled to Jeziory, to stay in a lodge and nature centre used by Henryk's school for research and field trips. The lodge, an intriguing and rustic place with dark weathered wood, shuttered windows, and a large veranda, was tucked among tall spruce trees on a secluded lake. A faculty member managed the centre and conducted local botanical and zoological studies. Marysia often crept into his study to inspect his collections of bones, nests, fossils, and insects.

One day, sensing her keen interest, the professor took her on a boat trip to collect water plants from the lake. She enjoyed learning how to gather and label the different specimens. He rowed farther to a sheltered platform, helped her ashore, and they climbed to a raised deck to observe a beaver colony. He warned her to remain silent and Marysia sat perfectly still, observing the adult beavers cutting branches

Marysia, Heniek, and Hela vacationing on the Baltic Sea, circa 1931.

from a felled tree and the young gathering to nibble on the bark. He allowed her to accompany him often after that.

The experience may well have sparked a deeper interest in animal biology, for Marysia began to gather her own specimens such as feathers, stones, and shells while on hikes and vacations. When her mother brought home a rabbit to make pâté, Marysia asked for the animal's head. She boiled it in water to remove the flesh, leaving a small, pure-white skull. All these she gave to the school museum.

Summertime also meant seaside vacations on the Baltic Sea or extended visits to health resorts. Fanny sometimes accompanied them to Druskieniki, a spa with healing mineral springs and mud baths, so she could attend to her arthritis. Marysia adored Babcia and made the most of their time together. An accomplished knitter, Fanny was pleased when Marysia expressed a desire to learn as well. "I think if a young lady wishes to learn to knit, then the best choice is to start off with a shawl," she said.

As Marysia continued with her knitting, she kept dropping stitches but was reluctant to unravel and start again. When her *Grossmutter* asked to see her work, Marysia tried to rearrange the shawl to hide the holes. "Hmm, that's very nice. You are making some progress," said Fanny, then raised her head and looked her granddaughter in the eyes, "but I see, Mi, that you have made some mistakes."

"Uh-hmm," said Marysia, eyes downcast.

"Well, it doesn't show too much. I see you were trying to hide them, but you have to decide what you are going to do now," she said gently. "You could leave them, and perhaps no one will notice, but you will always know they are there. Or you can unravel it and start over again."

Marysia realized if she settled for something that was not her best, the effort of hiding the mistakes each time she wore the shawl might outweigh the trouble of correcting the errors. It was a simple but valuable lesson, one she recalled regularly in later years while pursuing her own endeavours. She often repeated Babcia's words to others.

Fanny also appreciated the joys of cooking, often allowing Marysia to help her in the kitchen. Maria often said of her mother, "She doesn't cook, she celebrates." One day, Fanny gave Marysia a few

The Adler family:
Marysia, Henryk, Maria,
and Heniek, circa 1932.

coins and asked her to run to the bakery for bread. Inside, the bakery smelled of honey, caraway, and rye. The girl watched the baker as he removed loaves from the brick oven with a wooden paddle and set them out to cool. He then spread the base of his paddle with flour before sliding in more risen dough to bake. Marysia chose a warm loaf, fresh from the oven, and put it into her bag, carted it home, and tossed it on the table, flour side up. Fanny scolded the child for her show of irreverence.

"Bread is the most important thing we have to sustain life; you must always treat such things with respect to show you are grateful for this and appreciate the work that went into making it. If you ever drop a piece on the floor, you must pick it up and kiss it to apologize," she said sternly.

℃ℬ

As much as Marysia loved the women in her life, she felt most attached to her beloved father. Each day, he walked her to school. During these walks, she began to question what she saw in the world around her. He challenged her ideas, encouraging her to think for herself and arrive at her own conclusions. What with her father's love of books, travel, and spirited discussions, Marysia felt a great connection with Henryk. Her sense of self was so inextricably linked to him that, years later, she called him a soulmate.

Henryk, said to have a "golden mouth," was routinely asked to speak at public functions and to introduce travelling stage performers or dignitaries at the Grodno theatre. Marysia remembers the excitement of visiting the theatre, where the Adlers enjoyed an exclusive reserved balcony seat. The balcony was ideal for watching others, including her father, below on stage.

Henryk witnessed great poverty in his travels and felt sympathy for what was then termed the peasant class. His daughter noted how he showed equal respect and friendship to everyone he encountered, regardless of their social position. He saw those whom others overlooked. Entering the turnstile at the train station, for instance, as others pushed brusquely by, he paused to offer a cigarette and chat with the attendant.

Marysia spent many hours hiking with her father. The two would set off in the morning with rolls and chocolate and be gone all day. They developed a comfortable companionship. He answered her questions and never made her feel awkward for asking them. He told her that, with her talents, she could be anyone she wanted to be, do anything she set her mind to.

Early one morning, during a summer stay in Druskieniki when she was twelve, father and daughter followed a worn path through the forest. Pines stretched skyward, their bottom limbs trimmed by peasants for firewood or fencing. Sun stippled though the canopy, creating shafts of airy light, patterning the forest floor like the stained glass of a cathedral. Birdsong drifted downward from the choir loft of evergreens. Eventually, the path opened into a field of yellow lupines on the outskirts of a small village. As they ambled along the dirt road toward a cluster of primitive huts, her father explained that the lupines would soon be plowed under to enrich the sandy soil for growing flax and rye or other crops.

Entering the village, Marysia was taken aback by the signs of such a primitive lifestyle. Huts of horizontal slats and thatched roofs lined the rutted road. In the midst of dust and dirt, chickens bobbed for grubs, pigs nosed the ground, and goats tugged on islands of grass. She saw earthen floors, uncovered windows, open doorways, and holes in the thatch to let out smoke from indoor fire pits. Outside some huts, twisted piles of golden flax lay stacked like great plaits of brittle hair, and women with gapped smiles and bare feet sat in the sunshine deftly mangling the sinewy strands or weaving silken strings of processed fibre on large looms. Marysia watched the looms shuttle in a steady rhythm, creating a fine, soft linen just like the cloth Hela bartered for at the city market. Without thinking, she touched her fingers to her linen dress and smoothed out the wrinkles.

A young girl sat on a doorstep slowly eating spoonfuls of sodden bread from a bowl of milk. Her skirt hitched over her knees revealed dusty, calloused feet and mottled legs the colour of tea stains. Beside her coiled a metre-long snake, as thick around as an egg. Suddenly, its head darted into her pottery bowl, tongue snapping. Still chewing, the girl rapped the reptile's head with her spoon and it recoiled. A moment later, it made another attempt. Rap! Rap! It recoiled again. Her hand shooed it away like a troublesome fly.

Marysia stared with curiosity and tugged on her father's sleeve. "Tato," she whispered. "Why is she doing this?"

Her father followed her gaze. "Ah, Mi, good question. I would say that she is hungry, but the snake is also hungry."

"But why is she sitting with a snake?" she persisted, looking to see if other snakes lay nearby.

"Snakes are good companions. They catch the mice and rats," he said, moving down the dirt path, his attention distracted by a farmer mending a woven fence beside the road.

Marysia stared a moment longer at the girl and the snake, then ran to catch up as Henryk reached into his pocket, brought out his silver cigarette case, and offered it to the farmer. The man took one cigarette and, nodding his thanks, tucked it behind his ear, saying he would save this good tobacco for later and mix it with his own so he could enjoy it more than once.

Henryk extracted several more cigarettes. Handing them over, he said, "I have plenty. Take these and smoke with me right now." Taking the cigarettes, his new friend hefted them in his hand a moment and tucked them carefully into the pocket of his torn and baggy pants. "I can share these with my brother and brother-in-law later." The two men spoke together for a moment longer, and then he invited Henryk and Marysia home to meet his family. The man led them to a larger hut at the other end of the village. Marysia saw other women at their looms and several more snakes, though none as large as the one on the doorstep.

He invited them inside, and while the men sat at the table and talked, Marysia looked around. This hut was larger than some of the others and had glass windows, in contrast with the more typical covering of transparent membranes, such as cow bladders, stretched across the opening to block the wind. Wooden benches lined the walls, and in one corner was a bed piled with embroidered pillows — small luxuries. A loom sat silent in another corner. A gaggle of children peered shyly from a doorway.

After the visit, Henryk stood and took from his rucksack the chocolate they had brought for lunch. Nodding toward the curious children, he handed it to his new friend, emptied the silver cigarette case, and bid him good day. On their walk home Marysia asked why the man did not smoke his cigarettes right away. "Little Mi, he is a good, honest man who does not want to take all his pleasure at once. He knows how to make a little go a long way."

Henryk was a member of Poland's intelligentsia, a tiered class of white-collar workers and intellectuals. He would have cut an authoritative figure in Grodno, given his wide educational background and European travel experience. He became involved in social issues within the community, joined various committees, and met regularly with other patriots to discuss improving Poland's cultural development. Teachers were considered civic leaders of the community, and as such Henryk received much respect and esteem.

Henryk Adler in his school office in Grodno, date unknown.

He travelled frequently throughout 1935, and when the Adlers returned from summer vacation, he told the children he had been offered a position in a larger prestigious school in Chełm. The job would bring a lovely home with a garden, a carriage, and two horses. Marysia was excited about the idea of having horses, but little more was said regarding the move.

School commenced in September. Henryk resumed his custom of walking Marysia to her class, but she began to notice her father seemed preoccupied and distracted. He had little time for her. One morning, as she prepared for school, he failed to appear. Marysia went to find him. The door to his bedroom was closed. She dared not enter and left for school by herself, deeply troubled.

At school, her disquiet grew into a sense of foreboding. Noticing her upset, her teacher took her aside and asked what was wrong. Marysia began to cry, saying she wanted to talk to her father. The concerned teacher took her to the office, where she dialled Henryk's office at the school. A man answered the phone, and Marysia whispered, "Tatusiu?" Marysia listened a moment, then frowned, realizing it was not her father's voice.

"This is not Tata," she told her teacher, handing back the phone. Her teacher took the phone and spoke, "I have Marysia Adler here and she would like to speak with her father. Is he there?" After a pause, she handed the receiver back to the child. Marysia heard her father's voice across the line. He told her he would see her that night and not to worry. Marysia was not reassured. That evening, her father joined them for supper and all seemed fine. She did not mention the incident to her mother, something she later regretted.

The next morning, Hela told Marysia her father had gone on a trip. Since he sometimes travelled because of the upcoming job promotion, she did not think it was strange. But two days later, Henryk's sister Kazimiera arrived unannounced, looking for Maria. Hela replied that the master was on a trip and the missus was out with friends. The expression on Kazimiera's face and the tone of her voice frightened Marysia. She knew something was wrong.

When Maria arrived home, she sent Marysia and Heniek outside to play, and she and Kazimiera went into the sitting room and closed the door. That evening, after the family had eaten supper, Maria took Marysia aside and said, "You will not be going to school tomorrow as we are going on a trip to Warsaw with Kazimiera. Hela will help you pack."

Marysia did as she was told and prepared for her trip. She did not ask questions. They travelled by train to Warsaw and stayed with friends. Marysia could sense a terrible nervousness in the air. Conversations took place behind closed doors, with people coming and going. Maria told her daughter that she and Kazimiera had to leave for a few days. Marysia would remain in Warsaw with the friends.

And so Marysia waited. The people were kind, but she had no place to be alone. For the child who found such comfort in solitude, her world had upended, leaving her nothing familiar. She tried to come to terms with the growing uneasiness she felt inside. Three days later, Maria returned. She sat down with Marysia and delivered the news with an even, quiet voice.

"Your father is dead."

"Yes, I know," whispered Marysia, head down.

Her mother looked at her in surprise. "How could you know this?"

"I just knew."

Her mother nodded and asked nothing else. "I can't speak about it now, but I will tell you more later, when we get home." She stood up, smoothing her skirt.

Marysia sat numb, unable to comprehend what had happened. She did not cry, nor did she show emotion. But deep inside, she felt half of her had died.

After they returned to Grodno, Maria explained the dire situation to both children. "Your father is dead. He killed himself. We can no longer stay in this apartment. Kazimiera has invited us to stay with her and your cousin, Maja, at their home in Chełmno for a while. Hela and Heniek are coming with me, but Marysia, there is no room for you and so you will be remaining here in Grodno to finish the school year."

Marysia felt cold. "Alone? But where will I live?"

"I have spoken with the teachers at your school and made arrangements for you to stay in the boarding house with the student teachers. It will take us several days to pack our things here and you will just be in the way. You have already missed too many days, so you will go back to school tomorrow. Your teachers know what has happened, but I advise you not to speak of this to anyone. It is our private affair and no one else needs to know."

"But where is Tata?" asked Marysia. She needed to see him once more. She wanted to say goodbye.

"He is dead and buried in Sulejów, the same place where he killed himself," said Maria.[8] "Now, we will not speak of this again." She stood up and, with a brief glance at the children, turned and left the room.

Forced in this way to immediately leave the Grodno apartment, Marysia was deprived not only of her home and family but of all tangible reminders of her father: his clothes, his possessions, his pictures, his books, and, most dear of all, his scent.

CHAPTER TWO

Influences

Life is a tangle of things, and in my life, as you will discover, there are many tangles, many levels, many occurrences. To untangle all this and make sense of it is sometimes difficult. In a way you understand yourself, and in another way, you never will.

The temperatures have dropped to -36°C and the bay is broken into ice chunks and wreathed in sea smoke. Although the only heat in the old farmhouse comes from a woodstove in the living room, it is cozy and warm. Mary, dressed in a flowered housedress with bare legs and slippers, tells me it was 12°C in her bedroom this morning before David started the fire.

"It is very irritating that I am not physically able to do things I used to," she says. "This, maybe, is my greatest regret about old age — you want to do this or that or the other, but then you become physically exhausted. I used to be able to put my mind to something and work and work, but now I cannot do that. This is so hard."

Changing the subject, Mary points to another chair. "You should sit over there. You weren't comfortable the last time. No? You want to stay there? Here then, take this footstool."

After settling herself and ordering David to bring tea and cake, she looks down at her hands in her lap, then resumes her story about her father. "My life fell apart within a matter of days. It is still very painful and not something I want to talk about. I was made to feel like I shouldn't be talking about it, but I thought about it a lot. I still think about it a lot. I have a picture of my father in my bedroom and I look at him every morning. I am sure this is because I lost him so early. I miss him to this day."

She stares out the clouded window, glass stained with time and moisture. A thin pane separates here from there. For a moment, she watches the weather and the water, perhaps seeking insight, perception. And truth.

"I was actually saying goodbye all my life. The mourning never stopped. I lost my father, and it was deeper than you can ever imagine. My mother, probably not wanting to upset me, never even came to say goodbye. You must realize what she was up against. She was in a foreign country, left with two young children, and her husband took his own life. Her reputation was ruined. She didn't know what to do."

Two days after returning home from Warsaw, in shock over the sudden death of her father and understanding nothing, Marysia moved out of her home and into the school's boarding house. The single-level residence had a dining room, kitchen, and several large dormitories. Each of the fifteen student teachers sharing a dormitory room had a single bed, a night table, and a locker. A separate, detached building held sinks, showers, and toilets.

Marysia was the only child in the residence. Although the older girls treated her kindly, she felt isolated. She was used to having her own private space. Each night, she returned to the dormitory with the student teachers while her schoolmates went home to families. She sensed estrangement, a distance that hadn't been there before. She felt abandoned and wounded. She began to withdraw. School studies no longer interested her, and she stopped taking part in the activities. On days when the older girls went shopping in town, Marysia retraced the routes she and her father had once hiked, seeking comfort in the familiar pathways.

After several months, her teacher wrote to Maria, saying Marysia was depressed and lethargic. She was grieving. She needed her family. The school was no place for her. Maria made arrangements for Marysia's travel. On Christmas break, two teachers took her as far as Warsaw, where she boarded a train and travelled the rest of the way to Chełmno alone.

Winter moved to spring and the weather warmed. Maria hired a tutor to help Marysia with her schoolwork, and Kazimiera rented a larger apartment to accommodate her relatives. Among family again, Marysia began to heal. Kazimiera's new apartment faced a park, where Marysia, Heniek, and Maja played. One day, a shout from across the square drew the children's attention. Marysia saw a woman fall from a third-floor window. She watched, horrified, as the woman lay dying on the pavement. Afterwards, she was afraid to sleep alone. She grew quiet again.

Maria knew she had to help her daughter, but she still struggled with her own grief and anger. She appreciated her sister-in-law's kindness while she stabilized her life, but the apartment was cramped and the two women had different interests. Although she received only a small pension from Henryk's death, she decided to move to Częstochowa, where she had a network of friends. Perhaps they might help her find work as a tutor. She kept nine-year-old Heniek with her and sent Marysia to stay with her wealthy friend, Zofia Monikowska, for the summer. She trusted her friend to provide a stable home while she found suitable work and accommodations.

Zofia Monikowska's husband had died ten years previous, leaving her a pharmacy in Częstochowa. A cultured, pleasant lady, she lived with her daughter and son-in-law, Ewa and Edmund Kotlinski, on their estate, which was about five kilometres from Częstochowa on the road to Mirów. The family always referred to the estate as Mirów, the Russian word for "peaceful place," and the name came to have special significance to Marysia.

Zofia's son, Jurek, attended university but spent summers at home. Ewa worked as a pharmacist in the family business. Edmund held degrees in agriculture and agronomy and managed the Kotlinski estate, which consisted of a large house, barns, tennis court, gardens, pastures, and many cows, horses, chickens, hens, and pigs. Zofia's family treated Marysia with great kindness and compassion, never once mentioning her father or his death, and warmly welcomed her into their family routines. She followed Edmund as he worked about the farm and fields, asking questions about the land and agricultural practices. Although the Kotlinskis employed servants, Marysia helped with the household and farm duties. She learned how to plant vegetables, raise chickens, feed the pigs, and assist with husbandry.

The family pursued knowledge and culture. Visitors and lively conversation filled the home. Friends dropped in and stayed for days. They sat together each evening and included thirteen-year-old Marysia in their discussions of politics, war, sciences, and philosophy. During her stay, Marysia read books, listened to classical music, and heard stories of the family's travels abroad. These new diversions challenged her mind, helping her move beyond thoughts of her loss. She imagined her father's family might have lived such a lifestyle in Russia.

At the end of the summer, Marysia moved into her mother's apartment in Częstochowa and enrolled in school. While the summer had contributed to her healing, she still had not regained her confident, outgoing nature. She returned to school reticent and intimidated by the new surroundings. The school's strict code of conduct went against her free-spirited nature. Uniforms were checked daily for neatness. The children did not play games in the courtyard but marched in a silent, orderly circle under the watchful eye of the headmistress. The headmistress knew Henryk Adler and may have heard rumours surrounding his death. On several occasions, she muttered caustic comments within earshot of the young girl who cherished her father's memory. Marysia began to dread going to school.

She attended classes six days a week. Sundays were for church. Anyone absent had to supply an excuse on Monday. Church bored Marysia, so most Saturdays after school, she hitched a ride to Mirów on the horse-drawn milk wagon. Back at the Kotlinski estate, she explored the hilly countryside. She learned to ride a bicycle and a horse. She picked strawberries and raspberries, fed the animals, harvested vegetables, swam, and played tennis. She was much happier at Mirów than in Częstochowa, as Maria was too busy working to pay her much attention. The milk wagon brought her back Monday morning.

Once, when her teacher asked for her excuse, Marysia explained she had been at Mirów all weekend. Her teacher commented wryly, "You are like a cat who always travels its own paths."

While living in Grodno, she had on occasion tended to hedgehogs, stray kittens, or mongrel dogs, and surrounded by animals at Mirów, her compassion for them grew. When she spotted a jackdaw flopping frantically on the ground, flypaper stuck to its wings, she wanted to help. Taking the bird back to the farm, she carefully removed the sticky paper. She dissolved the remaining clumps of glue using kerosene and trimmed the damaged feathers. She put the injured bird in a cage and cared for it until it could fly again.

When she was fourteen, Marysia travelled by train to visit her grandmother, who was vacationing in Oskau, not far from her home in Olmütz. Her Aunt Herta, wife of Maria's brother Leopold, and her three children were staying there as well and Maria thought Marysia would be a big help with the chores. Each morning, Herta took the children to the village, leaving Marysia to make the beds, do laundry, wash dishes, and polish shoes. She often criticized the girl's work, and one day her comments brought Marysia to tears. "She told my grandmother I was lazy, so just to show I wasn't lazy, I went to a nearby farm on my own and said, 'I know how to work on a farm. Would you give me a job?'"

The farm owners agreed to let the girl work for trade, and each day she came home with fresh bread, butter, and vegetables. "My grandmother was triumphant because I had done this. She talked to my uncle and said, 'You see, Herta accused her of being lazy, but look. That girl works hard down at that farm and is treated well there, not constantly reprimanded.' I was very pleased to have my grandmother stand up for me."

That fall, Maria enrolled her in a girl's boarding school in Rabka. Located in southern Poland, close to the border with Czechoslovakia, between two mountain ranges, the town specialized in offering recovery and relaxation for children with chronic ailments. The purpose was twofold. Maria hoped the iron in the town's hot springs would help bolster her daughter's health and the school would strengthen her language skills.

At the school, Marysia continued to show a spirit of service. She volunteered in the nurse's office and tidied up after class, putting books away, straightening

Marysia (second from the right in the second row) with Rabka schoolmates, circa 1937.

chairs, emptying wastebaskets, and watering the plants. She despised disorder and was known to natter at those who messed up her work. She consoled and cared for the younger girls, tending cuts and bruises or washing hair. Sometimes she lined up three or four youngsters at the wash basin. One day, as she wrapped a towel around one wet head, the little girl said, "You are so nice, just like a *Grossmutter*." The moniker stuck.

A natural performer, she leapt on desks to give impromptu speeches or hilarious impersonations of teachers. Once, after reading a story about Japanese geishas,

Marysia stripped to music, throwing her clothing around the classroom to the horrified delight of her classmates. Some screamed and ran from the room as, caught up in the moment, she giddily threw her underpants after them.

Marysia instigated persuasive tactics when a change in school policy resulted in an extra day of classes per week. The girls stole a skeleton from the health classroom and set it up in the principal's office. They dressed the skeleton in a school uniform, put a petition in its hand, rigged puppet strings from the hand and jawbone to their hiding place behind a door, and waited, giggling, for the principal to return to her office. The girls won their case.

Although she assumed a leadership role easily, it sometimes embarrassed her when her friends looked up to her. She sensed she was attracting people who wanted to learn from her. "There was a time when I tried to be like the others, not saying the things I wanted to say, acting more dumb because I was embarrassed to be thinking I might be special. But to be somebody else is difficult."

At every opportunity, Marysia escaped the confines of the school. The students' dormitory was locked at night, but she swung herself easily from a second-floor balcony to the ground. She hiked along mountain pathways, often returning with wildflowers and quietly placing them throughout the school.

"For me, there was a strong pull toward freedom. I always wanted to do what I wanted to do. I didn't want anyone dictating to me." Once, she had just clambered in the ground-floor window of the study hall, her shoes covered with snow, when a teacher opened the door to check on the girls.

She looked carefully at Marysia. "You weren't here earlier. Where were you?"

"I was here all along," lied Marysia.

"Hmm, why then are your shoes filled with snow?" the teacher asked.

The next summer, Marysia was back at Mirów. She was fifteen by then and Zofia's son, Jurek, home from university, often took her horseback riding and dancing, swimming and collecting mushrooms. One day, she overheard Zofia and Ewa discussing Marysia's suitability as a wife for Jurek. She had often thought Jurek was the kind of boy she would like to marry someday, but because of the age difference, she had not considered him romantically. Now she noticed his handsome features, reddish hair, and blue eyes. They were already the best of friends; she sensed they would eventually fall in love. She began to dream of attending a school for countrywomen, where she would learn to manage the farm while Jurek worked in the pharmacy. Back at school, thinking her future secured, she felt no need to join in her schoolmates' conversations about boys. In her mind, she was betrothed to Jurek.

She did not realize it at the time, but she possessed a natural, healthy beauty

Marysia (bottom left) and her classmates from Rabka,
circa 1937-39.

and a strong physical presence. Beneath her jovial prankster exterior, an undercurrent of sadness remained, hidden to all but those with the keenest perception. While she paid little attention to her appearance, never taking an interest in stylish clothes, curlers, or makeup like her peers, there were certainly others who did.

Wilfried Gerhardt was her homeroom teacher. Singularly handsome in a self-possessed sort of way, he had a thick blond mane, the dreamy eyes of an artist, the heart of a romantic, and the intense charisma of a maestro. He was a photographer, an artist, a composer, a musician, and, of course, in a school of adolescent girls, the target of many a romantic notion. When he walked down the hall, girls pantomimed violins playing and swayed romantically, rolling their eyes and swooning in his wake.

In the autumn of her second school year, Marysia was on one of her secret walks when she encountered her teacher sitting on the mountainside, canvas on easel, paintbrush in hand. Feeling euphoric from her hike and confident she would not be reprimanded, she approached him.

He looked up from his painting, apparently not surprised to see her. "You are going to be late for supper," he commented.

"I know," she tossed back with cocky assurance, "but I have a way of sneaking in."

"Oh? And how do you sneak in?" he inquired, still painting.

She looked over his shoulder and studied the strokes of his brush. "I crawl up to the balcony of my room or go to the window of the study room. The others will open the window and let me in."

He stopped painting and turned to face her. "Are you not afraid I will betray you?"

"No."

He laughed and said, "You are right! Now tell me, where do you go when you walk?"

"Anywhere. I just enjoy being outdoors."

"The next time you go, let me know and we will go together," he said.

They began a weekly ritual of secret signals and discreet meetings in designated places. Having her popular, handsome teacher walking with her in the mountains was like having her father with her again. During their walks, he introduced her to native vegetation as they searched for rare plants and orchids. They talked of important things and of nonsense; they collected flowers, observed animals, explored the countryside, skied in winter. Her naïveté, her age, the unexpressed grief she still carried, all made her deeply impressionable, and his perceptions of nature, worldly opinions, and philosophical oracles influenced her views of the world. He created pencil sketches and a sculpture of her and called her his *Hexlein*, which meant "Little Witch." She always called him Mr. Gerhardt.

It soon became evident to me that this was special. When we were in school I could feel he loved me and I was afraid of that. I shied away from this emotion. One time we were somewhere hiking and we ran down a hill. We were laughing and when we finally got to the bottom, he grabbed me, embraced me, and said, "I love you." I said, "Shhh. Never say this again." And he never did. I was not ready, nor was I able to return his love. I did love him, but not that way — there are various ways to love and they are all very different.

It was a confusing time for Marysia. There was still Jurek — the man she assumed she would someday marry. Mr. Gerhardt was already married and his wife, Johanna, was expecting a child. Johanna was the headmistress of the school, a well-liked and motherly woman, warm and encouraging to her young charges, and Marysia thought highly of her.

Marysia was naive about the adult world and in many ways remained a child seeking affection, guidance, and parental love. Even so, she intuitively clung to ingrained standards of behaviour. "I didn't have a mother to watch over me, so I had to do it myself. Other kids were doing things, but I could not because such things might dishonour the family. I am a descendant of a proud family and had to behave as they would expect."

While her teacher's attentions helped her see herself as someone who could accomplish great things, nature still provided the solace and security that sustained her during her most troubled times.

> Because I lost my father, I had to find something else to support me. Nature was my support. It was a reliable and strong influence in my life. But this has nothing to do with animals or birds; this is almost like a religion. It is something I believe in, something that is with me all the time.

Marysia, age sixteen, circa 1939.

Within the mountainous landscape surrounding Rabka, there were plenty of trails to explore. One autumn day, she took the train to Babia Góra Mountain.

She hiked through stands of mustard-coloured beech, maple, and sycamore and walked alongside clear streams, still free-flowing in spite of the lateness of season.

Marysia visiting an alpine sheep farm during a mountain
hike near Rabka, circa 1937-39.

As she gained elevation, the trail transitioned from old-growth forest dominated by stately fir and spruce some centuries old and more than forty metres in height to stunted stands of pine and spruce. Finally, she emerged above the treeline in a landscape of scree and low shrubs.

The distant Tatra Mountains sprawled to the horizon. The play of light and shadow turned the peaks and valleys into a velveteen cloak lying rumpled on the land. The beauty of the scene made her knees weak. Marysia sat abruptly on a boulder and dropped her eyes. Slowly, she raised them again in reverence, comprehending small slices at a time. She sat without moving, feeling she belonged to the landscape, as surely as the fragrant and pitted bark belonged to the spruce, the sponge of moss belonged at its roots, the splatters of yellow lichen belonged on the boulder upon which she sat. The lines of separation softened and blurred, and she knew in that moment that she was as much in this world as it was in her.

It was a moment both shattering in its immensity and frightening in its clarity. Her response was visceral. She felt something shift deep within her.

During the years Marysia spent at Rabka, she split her summer breaks between Girl Guide camp, Mirów, and short visits to her mother and other family members. While at camp, the girls lived in tents, used outdoor latrines, cooked their own meals, and crafted makeshift tools. They received instruction on survival skills and then were abandoned a distance from the camp to find their way back. Marysia had become fit and strong during her time in Mirów and Rabka, and the survival training taught her resilience and fortitude. She learned to analyze her situation and react accordingly.

In the summer of 1939, perhaps there was a reason behind the rigorous training of these young girls. Hitler was a powerful force in Germany. But many in Poland believed that, in spite of Hitler's threats, Germany would never dare to instigate a war against their allies, France and England. When talk turned to such things, Marysia felt a curious tingle of excitement and expectation. Should it happen, war would, no doubt, be a great adventure.

When Guide camp was over, Marysia travelled north to visit her Aunt Kazimiera and cousin Maja for the remaining three weeks of the summer vacation. Although

Marysia and a companion at Guide camp in the summer of 1938.

Kazimiera still lived in Chełmno, she was temporarily working out of her estranged husband's office in the larger city of Kutno.[9]

On the morning of September 1, 1939, they awoke to the sounds of planes overhead and explosions in the distance. Kazimiera quickly turned on the radio. Her worst fears were realized.

Hitler was invading Poland.

෴

CHAPTER THREE

Surviving

In me there was a very quick way of shutting everything out, except for my own little person. I wasn't worried about my mother, brother. Those things were all gone. You become like an animal that tries to survive. All you think about is survival and will you have enough to eat.

Outside, a wild wind has whipped the bay and bare trees into a frenzy, but inside, the warmth of the March sunlight serves to awaken drowsy flies from winter slumber. A dozen or so jostle and bump fruitlessly against the windows, their noisy activity mildly distracting.

Mary calls out to David to bring the vacuum. He immediately emerges from his office, a battery-operated mini-vac in hand, and with a whirl of air, all is quiet again.

"Now take it outside and let them go," directs Mary. "They'll be food for the birds."

She returns her attention to the envelopes on her lap. Mary has received a letter from a Rabka classmate. Although they are scattered over two continents, they have held regular reunions through the years. They still call her *Grossmutter*, she tells me. Even the Gerhardts attended some of the gatherings, and on occasion Mary was a guest in their home.

Mary says that just once, Johanna Gerhardt spoke about her husband's feelings for his young student. "She told me, 'This did not bother me. He is an artist and musician, a special soul. I believe he needs to have a muse in order to create. He simply chose you as his muse.'"

During one such visit, he sketched her, calling her his Indian from Canada. She still has the sketch.

David, his duty of relocating the flies complete, brings in a tray with dainty china teacups and slabs of homemade cake with fruit and dollops of sweet yogourt. As he hands over pretty cloth napkins, the conversation turns to war.

"It is hard to explain what it is like to live through war," Mary says. "War means something much deeper to me. It's not just the war. We were just pushed into the water — sink or swim. Put in front of reality, you have to keep living; you cannot sit terrified, you would get cold and hungry. There comes a moment of crisis and you have to handle it. Now we have grief counsellors and support teams whenever there is a crisis. But then we had nothing. Where would I have been without my own resources?"

☙

Hitler's blitzkrieg assault on Poland began on September 1, 1939, and within seventeen days, the city of Kutno had fallen to German occupation. On October 6, the final Polish army surrendered and the country was divided between Russia and Germany.[10]

> One day, the Germans just marched in. There was no resistance; the Polish military wasn't even there. A friend phoned up to say there were German soldiers in the marketplace. We went there to see, and sure enough, there were all these young chaps, smartly dressed up in nice uniforms, good-looking. There was a water pump in the middle of the marketplace and they were pumping and drinking the water and talking to the people in German. Now we had to face the occupation.

Any thoughts Marysia had of reaching her mother disappeared. She felt more confusion than fear. The enormity of war was beyond her adolescent grasp. She went with Kazimiera, a pediatrician, to the hospital to help out and run errands. Unsure of how to act or what to say, she followed her aunt's lead. Dressed in a gown and cotton gloves, she cleaned and sterilized utensils and prepared the operating rooms. Absorbed, she watched the surgeries as they were performed.

At the hospital, she heard rumours about the persecution of Jewish families, but as a Catholic Pole she was not directly affected. Then one day she accompanied

Kazimiera to an abandoned sugar refinery that, with its surrounding walls, fences, and barbed wire, had become a Jewish ghetto.

> The first time I saw the ghetto, I was shocked. I saw the Jews just packed in there. They sent for my aunt because there was a sick baby. Later on, they would just let them die, but in the beginning, they made some effort to help — perhaps fear of epidemics. There was a young mother with her first child and he was dying. My aunt said, "I am sorry, I have no medication, nothing I do will help." I remember leaving the ghetto and asking her what would happen to the baby. "He will die," she said. "But I think it is better for him anyway." It felt so awful, but she was right. What was the point in keeping the child alive to suffer until he could die another day? Those were terrible times.

In the meantime, Maria and Heniek fled Poland to live with Maria's mother in Czechoslovakia, which had already surrendered to German occupation. Maria had remained in Poland after her husband's death to collect her widow's pension and keep the children in Polish schools, but when the government collapsed, her pension disappeared. With no means of support, she and Heniek crossed the border with little more than a suitcase of clothing, treasured mementoes, jewellery, and photographs.

Once she reached her mother's home in Olmütz, Maria was able to scrounge enough money to buy Marysia's way across the border. In March 1940, she sent money and instructions through friends to Kutno. Secrecy was critical. Marysia would take the train to Kraków. She would travel light and wear dark clothing; it was important to be as inconspicuous as possible. Reaching Kraków, she would go to the address given her and receive instructions for the next leg of her journey.

While apprehensive, Marysia was confident in her abilities. She was, after all, a Girl Guide. Just that summer hadn't she navigated her way back to Guide camp in the dark? How hard could a train ride be? She arrived in Kraków and found the home of her contact, a man who had already smuggled a number of people across the border. He showed her to a small hidden closet, gave her some food, and told her to sleep; he would awaken her at midnight. Marysia managed to get a little rest in the uncomfortable, cramped quarters.

At midnight, he awakened her and they walked the unlit streets to the train station. As they walked, he gave her instructions that she would have to follow closely. She would travel in an empty passenger train used to transport troops from

Czechoslovakia to the front line. She was to find a bathroom near the back of the train and lock herself inside. If the smell became too offensive, she could sit in the hallway, but she must be vigilant and not let herself be seen. The train would leave the station at 2:00 a.m. Whenever it stopped en route, she was to be well hidden in the locked bathroom. He told her that once the train passed Cieszyn, the next stop would be in Czechoslovakia. She should exit the back of the train without being seen and look for a small park with a pathway. By the time she followed the pathway back to the station, it should be approaching daylight. She could then go to the ticket window and buy her ticket to Olmütz.

At the station, he exchanged her Polish money for Czech currency and wished her luck.

Marysia boarded the train and found a bathroom. The floor was filthy so she sat on the toilet. To take her mind off the danger, she thought about seeing her mother and playing with her brother again. She was afraid to sleep for fear of missing her stop.

The train had just wound through the low pass between mountains that marked the border of Poland and Czechoslovakia and was approaching the Cieszyn station when she heard footsteps and doors opening and closing. The footsteps paused outside the bathroom door. She held her breath as the latch jiggled, then the footsteps faded. She exhaled in relief but almost immediately heard voices in the corridor. She heard the latch again, then a key in the lock. The door swung open and a railway official dragged her to her feet.

The railway officials turned Marysia over to the military police, who strip-searched and interrogated her. Was she smuggling messages? Did she work for the underground? Was she a spy? Sobbing uncontrollably, Marysia kept repeating she wasn't a spy, she had no messages for anyone. She was just trying to reach her mother.

After several hours of interrogation without gaining additional information from the distraught girl, the police officer stated, "You are not going to your mother. You have broken the law trying to smuggle yourself through the border. You are to be sent to prison." They transported Marysia by train to a jailhouse in Pilzno, south of Prague. Two women, who brought food for the prisoners, felt sorry for the young weeping girl and agreed to deliver a message to her mother. Marysia wrote, "I am sorry, Mamusiu, I was arrested."

The women also advised Marysia to memorize a new birth year, as it was safer to be a fifteen-year-old girl than a seventeen-year-old young woman.[11] For greater anonymity, she changed her name as well. Adler was known to have Jewish connections. Her mother's maiden name, Chorinska, was a name of some prominence, so they decided she should drop the C and go by Horinska, an innocuous, unassuming name. She did not possess any identifying papers to contradict her story, and so Marysia Adler became Emilia Horinska.

After two days in the jail cell, Marysia and the other female prisoners were packed into a train and transported to a large distribution camp in Vienna. Each prisoner received a card with their name and a number. Each day, they gathered in a central courtyard to listen for their number. The prisoners' biggest fear was being sent to a German factory that might be targeted by Allied bombs. That fall, after about seven months in the barracks of this camp, Marysia heard her number called. She was told to be ready at four o'clock in the morning.

When the trains arrived, she and the others were herded into cattle cars. They barely had room to move about. Two buckets were provided — one with drinking water and one for urination. There was no food. Marysia listened to the conversations going on around her. Despite unfamiliar languages, she discerned apprehension. Some were praying, others swearing. The passengers were cramped and cold. Before long, the train slowed to a stop. Marysia could hear sirens blaring, people screaming, and sounds of frantic movement outside. Some of the men lifted her up so she could peer through the slats at the top.

It was an air raid. Prisoners began crying out and banging on the sides of the cars to be let out, but the guards had abandoned the train. They huddled together and prayed for safety. Eventually, the furor outside died down and the guards returned. The tracks nearby had been damaged in the bombing. The prisoners would remain on the train until the tracks could be repaired; however, they were briefly permitted outside to relieve themselves in a field, while armed guards watched.

The journey resumed for another day, stopping frequently. Some found room to squat on the floor, but most just leaned against each other. Now and then, as the train slowed while passing through a station, the men would lift Marysia up to peer through the cracks for the name. They travelled through Linz toward Salzburg. It was welcome news to discover they were headed into the Austrian Alps, far away from falling bombs.

Finally, the train stopped and the prisoners were unloaded and repacked into trucks. They bumped along the road for some time, before coming to a halt. Someone called out the name of Ebensee.

The village of Ebensee was situated at the end of the long and beautiful Traun Lake, about seventy-five kilometres southwest of Linz, Austria. Surrounded by snow-capped peaks, the area had been known for centuries as a centre for salt production. Following Austria's surrender to the Nazis, the salt factory was used as a forced labour camp for prisoners of war.[12]

Upon arrival, the prisoners were measured and their facial features and bone structure carefully assessed as the Nazis searched for Jews disguised as Gentiles. Marysia was told she had Denaric features, a region close to the Austria-Yugoslavia borders. Because of her medical experience, they put her to work in the small hospital with about twenty beds, originally built to serve the needs of the factory workers. Her work was not physically hard, although she could see that factory labourers were beaten, starved, and subjected to horrific living conditions. Marysia put thoughts of family out of her mind. She learned to ignore verbal and physical abuse inflicted by the guards, submitting but refusing to be demoralized. She was acutely aware that she was one of many in the same situation.

Marysia lived and worked with about a dozen others from different cultures — Russians, Hungarians, Ukrainians, and Poles. Magda was another Polish girl her own age, and sharing similar backgrounds and interests, they struck up a friendship that would last many years. In this new existence, people who had been stripped of their identity, possessions, and security clung to an emotional attachment to others. Some might fight over a scrap of bread, but more often they shared what little they had. They found entertainment in recollections of past pleasures, and lying on wooden bunks in the darkened barracks at night, they talked about favourite recipes as if life was normal. Whenever possible, they sat outside in the fresh air, picking lice from each other's hair and clothing. Beyond the barbed wire, they could see the lake, the mountains, cows grazing, and people scything hay in the fields.

Marysia and three others cared for the occasional patient deemed worthy of medical attention, but mostly they helped prepare meals in the hospital kitchen for the guards and camp staff. Two Nazis oversaw the entire operation and made decisions on the food distribution. One heaped verbal abuse on the prisoners, calling them dirty pigs, which, Marysia thought, was exactly what they were, considering the poor living conditions, lack of proper facilities for sanitation, and the constant grovelling for food.

The prisoners collected slugs, worms, mushrooms, and berries to supplement their meagre allowance of food and made alcohol, a valuable commodity, by fermenting mountain ash and elderberries in bottles set on windowsills. Occasionally, someone received a package from home and these things were bartered. Meals mainly consisted of potatoes and turnips and a special beverage brewed from chicory and roasted barley. The barley grains were shaken with a thick beet juice the consistency of corn syrup, and then baked in the oven until a deep mahogany colour. Once the roasting process was complete, the dried grains were ground with chicory and used as a coffee substitute.

One day, Marysia and others were sitting in the kitchen. This was the only place they were permitted to gather. The open windows released the rich aroma of the roasted chicory and barley. The smell of the coffee roasting brought back fond memories of family outings to a restaurant when her father would place a drop or two of real coffee on a sugar cube for Marysia to taste. Marysia was lost in reverie when two SS guards walked by the open window. One stuck his head through the opening to comment on the wonderful aroma. The cook asked if they wanted some and, to Marysia's astonishment, the two men came inside. Everyone dropped their eyes and fell into an uncomfortable silence while the guards stood and quietly drank the brew.

Several days later, as evening shadows lengthened, they were back again, quietly drinking their coffee with the prisoners, exchanging the odd smile or nod. Those around the table watched them warily, confused at the unaccustomed behaviour. A week later, obviously feeling more comfortable with the situation, they sat down at the table and struck up a conversation. One prisoner, a doctor, found the courage to ask how they became SS guards. Was it a special distinction for past service and loyalty or was it earned through actions? They replied that most SS were recruited from *Hitler Jugend* (Hitler Youth), with preference for those with a higher education. The doctor then asked if they enjoyed what they were doing. All around the table went silent. The men looked at each other for a long moment, and then one said, "Nein. We don't like killing."

Marysia felt her heart begin to pound. Everyone knew people in the camp were dying, but it was truth better left unspoken. In the pause that followed, no one knew what to say. Marysia wondered if they might suddenly realize the repercussion of their words and shoot those who had just heard them.

The two soldiers stood abruptly and one said, "If you think this is a pleasure for us, you are mistaken." He gestured to his companion, and they walked out.

A week later, the two guards returned, asking if the coffee was ready. They entered the room, filled their cups, and then the one who had previously remained silent spoke. "We came to tell you if you say anything about us coming here to drink coffee with you, or if you speak of what we told you before, this would be the end for us. We would be shot. So, our fate is up to you." They drank the remains of the coffee and left without another word. What remained was a very profound and unusual gift; to this small group of people, stripped of every sense of control in their lives, they imparted a modicum of power.

The series of encounters gave Marysia a new perspective to contemplate. She considered the possibility that many of the SS were simply regular young men, recruited from the Hitler Youth, which had brainwashed its membership at a very impressionable age. They were cultivated with hatred and fed the propaganda of Aryan superiority. By the time they were recruited into the SS, for many this had become the only truth they knew. Still, there remained some who harboured remnants of compassion. They, too, were victims of circumstance.

Marysia realized there were many sides to truth. "Afterwards, whenever I met any SS, I always thought of those two soldiers and wondered if they were really doing this because of their idealism or because they were forced."

These were difficult months for Marysia as she struggled to adapt to her new surroundings and life as a prisoner. Her health was deteriorating; she had become thin, weak, and listless. Her menstrual cycle had stopped altogether. Perhaps someone took pity on her because one late spring day in May 1941, she was ordered to pack her belongings and before day's end was put on a train.

As Marysia travelled to her unknown destination, she contemplated the past six months and wondered what lay ahead. From Ebensee, the train headed south through Bad Ischl, Golling, Bischofshofen, and Schwarzach. At each stop, she listened carefully as a guard called out prisoner numbers. Finally, the train pulled into the station at Texenbach, Austria, and Marysia heard her number called. She stepped off the train and into the next phase of her life.

With most young people drafted for the war effort, Austrian farms supplying the German army needed labourers to continue producing food and goods. Marysia was sent to work on a modest alpine sheep and cattle farm located in the mountains surrounding the small village of Wörth, near the larger village of Rauris. The farm, owned by Franz and Hilde Walner, was a typical chalet-style with balconies. The Walners were plain, decent people who had accumulated cows, goats, sheep, and a single mule. They welcomed Marysia's presence, as the two Walner boys were too young to help with the hard labour. Another young lad of thirteen lived with them as well.

The Walners lived the subsistence life of the *Hochbergbauer* (highland farmer), an insular world of self-sufficient village folk. They had neither electricity nor plumbing, and a single telephone line connected them with the village below. They needed little money, as most food was produced locally and the farmers bartered for goods. The only real change the occupation of Austria brought to their lives was that the German authorities now demanded portions of their meat, wool, and cheese rounds. Whether Germany or the Allies won any particular battle was irrelevant to the immediate attention required when a calf was born or the flour bin was empty.

And so, in the midst of war, Marysia found herself delivered into a safe and uncomplicated life with a warm place to sleep, food to eat, reasons for laughter, and a family for company. Each morning, she rose at 5:00 a.m. to milk the cows, separate milk, churn butter, or bake bread. She carried fifteen buckets of water from a stream to the chalet kitchen, where a large barrel fitted with a nozzle held water for household use. Then she went to work in the gardens and fields.

One day a week, she and Hilde did laundry. Grasping a woollen ball woven with the long strands of a cow's tail for abrasion, she dipped it in homemade liquid soap and scrubbed the clothes on a wooden table, then boiled them in a large pot. After rinsing the clothes in the stream, she spread them on the grass to dry. Saturdays, she washed the house from top to bottom, scrubbing floors and benches with spruce or fir boughs. She removed the windows from their hinges and scoured them clean with balls of stinging nettles that had been soaked in water to remove the sting.

The family ate primarily smoked meat or sausage, potatoes, vegetables, or eggs. Hilde taught Marysia how to cure and smoke the meat and make sausage and how to make regional specialities like *Kaiserschmarrn*, a fried batter made of flour, eggs, and milk eaten with sugar or melted cheese. On Sundays, friends and relatives came for a special meal and Franz played the accordion. The Walners treated her well, and in the rhythm and routine of her daily chores, her health improved. In time, she grew strong again.

After the sheep were sheared in the spring, they delivered wool to the village, then on to the carding mill up the valley. Three or four times a year, soldiers came to the village to collect farm produce, meat, and cheese. The announcement would be made through the church, and on the designated days, the farmers gathered in the village square to hand over their goods to the Nazis.

The beautiful surroundings and the uncomplicated lifestyle, however, did not shelter them fully from tragedies. One fall, Marysia and Hilde were working in the fields, cutting and collecting hay for the winter months. Hilde was nearing the end of her pregnancy. On this day, she felt tired and was worried that she may have overdone it lifting heavy bales of hay. Suddenly her water broke.

In her work at the Kutno hospital, Marysia had witnessed childbirth. She had helped with the birthing of calves, goats, and lambs at Mirów, and sometimes she sat up all night in the barn with Franz when there was an expectant animal, in case there were complications. She knew what to do. She removed her apron, spread it out on the ground under Hilde, and positioned her legs. Labour did not last long. The premature baby was a girl — tiny, frail, and silent.

As Hilde sobbed, Marysia comforted her. "Don't worry, you can have another." She bundled the lifeless child in the apron and ran back to the farm to get Franz. The typical *Hochbergbauer* handled the cycle of life and death swiftly and moved on. There was no time for the luxury of grief; the cows must be milked and the hay stored for winter.

Spring brought preparations to move the animals to the alpine pastures, a festive ritual for which Franz and Hilde dressed in traditional folk costume. Franz placed a flower wreath on the horns of the lead cow and Hilde sprinkled holy water on the animals as the procession passed. By now, Marysia was well versed in the routines of the farm. She led the goats, the old hired *sen*, or cowherder, led the cows, and the boy herded the pigs. Everyone marched down to the village, through the streets, and then up to a high mountain pasture. Franz followed with a wagon carrying bedding, cheese-making implements, and food. They unloaded the supplies into a mountain hut, then the Walners and the young lad returned home to the farm.

For months, the old *sen* and the young girl lived together in the primitive hut, caring for the animals, moving them from pasture to pasture, and making hard, yellow rounds of Emmenthal cheese. Each day, the cows were milked morning and night, the milk was made into cheese, and the flattened spheres were flipped so they would ripen consistently. There was a steady, comforting tenor to these days as Marysia arose with first light to quietly complete her tasks by rote, and then as the shadows lengthened across the valleys, she crawled back into her bunk for sleep. She also took care of the cooking. The old man was not good company and mumbled constantly to himself, so she took her simple meals of milk, potatoes, and cheese outside to sit and eat in solitude.

In her quiet times, she hiked and explored the terrain, or she sat and gazed across the mountain ridges. Nature was a living companion, and she began to explore the mountain, coming to understand it as one would get to know a new friend. Sometimes, she ran through the pastures until she collapsed, exhausted. Then she lay in the grass, allowing the mountain breezes to bring a melange of scent that marked the season's progression. Just as she had done as a child in Grodno, she occupied herself by trying to identify the different smells. She felt the ageless permanence of the rock and the temporality of the grasses and flowers.

Once, she awoke at night and, unable to sleep, ventured outside. The moon was brilliant and the illuminated mountains so ethereal and ghostly in the moonlight that she began to quiver. "I stood there shattered by the beauty of it."

Marysia had been on the farm for four years when, one day, the telephone dispatcher called. "The war is over. Look down into the village, you will see the English trucks." Franz hung up the phone and ran to the cupboard to bring out a telescope.

"It's true!" he shouted, peering through the lens. "I can see the English!" Everyone rushed to the balcony to stare down into the valley. When it was Marysia's turn to look through the telescope, she could see soldiers with funny, flat helmets covered with netting. They were gathered around the village well, pumping water and drinking from cups.

One evening shortly thereafter, Marysia was in the barn milking the cows when Franz entered with three American soldiers. They did not speak German, but one spoke broken Russian and Marysia understood some from her childhood. He began to question her, taking note of her answers on a small notepad. They were canvassing each farm in the vicinity in search of escaping German soldiers.

Franz, intimidated and anxious to please, invited them to the farmhouse for a drink. He had a favourite whisky — very strong and bitter — that he brewed from mountain ash. The men stayed in the kitchen drinking, the Americans talking among themselves while Franz nervously smiled in response when it seemed appropriate. In the adjoining milk kitchen, Marysia remained out of sight, occupying herself with work. Hilde brought in her supper and the two exchanged glances as the laughter became boisterous.

As she had to rise early, Marysia ate and went to bed. Outside, the soldier who spoke Russian cornered the young farmhand and communicated to him that he wished to know where the young woman went. The lad pointed to the window of Marysia's room and indicated that she was sleeping.

The sound of her window opening awoke Marysia. The drunken American crawled inside the room and fell on top of her in the bed, placing his hand over her mouth and whispering in Russian, "If you scream, I will shoot you." He waved his gun close to her face and began to fumble with her clothing. Marysia screamed. Suddenly the door opened, and other soldier stood there. Marysia saw her opportunity. With speed and agility, she wriggled from his grasp, rolled out of the bed, and ducked under the arm of the soldier at the door before either could react.

She flew down to the kitchen, where the third soldier remained drinking at the table, turned at the sight of him, and bolted into the larder. She heaved the window open, climbed over the sill, and tore barefoot through the night. The air was cold and wet, but none of this registered. Finally, exhausted and gasping for breath, she stopped outside a distant hay barn. Her legs and arms were suddenly heavy as the adrenalin rush subsided. Awareness returned and she realized her teeth were chattering. She looked to the barn for shelter and warmth, but it was empty of hay as the winter stores were depleted. She groped her way to the back wall and sank to the floor. There, she huddled in the darkness, trying to calm her heart and retain some of the body heat generated by her flight. Her ears strained above their own roaring for any sounds outside. As her breathing calmed, she began to sob. Rarely had she ever longed for her mother, but at that moment, she desperately wished for her as all the fear and loneliness and sadness she had held inside for so long poured out.

The distant sound of a dog howling penetrated her consciousness. She listened to its cry, realizing the dog did not appear to be moving. Thinking it might be caught in a trap or crevice, she emerged from her shelter and began a barefoot descent through the meadows and scattered trees, picking her way along in the dark. After a time, she felt the cold mud of freshly plowed fields on her feet and came to the howling dog tied to a stake. The field had been recently planted with potatoes and the owner must have secured the dog to discourage deer from digging the tubers. Untying the rope, Marysia wound it around her fist and let the dog lead.

Soon she spied a darkened farmhouse in the gloom. She banged on the wooden door. Upstairs, a window opened and a woman called out, "Who is there?" "It is Emilia Horinska. I work for Franz Walner up the mountain, and I need help. Some American soldiers tried to rape me."

The woman brought her inside and held Marysia at arm's-length to inspect her mud-caked nightie, feet, and legs. "Oh my dear," murmured the woman, brushing the damp hair back off Marysia's tear-stained face, "we need to get you washed and dressed in something warm." She led the shivering girl to the kitchen woodstove and poured hot water from a large pot into a basin. She then removed Marysia's nightgown, sponged her down, washed her hair and rubbed her dry, and gave her a clean gown. She wisely asked no questions. She then tucked her into her own bed and lay beside her for the rest of the night, her arms wrapped about Marysia's body.

> This incident left a mark on my life forever. From time to time it simply comes back like déjà vu. Sometimes I wake up thinking about it, so it is still alive in me. It didn't change my character in any way, but I empathize more with others. You see, it's not about being assaulted; it's about being violated. As a woman you have a fear in yourself, for this is your most precious thing. It was very traumatic.

Having protected herself from assault led Marysia to thoughts of Jurek and marriage. Her dreams of becoming a countrywoman resurfaced. She had earned a good reputation as a hard worker, and the Walners had encouraged her to remain with them. She had no desire to return to Poland, but could envision a happy life as a farmer's wife in the Austrian mountains.

Immediately after the war, Marysia had sent a message to her mother through the Red Cross to tell her where she was. She wrote again to say she was content to stay in Wörth. Maria replied with a brusque message: "I don't think your father would have wanted you to become an Austrian farmer's wife. You need to come down from there and finish your education."

"It never even crossed my mind that I could disobey. Once she wrote this, I had no choice. Franz and Hilde understood this, although they wanted me to stay. I cried so hard when I left."

It was a cold, wet day in October 1945 when Hilde Walner helped Marysia — now a young woman of twenty-two — pack her few possessions for the journey to the Texenbach train station. Openly crying, Hilde stood outside the farmhouse and waved as her husband and young charge disappeared down the mountainside path with the pack mules. They never saw each other again.

Having nowhere else to go, Marysia returned to Ebensee, hoping to find familiar faces or perhaps a school in operation. She registered as a DP and was again given work in the hospital, which was by then being run by the American Red Cross.[13]

Outside the hospital, she reconnected with her friend Magda. They sat on a bench in the sun and Magda told her about the horrors and brutality that had transpired in the camp in the years since Marysia left, and the mass confusion in the days after the Germans fled and before the Allies arrived.

In exchange for her assistance in the delivery room, Marysia received food, a bed, and American cigarettes as payment, which she bartered for necessities. In the months following liberation, the delivery room staff were kept busy delivering babies of rape victims. Some had been raped by German or Russian soldiers, others by British or American soldiers. Some women refused to see their children. These babies were placed immediately in an orphanage to await adoption. Her own experience left Marysia with deep feelings of empathy and compassion for these women.

"It was so tragic. It was good for someone to be there to hold on to them."

An elderly Polish priest, who came to christen the babies, asked her to be a godmother. Over time, he commented that she had become a godmother to more children than she could ever name or would ever see again.

"When are you going to bring me your own child?" he joked with her one night.

"I don't want to have a baby the way they are born to these unwed mothers," Marysia protested. "I have to be married first."

"Ahhh, child." He nodded. "You will do that. You will find a good man."

As Christmas 1945 approached, to combat the loneliness, Marysia and the others brought in a small fir tree from the forest and covered it with cotton balls and snowflakes cut from tissue. Seeing how it lifted the spirits of her counterparts, she fashioned wall decorations with evergreen boughs and searched for more suitable materials for decoration. On Christmas Eve, doctors and nurses carried a homemade crèche with figures of baby Jesus, Mary, and Joseph from one room to another, singing carols.

> We were all in a foreign land, far away from our loved ones. Christmas under those circumstances could have been a very depressing time for us. Instead, although all of us were in tears, it was a great moment of relief, of sadness turned to joy. A new life was born, a star to guide us out of the darkness.[14]

The following spring, she moved from the hospital into a refugee house. She shared a kitchen and bathroom with the other tenants and kept a single-burner hotplate in her room for cooking her meals. The United Nations Relief and Rehabilitation Administration (UNRRA) provided a package containing army surplus blankets, a mess kit, foodstuff, and clothing to each refugee, and Cooperative for American Remittances to Europe (CARE) sent a package containing luxuries such as dried fruit, powdered milk and egg yolks, canned hash, rice, cornmeal, and oats. She traded the clothing for milk and butter from local farmers. She had learned to make a little go a long way.

As Marysia and her mother corresponded, she learned about her mother's life during the war. Her brother, Heniek, spent the war years at boarding schools, while Maria stayed in her mother's villa in Olmütz, Czechoslovakia. Near the end of the war, when the Russians drove the Germans out, many people fled the area in fear. However, Fanny, by then eighty years of age and crippled with arthritis, was too frail to travel so the two women remained. The Russian army confiscated the villa to billet their soldiers and threw the women out, so they took a few precious belongings and went to live with their long-time cleaning lady in her basement apartment.

At the end of the war, they returned to Fanny's villa, but new regulations required that foreigners return to their own country. Maria was told she would have to go back to Poland, although her family was in Czechoslovakia and her mother needed care. She wrote to Arthur Seidl, who had been married to Maria's late sister, Frieda, and asked if he could help. Arthur, a notary living in Schärding, Austria, promptly offered to marry her, an arrangement that would allow Maria and her mother to go to Austria. However, before this could take place, there were a few complications to be overcome. Austria was divided into French, American, and Russian zones, with all movement between them requiring passes and permissions. Schärding, where Arthur lived, was in the American zone, while Olmütz was in Russian-occupied Czechoslovakia. To be closer to Schärding while she awaited approval for the marriage, the two women stayed with friends in Linz. The Danube River, running through its centre, split the city into Russian and American occupied areas.

Linz was about eighty kilometres north of Ebensee, so the proximity enabled Marysia and Maria to arrange a meeting on the banks of the Danube in the spring of 1946. Maria was on the Russian side; Marysia was on the American side. They could not cross the river, but at least they would be able to see each other. As Marysia approached the riverbank, she saw her mother with Heniek, three hundred metres away on the opposite shore, waving a white handkerchief and calling, "Mi! Mi! Mi!" Sobbing, Maria clung to her son for support.

Marysia was ill-prepared for the shock of seeing her mother and brother after all those years. To be so close, but to remain separated, was crushing. This was almost more painful than not seeing them at all. Later, alone again in her small room, she buried her face in her pillow for comfort.

> The arrest, the separation from my mother, the whole thing was becoming difficult to live with. There comes a time when your experiences, your thoughts and depressions gather together and become overwhelming. And mulling through these things, you become more aware of yourself and what has happened to you…who and what you are.

A month later, Marysia was finally reunited with her mother after seven years of separation. The meeting took place in Schärding, just before her mother's marriage to Arthur.[15] She was relieved to know her mother and grandmother were now cared for and safe. Her grandmother took her aside as soon as she arrived. "You can stay here for a little while, but we are guests here in this house and we don't want you to be a burden on the rest." Marysia assured her she would stay only for a short visit before returning to work.

Back in Ebensee, Marysia was making a life for herself. She even acquired a black Hungarian sheepdog. Mori and Marysia became inseparable. She let her dog mate and sold the puppies to Americans for extra income. She had friends, meaningful work, and eventually earned enough cigarettes to trade for a bicycle. But she still did not have family. When she learned that a school across the lake in the village of Gmunden offered classes, she travelled the forty-five minutes by train to attend twice a week. After school, to fill in time, she volunteered at a small Polish newspaper, writing copy, setting print, and doing other odd jobs, and then took the train back home again.

> I remember the train track was higher than some of the houses that we were passing. Coming back from work at night, I could look down and see families sitting at the table through the lighted windows. How deeply in my heart I envied them. They had a home, they had a table, they had each other. These were units of people together. Families. I was alone, not a unit. I was lonely and very young. I had friends, but friends don't take the place of family.

One rainy day in October, she sat in a waiting area at the train station. A colourful magazine caught her eye and she picked it up. *Auslese — Das Beste vom Readers Digest* was blazoned across the cover. She began to read.

> *Das Beste* talked about heroes big and small, achievements, adventures, and places far away. It made me realize I, too, could be part of this magical world, dream courageous dreams, do great deeds and have a positive impact on people's lives.[16]

At Christmas in 1947, Marysia decided to visit Irma, Arthur's spinster sister, who lived in Salzburg, Austria. Communication was slow and unreliable, so Marysia arrived unannounced. She stood on the street and rang the bell for Irma's apartment. There was no answer, so she tried a neighbour across the hallway. The neighbour looked out the window and, recognizing Marysia from previous visits, called down that Irma was spending Christmas with friends in the country. Since she was acquainted with Marysia, the neighbour threw down a key to the apartment.

For the next week, Marysia stayed in the apartment alone. Throughout the war, she had thought only of surviving the day ahead, but the full import of her experiences began to take hold. Solitude gave her time to contemplate her future. She knew she could not continue to work at the hospital. She knew she had more to offer but had no direction. Until this point, someone else had determined her path — nannies, parents, host families, teachers, even the Nazis. Now, for the first time, she felt solely responsible for her choices, and the weight of the realization disturbed her. She sank into melancholy, feeling lost and utterly alone.

One day, while sitting at the back of a Salzburg bus, she gazed idly out the rear window. Two women were running for the bus with suitcases, waving their arms for it to stop. Marysia watched them as the bus pulled away, watched them stop with their cases in the middle of the street, watched their shoulders sink in disappointment. She was too intimidated even to call out for the driver to stop. Later, she felt ashamed for her inaction.

Near the end of her week alone, she awoke one morning and, after wrestling with her thoughts, prayed, "God, if you are really there, if you really care about me, you have to let me know. Give me some sort of sign." She stared up at a simple poem, hung on the wall above her bed. The poem asked 'Why look at the world through sombre eyes when tomorrow the sun would shine again?' Sunshine seemed a long way off. Outside, it was a typical Salzburg winter day, where the rain fell steadily. Donning a coat, she walked through the streets of the ancient city. At St. Peter's Abbey, she entered to escape the rain. The sounds of her wet footsteps floated upward as she walked down the central aisle, moisture trickling down her neck. She slid into a pew and sat quietly, head bowed. She could smell the musty odour of her coat. After the noise of the rain and traffic in the streets, the stillness of the church rang in her ears.

Suddenly, she heard voices in the choir loft. They sounded disjointed and hollow as they echoed through the rafters and porticos. A moment later, she heard shuffled movement and the air resonated with young, clear voices in perfect harmony. They stopped, interrupted, and she heard a single voice — an instruction — then they began again. The music of their prayer floated into the sanctuary.

Marysia closed her eyes, face uplifted, and allowed the melody to wash over her. A tear trickled down her cheek and a tremendous pressure rose in her throat. She could not discern the words, but the crest and trough of the melody flowed around her. She hung her head and sobbed. It was a moment of release.

After a time, she composed herself and stood to leave. Walking to the back of the church, a cascade of young boys tumbled down the stairs, running past her. She recognized the Vienna Boys Choir. It was a rare gift to have heard them practise, and she felt as if it were a private concert, just for her. The experience shook her, but she saw it as an answer to her morning prayer. Back at Irma's apartment, she read the poem above her bed again, realizing that yes, there would be days of sunshine and happiness ahead, even though she was alone and discouraged just then.

It was the first time I sat in a church and felt I was truly with God. I thanked him for shaking me up. It was like a sign from him, and to this day, I pray and I feel, always, the presence of God but not in a structured way. I feel that everything I do is somehow directed. I have a distinct feeling that many things would not have happened

to me without the direction of a higher power. Sometimes it is good
to be alone and lost. It forces you to make a choice.

Back in Ebensee again after Christmas, Marysia decided she had to pursue
her education. She received a letter from her brother, who was continuing with
his schooling in Poland. "Jurek Monikowski wants you to come back to Poland,"
wrote Heniek. "And I think you should come back, too." Marysia held the letter in
her hand, rereading the words. Scenes from Mirów played through her mind — it
seemed like a lifetime ago. She thought about Jurek, who she once hoped would
be her husband. She felt some sort of attachment, a strong sense of loyalty, but she
didn't think it was love. He was more like a big brother — someone toward whom
she felt great affection and gratitude. She wrote back to Heniek, "No, I am on this
side of the Iron Curtain now. I will never come back to the communist side."

That summer, through friends, she made contact with a couple in Linz who had a
son attending the University of Innsbruck. She travelled by train to meet with them,
and they offered to put her in contact with their son, Sławek Wondołkowski.

In Linz, Marysia stayed overnight in a cloister, where she was given a bed and
a meal. During a conversation with one of the nuns, Marysia expressed gratitude
for the peace and serenity she found there. As they talked, the nun suggested
she consider becoming a novice, if she felt she had a calling from God. Such a
life sounded attractive and Marysia briefly considered how she might fit into the
structure of such a community where everything would be decided for her. She'd
certainly lived within rules and regulations at Rabka. She finally decided that if she
became a nun, considering her leadership qualities, she would probably end up as
a Mother Superior. Perhaps university would be a better choice.

She wrote to Sławek Wondołkowski, who arranged for her to come to Innsbruck
for a visit and to meet the other students in the fall of 1948. She was impressed
with the city and felt very much at home with the people she met. They were
orphans of war; very few had parents. She instantly made up her mind about what
she needed to do. Returning to Ebensee, she packed her belongings, tearfully gave
Mori to a friend, and then in October 1948 boarded another train, heading west
across Austria to Innsbruck.[17]

CHAPTER FOUR

Drifting

We had no future, only the past, and that was something cruel and dark and you did not want to go through it again. We were young people lost in this world. We had no homes, no parents, no one to offer guidance. Nobody. Our planning of our future or destiny was a great big question mark; you just took the opportunities that came your way and followed the wind.

Our interview has been interrupted by a phone call, and when Mary shows no sign of hanging up soon, I wander about the room while she chats. Classical music plays softly in the background.

Her heritage home displays an eclectic mix of treasures, old and new, collectibles from trips to Africa, New Zealand, Fiji, Norway, Alaska. Small dolls in European costume dance across a low shelf; detailed carvings of a meadowlark and a plover share the window ledge with Canada geese, a cyclamen, and an orchid. A deer head hangs on the wall, a gift from a friend who taught her to hunt. I run my fingers over a stuffed eider duck, its white feathers like ruffled silk. It was preserved by well-known Grand Manan naturalist and taxidermist Allan Moses. Everything has a story.

Duct tape covers the arm of a worn flowered sofa, temporarily hiding the frays where Kitty sharpened her claws. Antique straight-back woven chairs surround a long dining room table, the same table Mary covered with paper-thin pastry when she made apple strudel. Now she orders most of her baking from a trusted baker, travelling an hour to buy a dozen or so loaves of rye bread at a time. Instead of an hour clock, a tide clock hangs over the kitchen sink. Crowded bookshelves line three walls. I scan the titles: *A Naturalist in Canada* by Dan McCowan, *The*

Snow Walker by Farley Mowat, *Watchers at the Pond, The Natural World of Louise Dickinson Rich, Song of the Whale, Of Wolves and Men.* There are also history books, biographies, fiction, and classics. I spot three books on Eleanor Roosevelt alongside the memoirs of Field Marshal Montgomery. James Michener's *Poland* stands out for its weightiness.

I'm drawn to a wicker stand displaying a collection of Hummel figurines, painted eggs, and exotic china; alongside, a charcoal sketch of a woman on yellowed paper hangs in a plain wooden frame. Her thin, spare face and hollow eyes are haunting. When Mary is off the phone, I ask her about the sketch.

She tells me a student in Innsbruck gave it to her. "He sketched portraits and this one was a girl from a concentration camp. I liked it and asked if I could have it. We framed it and hung it up. Many people admired it, so I came to treasure it."

∽

Enrolling at the University of Innsbruck in October 1948, Marysia was happy to be given a room in the officer quarters. The officer quarters was one of four barracks arranged with a centre courtyard. Although the best of the four, her living accommodations were still austere. Cheaply constructed of thin plaster board and wooden beams, they appeared only slightly better than the bare wooden walls of the infantry barracks, where students were able to pass newspapers and cigarettes to each other through the gaps in the walls. There was little by way of insulation against the winter weather. Each room had a bed, a table, a wardrobe, and a small tin stove. But it was home. And she was making friends.

For the first month, the room next door to hers remained empty. She learned it was reserved for a male student who would be returning soon from the sanatorium. One afternoon, as she was studying in her room, the noise next door alerted her that her neighbour had returned. She tried to ignore it; however, the disruption continued until, frustrated and angry, she banged on the wall and shouted, "Would you please stop this noise? I need to study!" There was a moment of complete silence and suddenly a group of young men stood at her doorway, laughing and apologizing.

"We are so sorry. We have all gathered together to welcome back our colleague, Mietek." With this, they drew forward a handsome young man with thick, wavy blond hair and serious blue eyes. He was of average height, slightly taller than she, pale, thin, and angular. His smile was shy as he extended a hand in greeting.

Marysia stood up from her bed and shook his hand. "I hope you will not always be so noisy."

Very seriously, Mietek bowed his head toward her. "I assure you, I am a quiet

Marysia with a dog belonging to the student home, Innsbruck, 1949.
She is still using the name Emilia Horinska, as evidenced by the initials on her dress.

man," which brought a renewed burst of laughter from his companions, who hustled him back to his room.

A short time later, Marysia switched her courses from biology to medicine to take advantage of her past hospital experiences and to give her more options for future employment. Now sharing some of her classes with her next-door neighbour, she began to see more of Mietek Majka. As spring approached in Innsbruck, they began walking together along the river, slowly developing an easy and comfortable familiarity in the routine. They discovered a shared love of the outdoors and natural things. They attended class, came home, cooked supper, and ate together. Mietek loved dancing, so they dressed up and went to the dance hall on Saturdays. They skied, walked, and rode bicycles together, but separately also pursued individual interests and activities. Mietek enjoyed mountaineering, so while he was scaling mountains, Marysia embarked on multi-day hikes alone, staying in mountain huts overnight. On the heels of a war that rendered their future uncertain, they lived completely in the present moment. Theirs became a partnership of choice, of mutual respect, and of the affection that comes of shared interests and common values.

Almost reluctantly, Mietek shared his past through comments that she pieced together over time. She gathered his childhood had not been happy, and while he was close and protective of his mother, he did not have strong bonds with his father or siblings.

His parents, Anna (née Chmura) and Michał Majka, had joined the flood of European emigrants who travelled across the ocean in search of prosperity at the turn of the century. They met and married in Massachusetts, where they both worked in factories. They endured the harsh conditions and meagre pay, living frugally in the shabby rooming houses supplied to the immigrant workers. Eventually, they were able to move into a small home and start a family.

During these years Anna delivered a daughter, Wiktoria, and a son, Roman. The American dollars they saved were of great value in Poland, so after they accumulated a tidy sum, they returned to their native country and purchased a farm on the main road that led to Tarnów, in southern Poland. In 1917, they returned to the United States, leaving Anna's parents in charge of the farm and the two children.

In 1921, Anna, again pregnant, returned to Poland, leaving Michał behind to continue earning money. Mieczyslaw Majka, called Mietek, was born on December 20, 1921. A sombre young lad, Mietek had thick, wavy curls, blunt bangs, a heart-shaped face, and sweetheart eyes. He was four when his father returned to Poland in 1925, and the family opened a store on the farm with their savings. Rural folk,

Marysia with Mietek
outside the dormitories
at the University of Innsbruck.

who walked into the city to sell their wares, stopped at the store on the way back home to purchase their produce, groceries, and sundries. The store thrived, but required much work. The couple had little time for their youngest son.

Mietek hated the back-breaking labours required of a farm, so he harboured few pleasant memories of his childhood. He graduated from high school in July 1939, and in September the Germans occupied Poland. These were uneasy and dangerous times for young men. If stopped by the SS, he ran the risk of being shot or sent to a work camp, but if he had papers identifying him as a student, it was marginally safer, so he enrolled in a business trade college, which continued to operate in spite of the war.

Many of the students in the school were already involved in subversive activities against the Germans and Russians, so Mietek followed suit and joined the underground movement of Poland's *Armia Krajowa*, or Home Army. He supplied his parents with products he acquired on the black market, biking down backcountry roads after dark to deliver such goods as meat, eggs, and vodka to the farm. When the Russians invaded Poland at the end of the war, he was blacklisted for his involvement with the underground and had to go into hiding. Mietek joined a half-dozen colleagues as they smuggled themselves across the border to Allied-occupied Germany, where England was financing the formation of a Polish corps under the command of General Stanisław Maczek to force the Russians out of Poland. The college education he acquired during the war afforded him the rank of officer. They assumed the Americans and Russians would go head to head and start another war, but his unit never saw action. Instead, they sat around barracks, bored, waiting for something to happen. In 1947, members of the corps were offered an opportunity to attend a university. Mietek chose Innsbruck.

Mietek adapted to the life of a university student but rarely spoke of his activities in the underground or of his family. It was as though he began a new life at university. He had always been interested in the sciences, so he chose medicine. He enjoyed his studies, served as a secretary-treasurer of the Polish student's union, made friends quickly. However, in the summer of 1948, he developed pneumonia and was sent to a sanatorium to convalesce. He remained there until shortly after Marysia's arrival at Innsbruck in December.

The Innsbruck students became like family. Most of them had lost everything. Although their education and living expenses were offered free of charge, day-to-day needs were dependent upon aid organizations such as CARE, International Refugee Organization (IRO), and student organizations in other countries that periodically sent parcels of food and clothing. The Red Cross operated a soup kitchen for the students, and it was there that they ate many meals. CARE parcels contained the items they took for granted in the pre-war world: soap, toothpaste, toothbrushes, powdered milk, cocoa, coffee, tea. These luxuries they shared.

Marysia's resourcefulness grew, and she became quite adept at turning second-hand clothing into new. There was a treadle sewing machine in the barracks. While Mietek cranked the wheel, she sewed. She made shorts from blankets, unravelled the yarn from sweaters to knit new ones, remodelled dresses to fit, sewed the legs of trousers together to make skirts. Once, she even dissected a torn and bloody leather jacket, turned it inside out to hide the damage, and then stitched it back together again.

That spring, Marysia decided to start a garden in the unused centre field of the student barracks, so she wrote to CARE requesting seeds. They sent such a large quantity that she was able to strike a deal with a local greenhouse grower. In exchange for the seeds, he propagated enough seedlings for her garden, provided potato tubers and fertilizer, and plowed the field. While her colleagues complained about the garden chores she assigned, they all enjoyed a healthy harvest of lettuce, peas, squash, carrots, potatoes, beets, cucumbers, tomatoes, and cabbage that autumn.

They sold the excess vegetables to purchase three piglets from a farmer. The Innsbruck students raised the pigs in old sheds on the property, fed them on garden and kitchen refuse, and eagerly slaughtered them in fall, a clandestine operation, as the pigs were supposed to be registered and the meat submitted for evenly distributed rations. Marysia had learned her lessons well in Wörth. A former underground bomb shelter with an emergency shaft made a perfect smokehouse for sausages, bacon, and hams; the remote location of the barracks meant no one discovered their secret.

Despite the sense of community she appreciated at university, her years at Innsbruck were a transitional time for Marysia. She was like a tree dug from the soil, its roots severed. Her future was uncertain and so she just took each day as it came. Although she clung to her Polish identity by way of language, traditions, costumes, and memories, she had lost much of her emotional attachment to the land of her birth.

In the summer of 1949, Mietek received a letter from an uncle in Canada who had agreed to sponsor him should he choose to emigrate. He told Marysia that Canada was a good country, a young country filled with mountains and miles of forested wilderness. It would be much like Austria but better. He planned to leave as soon as he graduated. In fact, his diploma would come with a proviso firmly

Marysia with her mother, Maria,
and Mietek in Austria, 1949.

stamped on the back. There were no jobs in Austria after graduation. Austria agreed
to provide schooling to refugees, but the jobs were reserved for their own.

Many of their colleagues had already emigrated to the United States, and one
wrote letters describing life in the land of plenty. The students in their draughty,
sparse accommodations were incredulous to read of excess fruit and vegetables left
rotting on the ground, good clothing thrown in dumps to disintegrate, and large cars
clogging the highways while old ones lay discarded and stacked in junkyards.

Marysia was also considering her future. The war had left literally thousands of
children orphaned or abandoned as the result of unwanted pregnancies. The New
Zealand government would accept orphans from Germany and Austria, but only
if they had volunteers to care for the children until they reached their adoptive
families. The IRO sent representatives to several universities with a mission to
entice young women for this purpose. As incentive, they offered the women full
scholarships and accommodations in New Zealand.

After the IRO representative left and the girls came back to the barracks, the
young men gathered around, curious to hear what had transpired. Mietek took
Marysia aside and asked her what she planned to do. Marysia shrugged, still
undecided. Mietek continued to quiz her daily, asking if she had made a decision.
Finally, he told her what was on his mind.

"You should come with me to Canada," he said.

"Are you proposing?" she asked.

"Yes." Mietek told her he hoped she might consent to emigrate with him. They were young, healthy, and well educated, making them prime applicants. If they were married, this would give them an additional advantage over singles in the application process. It was hardly a romantic moment, but then again, marrying Mietek was not a decision Marysia made based on love.

> I wasn't thinking about marriage, so I was surprised he would be so adamant about it. He was just a guy I liked to go out with. I certainly did not mean to pin him down. I knew I would have to go somewhere, and Canada sounded as good as New Zealand. Our state of mind was different then, we didn't plan into the future. We lived like that for years, allowing things to evolve as they came along.

They wanted a quiet wedding, away from the university friends and their expectations of a good party. Marysia remembered the Polish priest from Ebensee and his predictions that she would find a good man to marry some day. She knew her priest-friend was now a chaplain at a convent in Linz. Marysia wrote to him asking if he could perform the ceremony. Of course, he wrote back, with delight. Mietek asked their good friend Sławek Wondołkowski to be his best man. They could stay at his parents' home in Linz during the wedding preparations.

In November, Mietek and Marysia packed a few clothes and acquired the necessary permits for travel from Innsbruck to Linz in order to meet with the priest. Sławek would follow later.

Her old friend welcomed them warmly. "Well then, let's get down to the happy business at hand," he said, settling into his chair and smiling at the young couple. "Now, when did you have your civil wedding?"

Mietek and Marysia looked first at each other, then at the priest. "Our civil wedding?" Marysia asked. "We just want to be married in a church."

The priest frowned. "I'm afraid I could be arrested if I married you in the church without the proper civil wedding first. I don't have the authority to perform the legal ceremony. You will have to go to City Hall and get the proper papers before I can perform the church wedding."

In addition to the legal paperwork, they also required American authorization because Linz was in the American zone. Marysia entered the offices of the American consulate and stood patiently at the desk. Half a dozen young well-dressed workers lounged around the office, laughing and joking with one another in a language Marysia did not understand. None of them did so much as acknowledge her presence. Marysia stood quietly, shifting from one foot to the other, self-conscious in her second-hand clothes. Eventually, one girl glanced over her shoulder and asked in broken German what Marysia wanted. Marysia started to explain why she was there, but the girl resumed her conversation and the group continued to ignore her, leaving her to wait an hour and a half before someone took her papers to be signed.

> I was nobody. That's just the way things were. I will never forget this humiliation. Altogether, the Americans treated us all like dirt. It is easy for me to understand why Europeans hated them after the war. The English and French at least treated us with some dignity.

Finally, they had the necessary papers in order. The civil wedding was set for Saturday, November 5, 1949.[18] Maria arrived from Schärding. With organ music playing in the background, a justice of the peace performed the quick ceremony in a large room at the Linz City Hall.

The next day — the day of their church wedding — Mietek surprised Marysia with a bouquet of red and white carnations, the colours of Poland. Mietek donned the same second-hand suit that he had worn to all his exams, and Marysia wore a brown worsted wool jacket and a skirt that she had modified from a pair of men's trousers. Walking down the street to the tram, she glanced at herself and other passersby in the glass of a storefront, noting that the only thing distinguishing her as a bride was the bouquet of flowers.

At the church, the priest slipped five shillings to Mietek and whispered, "Give this to the custodian after the ceremony." Mietek and Marysia looked at each other with surprise. Why would they require the services of a custodian? The priest just smiled and told them the organ music was their cue to enter the sanctuary.

When the music began and they walked down the aisle, they were astonished to see the sanctuary filled with people and flowers. Who were these people? They were so confused that the priest had to prod them with gentle directions throughout the mass.

During the ceremony, the priest spoke of Marysia's commitment to the young women during the months they had worked together at Ebensee. He recounted how she had held their hands and comforted them in their fear, how she had cared for the unwanted babies. When the service was over, two children came forward with bouquets of flowers. The priest whispered that they were two of her godchildren from Ebensee.

Later, when he joined them back at the Wondołkowski home, the details of the story emerged. Wanting the marriage ceremony to be special, he had announced to his congregation that he would be conducting a Roman mass — a formal ceremony with all the regalia of the Roman Catholic Church. He requested the parishioners gather flowers and then he contacted several young women from Ebensee to ask if their children could participate. He asked the nuns from his convent to sing and play music, bought small bouquets from his own pocket, and, in spite of the shortages, scrounged a box of food for the celebration. His kindnesses overwhelmed the newlyweds.

Back at the university, Marysia and Mietek settled into their two rooms as a married couple. Marysia turned their space into a home with hand-me-downs salvaged and traded. She covered wooden tables with fabric skirting to hide extra storage space beneath. Plants and bouquets of flowers adorned every surface, and curtains covered the wood-framed window. Their plain bed with its throw pillows doubled as a settee. A child's wooden straight-back chair provided seating for a guest. Rugs hung on the walls to insulate from the cold and hide the blemishes. They also had an aquarium of fish, one important concession to extravagance.

A year and a half later they had finished their studies. They had all their interviews, medical checks, and papers in order for emigration, and following the graduation ceremony on July 17, 1951, they packed their belongings in a wooden crate constructed from old tables and broken furniture, gave away the aquarium and other things they couldn't take, and bid farewell to their friends, promising to stay in touch.

They proudly boarded the section of the train marked Canada. Looking out the window at the Austrians standing on the station platform, Marysia imagined they must be very envious of her. Her excitement diminished as the train travelled through the devastated countryside of Germany. Six years had passed since the end of the war, but she saw charred forests and towns of rubble, bombed-out buildings, and lonely chimneys marking the spot where someone once lived.

In Bremen, there were several refugee camps operated by the International Relief Organization. Marysia and Mietek were assigned to Camp Lesum, where they stayed while awaiting transport to the port of Bremerhaven — the final stop before their journey to Canada. The very first experience, after entering the camp, was the humiliation of the disinfectant station, where everyone was sprayed with DDT.

> The men had to open the zipper on their pants, and it was sprayed in
> there and into their leggings. The women had to lift their skirts. You
> just did everything you were told to do. A woman was carrying a box
> and inside was a budgie. She was afraid to take the budgie through,

so I offered to take it in my blouse where it would stay hidden. The budgie started biting me, and all the while they are pumping DDT into me and I am trying to hold the budgie still. After we were sprayed, I gave her the bird back. Later on I saw her on the ship and she told me she opened the box and the budgie flew away.

American patriotism saturated the camp. They ate American food, listened to American music, and watched, morning and night, as the American flag was raised and lowered to the American anthem. Marysia and Mietek couldn't believe the amount of food provided. With each passing day, their excitement grew.

On August 14, 1951, the day of their departure, the clouds gathered offshore. Marysia and Mietek carried one small battered suitcase each containing the clothing and personal effects they would need for the voyage. The rest of their possessions were stored in the wooden box. Earlier that week at the IRO camp in Bremen, Germany, they had learned they would be travelling aboard the Swedish vessel, *Anna Salén*. But following the short train ride that transported them to the coastal port of Bremerhaven, they were held back as the other passengers boarded the ship.

Hastily reassigned to the USNS *General R.M. Blatchford*, which was sailing direct to Halifax to drop off passengers before continuing to New York, they were the last to board. The *Anna Salén* was already out in the harbour. Their own ship's engines rumbled, and the water frothed up around giant propellers as they slowly began to turn. Mietek fumbled with his new Kodak camera to take one last picture. He had spent the last of his Deutschmarks on the Kodak. While waiting, Marysia looked up through the shadow of the ship. The *General R.M. Blatchford* was almost new. An American C4 troopship built in 1944 and decommissioned at the end of the war, it was brought back into service for the postwar transport of emigrants to North American ports.

Without a backward glance, Marysia strode firmly forward up the metal ramp. It was time to move on.

∽

CHAPTER FIVE

Transitions

Before coming to Canada, I dreamed that I would be useful to some people; that I would be liked by some other people; that I could do something for them, and in return they would like me. And I wanted to be in nature; in the country, not the city. These were my dreams.

Spring is a vibrant time at the edge of the Bay of Fundy. I stop to watch a pair of eagles that appear to be playing on the currents of air. As I drive through wide greening meadows and marshes, Savannah sparrows flit across the road ahead of me. I notice Mary has posted a hand-lettered sign at roadside:

CAUTION! Birds on the Road. Baby Geese.

I slow down and peer into the fresh, new growth creeping up last year's cattail stalks. No sign of young goslings, so I continue on.

"Come in, come in," Mary sings out when I knock. The sun is shining, and as usual she is already in her armchair on the Bridge. The windows are open and the cool June breezes off the bay bring the chits and mutterings of a flock of songbirds gathering in the budding bushes and trees.

"I'm reading Harry Potter," she tells me. "I want to know what all the fuss is about. I think it will be a great impact on the next generation. It has influenced teenagers in a profound way, just like Nancy Drew did to your generation. This is an age when you get very easily influenced for your entire life. You make friends who last forever, make decisions on how you are going to live." She sets the book aside. "The next generation is going to be very much a Harry Potter generation."

I think for a few moments about transitions and change. About an eighty-year-old lady reading Harry Potter, with its underlying themes of tolerance. I wonder how a tolerant generation with a belief in the power of possibility might change a society. How that, in turn, might change a future.

Although it was Europe's very battle with intolerance that had opened up a future filled with possibility in Canada, leaving family and cultural familiarity must have been difficult.

She waves off the suggestion. "For me, to leave my mother and grandmother was not a tragedy or something I suffered from. You must realize we had been apart so much, and I had to rely on myself. What I suffered from was that I missed the way of life...the surroundings, the mountains. It was hard living here at first."

∽

When she and Mietek had first boarded the ship, Marysia wondered how she would survive the voyage. Two fellow passengers had taken them immediately below deck. They were disconcerted to discover they would have separate quarters: men to the right, women to the left. Marysia and her companion descended to the lowest level of the ship, stopping at a rounded metal door near the engine rooms.

Inside, the large room was hot and humid and filled with women of all ages and nationalities. They had shed their clothing and were standing about in white brassieres and underwear. Marysia thought they looked like floating angels. The only unclaimed bunk had a speaker and a red EXIT sign overhead. As the ship moved out of the shelter of the port and into the sway of open water, women began to get seasick. Many never reached the toilets, so threw up in the basins. They ran water but soon the drains were clogged and the water overflowed to the floor.

> The water was sloshing back and forth, so if you wanted to use the bathroom, you had to wait until the water sloshed to starboard, then quickly run and jump onto the toilet and then sit there and crouch. I remember the smell. Later on the fans started to work and move the air a little better, but it was still hot. I laid down on my berth and fell asleep, but I was wakened several times during the night when the crew communicated through the loudspeakers...they spoke in English, so I couldn't understand anything.

The passengers were to work for their meal rations, but many were too seasick to care about eating. Marysia, anxious to escape the cramped, reeking women's quarters, marched up to the employment office and told the clerk that she was a recently graduated medical student. The clerk assigned her nursing duties in the ship's hospital in the midsection of the ship, a position that afforded her an unexpected advantage. She was given one of the two bunks in a room with a private bathroom. With great joy, she collected her personal belongings from the quarters below deck and settled into her new room. She asked the others if Dr. Majka had registered for work. No one had heard of him.

She later found Mietek outside on an upper deck, sweeping up paint chips another worker had scraped from the vessel. Marysia was astounded that he hadn't told the ship's crew he was a doctor. Mietek assured her that he was content to be working outside in the sun and sea air. Several days later, however, he took his sunburned, peeling face and the long cardboard tube containing his parchment graduation certificate to the employment office and was reassigned to hospital duties. By then, the hospital accommodations were all taken, so he had to remain below decks in his berth. It really wasn't so bad, he said, except on Sunday when everyone prepared for chapel. The smell of shoe polish and old socks hanging to dry was so strong that he could hang an axe on it.

During their off hours, Marysia and Mietek sat outside in the sun and talked about their future. For the first time, Marysia allowed herself to imagine a new life. She pictured mountains, trees, brooks, rivers, and lakes. She saw herself living simply, raising a family, sharing her love of the outdoors with others. She already knew that she did not want to continue her medical training; she had seen too much of sickness and death. It had been so long since she had a real home, she just wanted to be settled.

After only a few days at sea, a storm struck. The *General R.M. Blatchford* forged ahead, but the *Anna Salén*, which had been accompanying them en route, turned back. Marysia watched the ship they might have been on head back toward Europe.

On August 22, 1951, after eight days at sea, Marysia spotted a gull, signalling their journey was nearly over. Shortly, an announcement over the loudspeaker brought crowds of passengers to the rails on the deck. Marysia never forgot her first view of Canada.

When we first saw land, when we heard the buoys — clang, clang — then briefly, we could see the shore faintly through the fog...it was tantalizing. Then the rain started and we couldn't see anything.

When it cleared again, we could see the green grass of Nova Scotia. Oh, it was so wonderful after all those days at sea. We were finally here. This was the end of our travels; we had come to a safe haven. We were very moved.

Disappointments followed. The *General R.M. Blatchford* remained anchored in the harbour while another ship unloaded its cargo. The passengers destined for Canada waited, huddled in groups with their possessions, the delay slowly draining the excitement from the experience. Eventually, the ship sidled up to the dock and the passengers disembarked, entering Canada through the gateway at Pier 21.

It was a very sad welcome. When you come to a strange land like we did, you have great expectations and they were immediately dashed because everything was dingy and dirty, full of garbage. The officials, who were pushing us through like cattle, seemed sick and tired of all this humanity passing through. We were handled impersonally. I've read in books about Pier 21 that they were offering toys to children, housing the sick in hospitals, but I did not see anyone being taken care of. As a Canadian now, looking back after all these years, I feel embarrassed that it was like that.

Once their immigration papers were in order, the new arrivals were led to the trains that would take them to their final destinations. These postwar trains were in wretched repair. Windows were painted shut, the cars stifling in the August heat. Tired immigrants crowded together on hard wooden benches with no place to lie down. Marysia and Mietek chose seats opposite each other so they could put their feet up. They stared out the windows at the passing landscape, comparing the size of North American cars and the plain, straight streets and uniform homes with the small vehicles and the cultural diversity and aesthetic beauty of European cities. They were mildly disappointed that the scenery was not as spectacular as they had expected.

At station stops along the two-day journey, Canadians boarded the train to sell milk and bread, sometimes asking as much as one dollar for a loaf of bread or a quart of milk. Mietek's uncle, who had sponsored them, had sent a few Canadian bills, but this was the only money they had. They grudgingly handed over their precious few dollars for food. Marysia and Mietek had never seen milk in paper cartons before and they admired the white softness of the bread.

With a few hours to spare in Toronto, before continuing to Hamilton, Mietek and

Marysia walked the city streets. Marysia, embarrassed about her dirty blouse, asked Mietek if she could buy a new one. She wanted to make a good first impression when they met his aunt and uncle. She wandered through a department store, fingering the textures of the clothing, amazed at the quantity and variety of goods. She selected a blue blouse trimmed with lace, which she purchased for three dollars.

They reboarded the train for the short haul to Hamilton. Mietek's uncle, Walter Majka, his wife, Sophie, and their son, Stephen, were waiting at the station. Walter and Sophie did not move, but Stephen came forward eagerly, embracing Marysia and Mietek, welcoming them in Polish. He picked up their suitcases and together the three made their way toward Walter and Sophie. As they drove to the Majka residence, Marysia wondered about the tension she sensed right away. It was a strange and uncomfortable beginning.

After being shown their room in the two-storey red brick house, Marysia and Mietek begged for a few hours to catch up on their sleep. They washed and climbed into bed, thankful for a soft place to lie, but the stifling August heat kept them tossing and turning. When they rose, Marysia was anxious to go for a walk to explore their new surroundings. They dressed in their nicest clothes for the stroll, as was the custom in Europe, and headed in the direction of Lake Ontario. They could see its blue water sparkling in the distance, but reaching the water's edge they saw only dirty wharfs, piles of refuse, and huge factories pumping out debris and smoke — a stark contrast to the waterside promenades of Europe. Their visions of the Canadian wilderness were dissipating quickly.

Walter and Sophie lived a quiet, uncomplicated life among their own tight-knit Polish community and earned extra money by renting the rooms they didn't use, the same rooms now occupied by Marysia and Mietek. Marysia found the atmosphere within the home oppressive. Walter treated her disrespectfully and often complained to Mietek about her. Sophie was subservient and unobtrusive. Stephen made a life for himself outside, achieving some local success on the football field, so he was rarely home. Marysia eventually discovered the reason for Walter's moodiness. When he had agreed to sponsor his nephew's emigration, he had harboured hopes that Mietek might arrive and marry a Polish doctor's daughter he knew, a union that would elevate the family's status in the community.

Although both Mietek and Marysia had acquired intern positions at what was then St. Joseph's Hospital, Mietek seemed to be fitting in better than she was. In 1951, the average annual salary of a single person in Canada was eighty-five hundred dollars,[19] but as interns, each received only one hundred dollars a month. This was barely subsistence, so Marysia thought she should find employment that paid better. They hoped to quickly become self-sufficient and move out of the

Majka household. This plan had one major flaw; there was little work available for a woman who did not yet speak English.

One afternoon, just after Thanksgiving, Marysia walked into a pet store to look at the tropical fish and found a very beautiful handmade tank, its plate-glass panels joined by scrollwork pewter. She admired it, thinking how much Mietek would also like it; however, the price tag of thirty-seven dollars placed it far beyond her reach.

As the days passed, she came up with a plan. She spoke to the owner of the store. "I don't have money to buy this right now, but I could pay you every week five dollars," she propositioned with her few English words. The owner agreed and she gave him seven dollars as a down payment. Each week, Mietek brought home his salary and Marysia sometimes went without food so she could tuck the five dollars aside.

Just before Christmas she made the final payment, proudly bringing home her husband's gift and several fish to inhabit it. Their first Christmas in Canada held this significant connection to their life in Innsbruck and served as a reminder that there would always be room for a small bit of luxury and pleasure.

The spring of 1952, Mietek heard that a plastic surgeon at the hospital, Dr. Wallace McNichol, was looking for a cook for his household. He arranged an interview for Marysia at the McNichol home, a stately red brick mansion surrounded by acres of beautifully landscaped grounds with rose and water gardens, orchards, and pathways. A uniformed servant greeted them when they rang the bell and showed them to the library, where the doctor was waiting for them. After a brief chat, Dr. McNichol offered her the job. He would pay her seventy-five dollars a month, plus room and board. To Marysia's shock, he told her Mietek could visit her on her days off. After some discussion in which Mietek explained they would not live apart, the doctor reluctantly conceded that both could move in.

Marysia in the kitchen at the McNichol residence,
Hamilton, Ontario, 1952.

Mary on the shore of Lake Ontario, while at the McNichols'
summer residence, circa 1952-53.

In a short period of time, she had gone from poverty salary to a job doing something she enjoyed, with wonderful accommodations and the privileges that accompany wealth. During this time Marysia became known as Mary, although Mietek continued to call her Marysia. She wore a uniform while working, but with her first paycheque, she splurged and bought herself a couple of new dresses and a purse. On each payday, she set aside money for nylons. These she carefully placed in an envelope and mailed to her brother in Poland. The money he earned from selling this valuable commodity allowed him to pay for his studies. Any money she had left over after their personal expenses she spent on postage to send used clothing to her friends and family back home.

During the summer, the McNichol family moved to their summer estate in Burlington, overlooking Lake Ontario. The servants travelled with them and shared a small cottage on the property. It was a beautiful location, and every day Mary swam from the dock. Remembering her own childhood joys of water, she was surprised that the children seemed more interested in the new television and their playhouse than swimming in the lake.

As long as meals were delivered with perfection and on time, the McNichols made few other demands on Mary. The McNichols had four girls under the age of twelve and a baby boy. She often took the children for walks and helped the oldest with her math assignments (the numbers were the same in English or Polish), which also helped her to become more fluent. To further improve her English, Mary listened to the radio and read *Reader's Digest* magazines, looking up each word in a dictionary. Her employer gave her a copy of the *Joy of Cooking*. As the new language became clearer, she tried to guess what the sentences meant, then consulted her dictionary to see if she was right. She was learning much about the Canadian lifestyle.

For his own part, Mietek was also learning the language. His colleagues, unable to pronounce his name, simply called him "Mike." He ticked off the words he had learned in his dictionary and had plenty of opportunity to practise them at work. He was single-minded in achieving his goal and studied endlessly each evening.

As they worked to adapt to the culture, Mike's future became clearly mapped out: once he completed his internship, he would continue with a year of residency, followed by his exams. They both knew it was just a matter of time before he was licensed to practise on his own. Mary was less content. She disliked Hamilton. This new environment was such a contrast to the spacious freedom of Austria that Mary found herself battling unaccustomed homesickness and depression. Hoping for some kind of peace, she walked often, seeking open spaces. Sometimes she looked to the clouds on the horizon and imagined they were the mountains of Austria.

That Christmas, she made a photo album as a gift for Mike. On the opening page, she pasted a photo of a night scene taken in Innsbruck, showing ice-crusted trees with a softly lit church in the background. The inscription read, "To my husband — my friend and companion of my good and bad hours, with gratefulness for his understanding and good loving heart."

Although life was pleasant at the McNichols', Mary didn't want to be a cook all her life. The time she spent with the children made her anxious to start her own family. Whenever she spoke of these things, Mike told her she must wait. His only thoughts were on building his career and supporting his wife with a decent salary.

Even then, Mary was not one to bide her time; as she recalls, "From the beginning we were partners in the same situation. There was no boss. We were equals. We discussed and decided things together. But this time I decided myself."

When she told him she was pregnant, Mike accepted the new situation. However, her employers were annoyed. They told Mary she would have to leave. She hadn't counted on this when she chose to get pregnant. On her final day of work in January 1954, Mary was instructed to be out of the house by 3:00 p.m. She had to sit outside on the step to wait until Mike picked her up after work. No one even came out to say goodbye.

Forced to return to Walter and Sophie's home, Mary continued to feel the strain. Their first child, Christopher George, entered the world on February 10, 1954, a whopping ten pounds, eleven ounces. Mary delivered naturally; her labour was long and hard. The baby suffered a collapsed lung, and it was twenty-four hours before she held her first child. She gave him the Anglicized name George in memory of Jurek Monikowski.

Throughout the lengthy labour, Mike had hidden away in a separate room, chain-smoking. Nothing in his medical training had prepared him to deal with his wife in pain. Whether it was an overdose of nicotine or a desire not to harm the child that prompted the decision, when Mike went in to see his wife following the delivery, he announced he had a present for her. He was quitting smoking.

Walter was ungracious about the new arrival. He did not want the baby buggy cluttering the hallway, so Mary left it on the veranda. Whenever she wanted to go for a stroll, she lugged it upstairs to warm it first. He complained about the cost for heating and limited their baths to one per week. One day, upset with a particularly high bill, Walter blocked the heat from the upper floors. After several days of bitter cold, Mary sat Mike down and said they had to find somewhere else to live for the baby's sake.

Mike summoned his nerve and successfully asked for a raise. Another fifty dollars a month enabled them to rent a very modest apartment in the attic of a single-family home. Even after they moved out, Mary continued to hold a deep resentment against Walter. His puzzling rejection and appalling treatment of her were among the most difficult things she ever had to reconcile. It would be years before she would find it in her heart to forgive him.

For the next year, they lived in two rooms and a small half-bath containing a toilet and a tiny sink. An old unpainted chest of drawers with a two-burner electric hotplate allowed the bathroom to double as a kitchen. They washed dishes in the bathroom sink and at meal times converted the sink to a table with a plywood sheet. One sat on the toilet to eat, the other on a rickety wooden chair. Their bedroom, furnished with one bed, a low coffee table, and an easy chair, doubled as a living room. The second room held Chris's crib and the old wooden trunk they had made in Innsbruck, which they used as a changing table. A small icebox was on the stairwell landing for their use. In the cramped quarters, Mary kept meticulous records of her baby's development, using notes and symbols to record everything about nursing, bowel movements, growth, fluid and food intake, changes in behaviour.

While her infant thrived, her own health suffered. Mike's meals were supplied at the hospital, and although he brought home sandwiches or muffins for Mary, she often went hungry.

We lived about a year in this apartment. I was happy and satisfied, except my health was poor because I was nursing and did not have the proper nutrition. I could see I was going downhill physically, but otherwise I was happy because I had the baby and the baby was everything. I went for many walks with him and watched him develop. This was always a tremendous pleasure for me. He was just starting to walk at twelve months, and one night my husband came home with great news. "Because I am now a resident, I will get a salary of $350." If someone had given us a million dollars, I could not have been happier.

Mary with her first son, Christopher, Hamilton, Ontario, summer of 1954.

The raise meant a one-bedroom apartment with a real living room, a proper kitchen, and a separate bathroom with a tub. But for Mary, the best part was that the building, located at the edge of the Niagara Escarpment on what was called "the Brow," afforded a panoramic view of the city and Lake Ontario. A park was nearby and a walking path followed the crest of the hill for several kilometres. During the summer, she pushed Chris in his stroller to a nearby park every day. Spreading out a blanket, she sat and knitted baby things and dreamed of another child.

She often met the same elderly couple walking through the park. They always exchanged pleasantries about the weather and the baby's progress. One day, as they chatted, another couple joined them and the elderly lady quickly introduced Mary, adding, "This lady is a foreigner — a DP — but still, she is very nice and speaks good English. And look at the baby and how clean he is."

Mary walked away feeling hurt and confused. When they arrived in Canada, they were proud to tell people that they were DPs. They quickly learned that this carried negative connotations. She had grown accustomed to the barriers and reactions of others when she was trying to learn English but hoped that, eventually, she would fit in.

In March 1955, Maria wrote to tell her that her second husband had died. By then, her mother, Fanny, had also passed away, and Heniek was married and living in Poland. Mary suggested she come live with them in Canada. After a time, Maria accepted her daughter's invitation. To accommodate another adult, the Majkas quickly found a new apartment on the outskirts of the city.

In 1957, Maria arrived and stayed with them for a year, but it was difficult for everyone. She was set in her ways. Mary, for her own part, had grown into a very resourceful and determined individual. Two strong female personalities in a confined space were bound to create tension. Maria, who felt guilty because of the financial burden she was placing on her daughter, decided she would return to Austria. She and her brother, Leopold, moved into a seniors' manor run by the Catholic Church.

When Mike finished his residency, a colleague encouraged him to join him in a private practice. Mike was torn between earning a good income and continuing his studies to specialize in pathology. If he chose general practice, all their financial worries would be behind them. If he chose pathology, it would be another four years of study. He and Mary discussed the options at great length and in the end, she told him, "We have already struggled through many years without money. We can certainly wait another four in order for you to become what you really want to be. We will get by. As long as we have a roof over our heads and something to eat, the important thing is for you to be who you want to be."

Mary desperately wanted another baby, but each time she brought up the subject, Mike opposed it adamantly. He still wanted to wait until they were financially secure. Once again, Mary made her own decision and soon she was pregnant. That spring, Mike accepted an offer to study pathology at what was then called the Westminster Hospital in London, Ontario. Mary was looking forward to moving out of Hamilton.

In May 1958, just before their second child was born, Mary and Mike Majka received their Canadian citizenship. They stood with others in front of a judge who questioned each one of them, asking if they had ever been in trouble. When he came to Mary, she patted her very large, protruding belly and smiled, "Your Honour, I'm in trouble right now!"

A week and a half before her due date, they were picking wild strawberries in a large field. Mike and Chris were a distance away when Mary felt her water break. She gestured wildly that they should come back in a hurry. "Yes, yes!" Mike called out, seeing her waving her arms but unable to hear what she was shouting. "We have lovely big ones down here too!"

The next morning, June 24, 1958, Marc Stephen pushed his way into the world, another very difficult delivery. Like his brother, Marc was a large baby and filled his infant bassinet with little room to spare. Mary and Marc stayed in the hospital for the next ten days, while Mike and Chris moved their things to London. The residence house had two stories and a veranda. To celebrate the move and increased salary, Mike bought his wife a washer and dryer and bought himself a 1959 Nash Rambler station wagon.

Despite their desire to fully integrate into Canadian culture, preserving their cultural identity was paramount. The Majkas spoke Polish at home and proudly adhered to their Polish customs. They had made a number of close friends in the Polish community, but social relationships with Canadians remained elusive. Once settled in London, Marysia hoped she would feel more welcome. Mike, accepted in the hospital as a professional pathologist, had daily contact and interaction with his peers. At home, Chris played with neighbourhood children, but in spite of her efforts, Mary regularly felt the sting of rejection from her neighbours. She often complimented one neighbour on his rose garden. But, as many times as they spoke, his wife never joined in the conversation. One day, a bee stung Chris and the gentleman rushed over with an antiseptic spray that took away the sting. When Mary saw his wife next, she commented on her husband's helpfulness.

The woman shrugged, "Oh, he is always very friendly and will talk to anyone. Even the black porters on the train."

On another occasion, Mary had crafted a Christmas decoration for the front of the house and a different neighbour commented on her talents. Mary decided to make another as a gift. She took it over and gave it to his wife, then invited her to come for a visit. The woman looked momentarily taken aback and quickly made up an excuse. It was obvious to Mary that she simply did not want to enter their home.

Mike with his second son, Marc,
London, Ontario, 1958.

You had to be strong not to get discouraged. But in a way, that produced a great resolve to show that I was as good, if not better. And perhaps this is what drove me. I tried, for example, to be a perfect mother. My children were always perfectly clean, my house was always perfectly orderly, our behaviour was always as perfect as we could manage. It wasn't so much that we wanted to vie for other friendships, or acceptance, it was for our own morale. I felt I wanted to prove to myself, more than anyone else, that I was just as good. I had been shunned and treated as a second-class citizen, but I determined I would not feel like one.

Mike, who attended the University of Western Ontario, received his licence to practise pathology in 1961. He subsequently received seventeen offers of employment. Mary wanted to live near the mountains, but Mike said, "We have already lived near the mountains. New Brunswick offers a new environment, close to the ocean. It will be something different for us. I think we should move to New Brunswick."

Mary shrugged, not really caring one way or the other. "Okay, Moncton, it is." They packed up the station wagon and headed east.

CHAPTER SIX

Aquila

There are many things in nature that remain unspoken and cannot be written about or explained. You have to live in nature to experience it. It is like being a guest in someone's home. You can visit and become familiar with the layout and habits of the occupants, but until you live there, you cannot hear its heartbeat.

Our regular weekly interviews have led Mary not only into soul-searching but into house searching as well. Today, she has a box of mementoes and papers brought down from upstairs. Rummaging through it, she finds a letter Chris wrote to his grandmother at Easter. He tells her they had been stranded on Caledonia Mountain in a snowstorm for several days with blocked roads and no electricity. "But we do not worry," he wrote. "We have oil lamps and cook on our woodstove."

"I wonder when that was," she muses. "Dave! When was that Easter snowstorm on Caledonia...the one that lasted several days?"

"It might have been April 1966," David calls from his office after a brief pause.

A few moments later, he emerges with a long weathered plank. There are handwritten notations scratched down the length of it: March 18, 37 cm of snow in Moncton, 50 cm on the mountain. April 13, snow-covered windows; April 28, tree swallows returned; May 7, first ants. It is a weather and wildlife record, part of a doorjamb that they brought from their former home on Caledonia Mountain. A reminder of the snowstorms and spring thaws, the wildlife and visitors.

"It is hard for people who have not lost everything to understand how precious it is to have a new home — to have your roots somewhere," says Mary. "I have my roots in Canada, and I will never cease to thank Canada for the chance to have this. I am very grateful."

⅓

For the Majka family, the hot July day in 1961 when Mary's curiosity first took them down the dusty road to Caledonia was a turning point. She had spied the advertisement under the section "Cottages for Sale" in the local newspaper. It read, "Year round cottage, executive type, secluded. Half hour drive from city. Next to TV Tower Caledonia Mountain. 30'x40', insulated, large picture window, screened in porch, stone fireplace, 220 wiring, beautiful view. Approximately 10 acres."

"It says, 'beautiful view.' We should drive out to see this view," Mary suggested, thinking it would make for a good family outing and an opportunity to explore the countryside.

Mike, Mary, and the boys stopped for ice cream and directions in Riverview, and then, armed with cones and the assurance that the scenic drive to the mountain was worthwhile, they turned down Pine Glen Road. As they left the outskirts of the town, the gravel road lined with mature pine trees opened into wide fields with a few scattered clapboard farmhouses. When a gust of hot air whirled a thick fog of dust through the windows, Mike pulled the car over until the visibility cleared. He complained that the boys would have grit in their ice cream. A few more kilometres and he once again stopped the car, this time for a lone man coaxing cattle across the road. Mike shook his head; Mary was enchanted.

They found the Caledonia Mountain road, then a hand-painted For Sale sign signalled their destination. Turning off the road, Mike eased the car along a dirt track through a large clearing spotted with small spruce trees until they spied the cottage, a small storey-and-a-half structure with checkerboard shingles, clapboard siding, shutters, and a fieldstone fireplace. It had been recently painted. Mike parked the car and the boys piled out, excited and anxious to explore. Seven-year-old Chris ran to the house, Marc, four years younger, tried to keep up. They stretched to peer through the picture window; Marc couldn't reach so he jumped up and down. The interior was furnished, neat and tidy.

The sloped meadow in front of the cottage bloomed with sweet clover, cow vetch, hawkweed, buttercups, and daisies. It was a field in transition; small spruce trees and saplings appeared here and there above the waving grass. There were no tracks to indicate anyone had been there recently, just grass and wildflowers billowing in the breeze.

Chris was excited. "Let's buy it, let's buy it, Mamusiu."

Mike was quick to set him straight. "Get this out of your head. We are here to see the view, not buy the cottage."

But that view had captured Mary's attention. Standing in the meadow, breathing in the evergreen scent of sun-warmed sap, listening to the frenzied hum of bees and the electric whirr of cicadas, she fixed her gaze on the distant glint of sunlight on water and the violet shadow of land against sky.

She had to have this place. It was her mountain. She could hear its heartbeat. She could see horizons from here.

When Mary convinced Mike to buy the cottage on Caledonia Mountain, the Majka family had been in New Brunswick barely a month and were temporarily renting a beach cottage in Shediac, a coastal summer haven about twenty-five minutes east of Moncton. Having just moved from Ontario, they had been looking for a house in the city so Mike could be close to the Moncton Hospital, where he had just accepted a position as pathologist. Finding the Caledonia Mountain cottage seemed a good omen; however, Mike felt the drive was too long for a daily commute. So they compromised and rented a bungalow in a suburb of Moncton. They enrolled Chris in school and began to settle into their new environment. They joked that they had come from a state of having nothing to having both a house and a cottage.

Mary and Mike never knew that their eventual home on Caledonia Mountain began as a humble holding pen; a small structure used to house hogs awaiting slaughter at the Swift's meat-processing plant in Moncton. When it reached the end of its usefulness, Ron McLaughlin, a general contractor, had purchased it from the processing plant, dismantled it, and then transported it to his land on the mountain. There he reassembled it, converting it to a comfortable family camp. It had electricity but no running water when, on a handshake, he agreed to a one hundred dollars per month rent-to-own arrangement with the Polish couple who answered his advertisement in the paper. They wouldn't have cared had they known of its history. And although later someone opined they'd paid far too much for the property, they considered three thousand dollars a fair asking price for their four-hectare mountain hideaway. Faithfully each month, they drove to Ron's home in Meadow, nearly an hour away, to hand over the monthly rent in cash until it was paid in full.

Before they moved to the mountain permanently, the cottage served as a summer and weekend getaway. It would become the first real home and security Mary would experience since her childhood in Poland. There were more good things to come.

Since arriving in New Brunswick, they had encountered genuinely friendly people who seemed intrigued by their Polish culture and accent. Neighbours and strangers went out of their way to extend offers of friendship and make the Majkas feel welcome. Immediately, Mary and Mike began talking to acquaintances about starting a local nature club. In December 1961, a small group gathered in the Majka's living room to form the Moncton Naturalists' Club.[20] The Majka family made up almost half of the original membership. Soon, the group grew to fifteen members, and they started meeting more formally in the boardroom of the local newspaper office, looking down through a plate-glass window on the presses and machines in the production room below.

That winter, the Majkas spent most weekends on the mountain. The government trucks plowed as far as a television tower located about five hundred metres behind the cottage, so the Majkas parked their Rambler on the cleared tower road. Pulling Marc on a wooden toboggan through the deep drifts, they snowshoed to the cottage on a trail cleared through the maple grove.

They spent their first New Brunswick Christmas at the mountain cottage, celebrating the Polish tradition of Wigilia on December 24, beginning with the breaking and sharing of the sacred Christmas wafer, *opłatek*, as they wished each other Merry Christmas. The meal followed, with *barszcz*, a fragrant ruby broth made from beets, and platters of perogi, baked fish, potatoes, sauerkraut, vegetables, dried fruits, and nuts. The finale was a nut torte, made with hazelnuts, chocolate, jam, and cream, a specialty of Maria's. Following the meal, the family opened gifts in front of the stone fireplace and the Christmas tree they had cut on their own property. Christmas would always be a celebration of Polish tradition — one they would frequently share with friends — but certainly during that first one in their mountain paradise, Mike and Mary had much to be grateful for.

The following summer, Mary stayed on the mountain with the boys while Mike commuted to work. They dug a well and installed an outdoor shower. But even with running water, they continued to use the existing outhouse — a two-holer in a three-sided stall without doors — for several more years.

"Our outhouse was a pleasant little place to contemplate nature," Mary recalls. "One day a woodpecker came to bang on the walls as my husband was sitting there. It wasn't just a place to relieve oneself, but a good place to watch birds. People have alcoves or bowers... well, this was our bower."

Mike was earning a decent salary and making a name for himself with his dedication to research. The young couple was financially better off than they'd ever been. When Mike told Mary he had a little money saved for improvements to the cottage, he asked which she wanted: the picture window replaced or an addition built for a bathroom. "The picture window," she said. "Of course."

Forests of spruce, pine, and maple stretched toward the tidal waters of the distant Bay of Fundy. The old logging roads, gullies, and steep ravines begged for exploration, and the Majkas soon discovered the veritable bounty the mountain provided. Buckets of wild blueberries, raspberries, blackberries, strawberries, and elderberries lined the kitchen counter in season, and Mary made jam and jelly from the excess. Throughout the countryside, a cornucopia of wild edible mushrooms awaited; over a number of years, they discovered more than four hundred varieties, some of them poisonous. Mushroom picking was a European tradition, and they called them by their Polish or German names. Among others, they carefully, and almost reverently, gathered *rydze*, *Steinpilz*, and *prawdziwki* in large wicker baskets. The boys, as young as they were, quickly knew which ones were edible and which were not. When Chris was less than discriminate with his picking, Mary secretly threw the damaged, dirty mushrooms into suitable growing areas, so the spores would develop into new patches. What they didn't eat immediately, she cut into fine slices and dried on wooden planks or window screens in the sun. Others were pickled or sautéed lightly and frozen for use in the fall and winter months.

They were surprised to learn very few people in the area picked wild mushrooms. On occasion, Mike would take a small terrarium of edible and poisonous specimens into work, displaying this on his desk, then asking those who came in his office which one they would choose if they were in the woods with nothing else to eat. At home later, he would chuckle, "They always pick the deadliest ones."

In winter, they broke snowshoe trails through the woods. In spring, they tapped maple trees, fished for brook and speckled trout, gathered tender cattail shoots, and picked fiddleheads by the streams. Sometimes a distant neighbour's cattle wandered from their pasture to the field in front of the house and Mary might awaken to a dozen or so cows grazing around the home. It reminded her of life in the Austrian Alps.

They called their new home "Aquila," the Latin word for eagle and the national emblem for Poland. Chris, the real patriot of the family, painted a white eagle on a plank and hung it over his bedroom window. For Mary, it was more than appropriate, as the cottage represented the place where she found true freedom and independence.

"On Caledonia, I lived the life of a person who is completely free of social commitments," Mary says. "I loved my children and husband, and I liked my friends, but I did it all my own way. I did not follow anyone's rules." After so many years of poverty — and the loneliness of Ontario — it would have been understandable had Mary chosen to live a socially active life like the other doctors' wives she had met. But something deeper called. "I told myself this is not how you want to live for the rest of your life. I want to do what I like to do, not what society dictates. I wanted to be me."

Her gregarious nature drew an ever-growing circle of friends in Moncton, and her penchant for hospitality ensured a steady stream of guests in their home. It was not her nature to issue vapid invitations out of a sense of etiquette — hers were genuine. The Majka family was so warm, their interests so diverse, that people often took her up on her offer.

Visitors felt a part of the household, and even when they dropped in un-announced, they were included in whatever planned or impromptu outing Mary devised. She made sure that even the most commonplace activities, such as berry or mushroom picking, a birding expedition, or a picnic, were events of great importance and fanfare. Friends were often invited to spend weekends with the family on Caledonia, many of them enjoying the novelty of the cottage in the wild, an adventure in the making, and Mary's lavish cooking. Such gatherings must have evoked her memories of the fine times at Mirów.

Members of the Moncton Naturalists' Club were frequent guests at Aquila as the entire area afforded many opportunities for birdwatching. Mary often remained home with Marc, but Mike and Chris were faithful regulars on club outings. Next to Chris, Peter Candido and Alan Madden were the youngest members. Mike sometimes drove into Moncton from Caledonia Mountain to pick up the boys for a field trip or bring them back to the mountain for the weekend, a lengthy round trip. Alan, who was nineteen at the time, remembers warm hospitality, climbing trees after dark to listen for owls, hiking through the woods, and the array of food presented to assuage his voracious youthful appetite during weekends spent on Caledonia. He also remembers Mary's first call to action.

On December 28, 1962, the newspaper printed a photograph of a man holding a dead eagle, with the caption, "Shoots Big Eagle." The story went on to say the

Mary baking in the kitchen at Aquila, early 1960s.

Aquila,
Caledonia Mountain.

man had skilfully brought down the eagle with a single shot from a .303 calibre rifle at a distance of two hundred yards. The magnificent bird, with a wingspan of seven feet, would be mounted and displayed in an unnamed Moncton store with an identifying plaque.

Mary was horrified at the senseless shooting of a bird that she knew to be endangered. The next day, she called the Department of Lands and Mines. "Is this legal?" she asked. They told her it was. At the time, a federal migratory bird act protected many birds but not raptors or those birds considered to be a danger to domestic fowl or a nuisance to farmers.

This has to change, Mary thought. She immediately wrote a letter to the editor of the newspaper, protesting such needless action and signing it on behalf of the club. She discussed it at length with club members. At the time, there seemed to be little else she could do, but a year later, she would be found resurrecting the issue once more.

By the spring of 1963, Mary had decided they would move to Caledonia permanently. They left the house in Moncton, enrolled Chris at the school in nearby Hillsborough, and moved their belongings to the cottage in the meadow. Mary immediately set to work transforming it into a comfortable family home.

Disregarding Mike, who maintained that nothing would ever grow in the miserable rocky soil, she built flower and vegetable gardens. She lugged stones from the woods to build a patio and dragged a picnic table under the grand maple tree behind the cottage, where they would most often eat their meals, all the while attuned to the surrounding birds and wildlife. Soon after the Majka family was settled on the mountain, a Samoyed dog, Eski, and a horse, Stormy, took up residence as well.

They had already worn a network of trails through the forest, and the contours of the land became as familiar as the contents of her baking cupboard.

Mary with Eski,
Aquila, circa 1964.

She and Marc travelled the forests of Albert County while Mike was at work and Chris was at school, ranging ever farther from their home base. Mary fell deeper in love with her surroundings. They drank from clear streams, scrutinized unfamiliar plants, watched for birds, and inspected the droppings of porcupine and moose. They picked wildflowers and collected lichens, grasses, and birchbark to decorate the house. Sometimes, she and the boys hiked several kilometres through the woods road to Stanyard Lake or drove to Ings Intervale for a picnic and swim. She carefully observed the progression of the seasons in the forest — her forest — and allowed the contours of the mountain to draw her through itself, guiding her step around this rock or down that gully, or across this clearing.

Gradually, through the medicine of the land, the give and take of it, she had found a quiet place for her roots to take hold. A place to call her own.

Reid Parker, one of three transmitter technicians who staffed the television tower near the Majka home, was one of their first neighbours. He enjoyed the ready companionship offered by Mary, regularly stopping for coffee or breakfast with her. He forged an easy friendship with the entire family.

When Chris got home from school in the afternoon, the two brothers raced up the trail to the TV tower to watch television and hang out with Reid. Reid and his wife, Wanda, did not yet have a family and he thoroughly enjoyed the Majka boys' visits. Chris and Marc had complete freedom and travelled the woods as adeptly as if they'd been born there. Reid never knew either of them to get lost. Chris was studious and fascinated with insects. He had an extensive butterfly collection. Marc, on the other hand, was insatiably curious and active. He always wanted to tinker with the transmitter panels, so Reid made him a board with knobs and buttons. It was Marc's favourite plaything.

Mary and Mike taught Reid about mushrooms and birds. "They really awakened new interests for me," he recalls. "The first bird we saw together was a pileated woodpecker. Afterwards, I got a bird book and a set of binoculars. And this mushroom business really intrigued me. No one picked wild mushrooms. We didn't realize there were so many kinds. She dried them and made soups."

When Mike bought Mary a brand new blue Volkswagen Beetle — the first of several — Reid accompanied her as she learned to navigate the twisting, narrow dirt roads of Albert County.

"We had a few scary moments," he recalls. "She was a hard student. She acts before she thinks. That's her type of personality. She was...I don't know how to put it...a free spirit." Indeed, it was nothing for Mary to veer across a field for a shortcut or barrel up a woods trail that was more rockslide than road. When she took her Beetle in for repairs, the mechanics never knew what they might pry from the undercarriage.

When Mary decided she wanted to learn to hunt, Mike bought her a rifle and Reid taught her how to use it. He doesn't remember that she ever shot anything, but she seemed to enjoy the long rambles as they searched. They joked that the Caledonia deer couldn't have been safer.

Reid introduced Mary to his brother-in-law, Ted Fenton, a seasoned hunter. Ted had spent many years working in a northern British Columbia mining camp. He was the only white man among a number of Aboriginal people hired to supply venison for the miners. He had learned much during this time, honing his hunting, trapping, and fishing skills in the traditional ways taught by his companions. Short and wiry, his unhurried gait was that of a hunter: deliberate and silent.

For the next several years, Ted and Mary travelled the autumn woods together, hunting for animals. Sometimes, Ted would leave his home in Albert Mines and Mary would leave Caledonia. They'd both walk cross-country through the old logging roads and meet each other partway, then spend the day tramping the forests. He called her "Mountain Mary," and the name stuck.

Ted introduced Mary to the intricacies of the wildlife community and showed her how to read the forest. He pointed out tracks, signs of passage, and droppings. He showed her indentations where animals had lain. He taught her how to think like an animal, to consider where food and water might be found, where to walk, or how to hide.

Nature spoke to me in a very different way during this time. After this, I learned to walk in the woods. When you can live with nature, experience it first-hand, and be very aware and sensitive, all of a sudden it is like an open book.

She observed Ted the same way she observed nature. She noticed that he exhibited a quiet respect for living things, at times seeming almost apologetic after a kill. "I felt sad when he shot something — I didn't want to see animals die — but I respected his judgment. I thought, 'If Ted thinks this is all right, then it must be all right.'" She watched many times as he lowered his rifle, refusing to take a clean shot because it didn't feel right, almost as if it were a decision of his heart as much as his mind. Once, after finding a fox with his neck trapped in one of his own snares, without a word of explanation, he cut the wire and freed the creature.

On another day, when Mary was hiking alone, she found herself in the same situation. She cut the wire to free the fox, then took the damaged snare with her. Walking on a bit farther, she spied a mother and baby porcupine. The mother quickly climbed a tree, but the baby had not yet learned to do so. It clung to the bark partway up the trunk.

Since I had the snare with me, I thought I should catch it. It looked so soft and fluffy, but the moment I put the snare on it, it let out such a miserable yell that I let it go. Besides, when I looked closer, I could see already the spines coming out. We wouldn't have been able to play with it or anything.

Mary was interested in all aspects of life and death in the wild. An expert trapper, Ted also taught her how to skin animals. He kept the skins and she kept the flesh. Once, Ted shot a porcupine and she cooked the meat, finding it tasted much like chicken. Reid remembers one occasion when she offered him wildcat. "I don't know what part of it she cooked. I had a taste, just to say I did, but I couldn't stomach that," he says, shaking his head. She even helped Ted and Reid trap a bear and then skin it for its meat. She kept the bear grease to rub on sore joints. Reid recalls, "We took the skin to a taxidermist and I had a rug made from it, but every time I got up in the night, I'd end up sticking my foot in its mouth, so I finally gave it to the Majkas."

The strange habits of the Majkas provided much fodder for talk among their neighbours in Albert County. They couldn't fathom why anybody would choose to live in such an unsettled area. They didn't know what to think of this odd foreign family who ate bear and porcupine meat, showered out of doors, and picked wild mushrooms. And "that Mary" — the one who ran barefoot through the meadows, kept a bearskin rug in her living room, and barrelled about the county in her Beetle — well, she certainly didn't fit their paradigm of "woman of the house." Quite frankly, the good women in the local sewing circles and ladies' groups had their own ideas about a woman who travelled the woods with a man other than her husband, and they were not afraid to share them.

What may have seemed strange to Canadian culture and sensibilities was perfectly natural to Mary, who finally felt she was able to be herself, to reclaim her identity and exercise all the joys of living she had enjoyed during her childhood in Poland. Her Polish culture and European ways soon brought other cherished friends and mentors into her life.

Shortly after the Majkas moved to the mountain in 1963, they met Frieda Gamble, the Polish widow of a New Brunswick-born Methodist minister. The couple had met and married in Poland, then returned to Canada in 1953, settling not far from Caledonia Mountain. Mrs. Gamble was left alone when her husband died five years later.

Tiny, but not delicate, the sixty-eight-year-old was not one to sit and lament her circumstances. She mowed her own lawn, repaired her house, picked mushrooms, planted and maintained extensive flower and vegetable gardens, raised chickens, and cared for her pets. In the summer, she filled the church with flowers on Sunday, and in the winter, she embroidered floral gifts for others. She adored children and made it a point to hire them to do odd jobs around the house. Everyone called her Mrs. Gamble.[21]

Mrs. Gamble filled an empty place in Mary's life, becoming like a mother to Mary and a grandmother to her sons. They shared their Polish roots, a love of the outdoors, of flowers, of cooking and hospitality. When Mary spoke Polish to her sons, it brought tears to Mrs. Gamble's eyes. Like the Majkas, Mrs. Gamble lived simply compared to the world's standards. She frequently spent her modest pension on the needs of others, quietly, without fanfare. She exhibited great Christian love for all living things: people, animals, birds, and plants.

In 1967, a young student minister from Salisbury named Roland Hutchinson came into Mrs. Gamble's life and, soon thereafter, Mary's. He was to assist with three churches in the area for a two-year period, and one of them was Mrs Gamble's. The two became very close, as Roland sat in Mrs. Gamble's kitchen, eating her Polish chicken stew, perogi, and cabbage rolls, and listening to stories about her life.

He remembers the first time he drove Mrs. Gamble to visit with her Polish friend on Caledonia Mountain. He had heard stories of the family who collected edibles from the forests and meadows of Caledonia Mountain and was looking forward to finally meeting them. During his first visit, he was fascinated by the Norfolk pine tree growing in their living room, but rather sceptical of the idea of pickled mushrooms. He also observed the obvious respect and affection Mary had for Mrs. Gamble.

"The visit left me captivated by the welcome and down-to-earth-ness of these extraordinary people. I was eager to return to the nurture of this 'learning centre,' to know this family better, and to hear more of the Polish language which Mary and Mrs. Gamble spoke at times, and which had a drawing power upon me for some unknown reason," writes Roland. It was just the first of many visits through the years as his friendship with the Majkas grew. That day in the Majka kitchen, none could foresee how the relationship developing between these three friends would, many years later, set in motion an extraordinary chain of events.

While Mrs. Gamble certainly taught Mary the softer virtue of looking for the good within people, two other strong and capable women entered Mary's life at the same time, and they showed her the merit in tenacity.

Muriel Lutes Sikorski was a consummate entrepreneur with no shortage of tourism savvy. A descendant of one of Moncton's first permanent German settlers, she married Lou Sikorski, a Polish immigrant who worked on her uncle's dairy farm, and together, they grew Muriel's first business venture, The Shanty, from a modest ice cream stand into the Magnetic Hill Inn, including accommodations, restaurant, and gift shop. Her enterprising spirit made Magnetic Hill, a topographical illusion where cars appeared to coast uphill, into one of the most popular and well-known tourism attractions in the province.

When a mutual friend mentioned Lou's Polish background, Mary contacted the Sikorskis and the two women became fast friends. Mary admired Muriel's self-confidence and fearlessness. She reinforced that Mary should be bold, work hard, and fear nothing. Both had a deep appreciation for their European roots. Through the years, they would celebrate many Christmases, Easters, birthdays, and anniversaries together. Mary opined that Muriel, who had never had children, came to think of her as a daughter. The Sikorskis most certainly played a role in making the Majkas feel that they had finally found a true home in New Brunswick. Indeed, years later, the two women would make several trips to Europe together in search of clues to Muriel's ancestral roots.

Through Muriel, Mary met Lois Cook. Lois and her Lebanese husband owned a chain of fourteen retail and wholesale shoe stores across the Maritimes. Like Muriel, Lois was a confident woman with tremendous willpower. Mary admired

Lois's achievements and her determined spirit. Up until her death in 2005, Lois remained one of Mary's closest friends and most fervent supporters.

"I will never forget one of the very first times I visited Mary," recalled Lois, a year before she passed away. "She took me for a drive in that Volkswagen and we went right through a blueberry field. Oh, how she drove through that field! That was one of my early experiences. She was rugged. She'd be outside in the snow in her bare feet, gathering maple syrup. Everyone was astounded by what this woman did; she was different than anyone I had ever met."

Throughout the 1960s and into the 1970s, as Mary was establishing her identity as a passionate advocate of nature, her friendship with these prominent business-minded women reinforced her own determination and persistence. Each provided crucial support and encouragement while she began to carve her own path in the emerging field of conservation.

As Mary's circle of personal friendships grew and her contacts through involvement with the Moncton Naturalists' Club expanded, so did her confidence. She decided to persevere with the incident that drew her ire when a bald eagle was shot for a trophy and the story ran in a local newspaper.

In the summer of 1964, she sent letters to a number of people she thought might support an attempt to change the wildlife protection laws, inviting them to a meeting. On September 1, 1964, representatives from the New Brunswick Museum, Canadian Wildlife Service, Fundy National Park, and the Moncton Fish and Game Association finally met to discuss the lack of protection for birds of prey, share information, and propose a solution.[22] They learned that New Brunswick, Yukon, and the Northwest Territories were the only jurisdictions in all of Canada and the United States without any protection for birds of prey. Mary compiled a brief on the subject, included supporting letters from members of the group, copied the submission for herself, and sent the originals by registered mail to the Minister of Lands and Mines.

After months passed without response, Mary drove to Fredericton. She presented her copy of the brief, along with the post office receipt, and politely asked what had been done with her request. "There was great consternation," she recalls. "People fumbling in drawers, talking among themselves, and finally out of someone's drawer emerged the package." They apologized profusely, and then assured her it would be reviewed and she would soon hear a response from the minister. Wheels turn slowly, but three years later, the provincial government amended the Game Act to include a blanket protection for the birds and mammals not covered by hunting or trapping seasons, becoming the first legislation of its kind in the Maritime provinces.[23]

It wasn't that she was a nature nut, she later explained, nor was she adamantly against hunting. It was the senseless killing that she abhorred. "Our life is a treasure, and we can afford that same feeling to other creatures who have to share the earth with us. We have passed the pioneer stage where anything that lived was our enemy or competition for our livelihood."[24]

From Mary's first experience in the field of conservation activism, she learned the value of persistence and careful preparation, along with authoritative support from all sides of the issue. With this success, she realized she could make her voice heard.

Another voice was also being heard in the early 1960s. American biologist and writer Rachel Carson had published *Silent Spring* in 1962, which informed the public of the cascading effects of chemical sprays on the environment. Mary heard about the book on the radio and ordered a copy from the library. Before immigrating, Mary had long observed nature's struggles with human interventions. There was no doubt in her mind of the importance of Carson's work; she had already questioned the use of pesticides in her own mind, fearing such things would do more harm than good. She predicted *Silent Spring* would not only create a sensation but would also stir up controversy from the proponents of chemical insect and plant control.

She was right. In the coming years, Carson came under attack from industry and governments, but she never once wavered from her convictions. Her proposals were well researched, reasonable, not radical. With a background in science and a reputation as a lyrical writer, she calmly put forth the facts, interpreted their significance, allowing others to make their own decisions. Today, she is credited with raising public awareness that what humans do to nature they also do to themselves.

> All of a sudden, my eyes were open. I thought this is exactly what is happening. That book influenced me more than anything else. I was very interested in nature, but it was my own private thing. I loved nature but until then didn't realize that I could, as an individual, act in nature's defence. *Silent Spring* became a catalyst.

Mary's mission took shape. Three decades later, she would tell author Harry Thurston that being a conservationist "is more than a profession. It is a lifetime occupation. I feel almost like a nun."[25]

෨෬

CHAPTER SEVEN

Family

*I have this tremendous sense of community, to take care of other
people. No matter if they are related or not, nice, young, old, poor —
it doesn't make any difference to me at all. It is the human beings that
I need to care for; I feel responsible to take care of things. I cannot pass
by and say let someone else do that.*

"I didn't have much family, except for the one I built myself. That is why I had all these adopted friends. They were my sisters, mothers, extended families." Mary is methodically folding 250 Christmas letters and sliding them into envelopes. She's been keeping friends annually updated on the activities at Mary's Point for more than twenty years. "This is a tremendous job," she says. "Writing text, choosing pictures."

She dictates her letter and David types a draft and inserts the pictures. She writes better than she talks, she tells me. It is a skill she inherited from her father. "Poems are even more amazing," she says. "Often I would write a poem and it was almost perfect. It just comes out of my head." Sometimes she sends her poems to friends, just to let them know she is thinking about them.

She still corresponds with colleagues from university and with friends all over the world, many who have visited her in Canada. "I seem to remember the whole story of a person. I want to see the whole person. Because of that, I think these people remain close to me."

Countless times through the years, Mary has opened her home to complete strangers, arranged parties and gatherings, travelled great distances to deliver thoughtful gifts, helped refugees settle in Canada, provided guidance and support to other immigrants, and given money, time, and resources to people in need. Now that her mobility is limited, she sings with a group of Polish women and spends long hours knitting, quilting, and embroidering gifts for her friends.

She reflects on the question as to why she and Mike never had more children, since she enjoys them so.

"My husband never wanted to have more, so I found a way to have more anyway. He used to joke about it, saying I cheated him into all these other children. I remember once he said, 'You are taking such good care of them all and who knows whether they will ever appreciate it.' I think maybe they do."

She reaches back in her memory to recall the first of these. "Wendy came to stay before David moved in. We saw her recently and we talked about those times on Caledonia Mountain." Mary pauses, her hands idle, eyes cast to the bay. "What a pleasure this is for me," she continues, still looking into the distance, her voice softening to a murmur. "She calls me the other mother. I love her very much."

∝

Caledonia Mountain was wrapped in one of its rainstorms in the summer of 1963. Wind blasted the television tower, each gust sending bullets of rain against the windows. Reid was hunkered down, playing a game with his ten-year-old niece, Wendy Stevens, when the power and telephone went out. Wendy had been staying with Reid and Wanda for a few months. Her mother was a single parent, working in Toronto and dealing with significant health problems. She couldn't afford the extra expense of a sitter for Wendy during the summer months, so she sent her east to stay with her sister, Wanda. Reid usually brought Wendy to stay with him during his shift.

He had to notify his office that the tower was no longer transmitting, so he sent Wendy down the path in the woods to the Majkas' home to see if their telephone worked.

This was Wendy's first introduction to the Majka family. "I was nervous about going," remembers Wendy (now a nurse living in Toronto), "but when I arrived, Mary was so warm and friendly. I told her who I was and she was all excited. She invited me in, and then had Chris walk me back to the tower."

Chris and Wendy hit it off immediately, as they were both the same age. Wendy may have lived in the city, but she felt more at home in the country. Chris showed her his mountain. They explored trails, cleared new ones, swam in Crooked Creek, romped with the dogs, buried dead birds and mice in the garden, and took great pains to hide from Marc, whom they considered a nuisance. When Wendy went

From left to right: Marc, Chris, and Wendy Stevens with the Majkas' horse, Stormy, 1964.

home, she corresponded through the winter. The following two summers she would return to stay with the Majkas.

The house was not large, but no one seemed to mind the cramped quarters or the extra child at the dinner table. Both Chris and Marc enjoyed having a playmate, and Wendy was happy just being there. Mary made her part of the family, drawing the child out of her shyness and helping her find self-confidence and self-acceptance.

"Mary was so different than anyone I knew. She was really good to me and so kind. I remember her taking vegetables to Mrs. Gamble so she could check on her. She had a flair for the dramatic. People called her Mountain Mary and some made fun of her because of her accent and flamboyance." Wendy smiles. "I remember getting angry at someone for this and telling them off.

"As a kid from the city, it was wonderful to have a totally different life. She told me once she had wanted to adopt me as her daughter. Through Mary, I learned that it was okay to be who you are, to have different interests. She gave me another piece of my life that I would not have had."

Wendy was the first of more than thirty children who moved through the Majka household. For her part, Mary never forgot the atmosphere of inclusion and comfort she found at Mirów in the tender years following her father's death. She felt such gratitude for the blessings and richness of her life that she wanted to pass it on, opening her own home whenever she felt a safe, peaceful place was needed.

Soon, she had the opportunity again.

By then, Moncton, Saint John, and Fredericton all had fledgling naturalist clubs that gathered for outings and to share information. The early bridges built between these three small groups initiated what would become a widespread community of people who were concerned with the environment and who discovered there was strength and purpose in numbers.

In April 1964, members of the three groups convened on Shepody Marsh, not far from the Majkas' home, to observe thousands of migrating geese. The entire Majka family was there. Mike gestured toward a young man driving a very large Buick, telling Mary that he and Chris had met the fellow during a previous birding trip. While only twenty-two years of age, the young man already possessed an impressive knowledge of biology, he said, and was the president and a co-founder of the Saint John Naturalists' Club.

Mary stared at the slight figure behind the wheel. "Does this boy even have a licence to drive?" she asked.

The boy's name was David Sinclair Christie.

David Christie grew up along the Kennebecasis River near Saint John, the only child of Charles Stuart and Mary Louise Christie.

Charles, a Saint John area businessman, along with his two sisters, owned Christie Woodworking Company Ltd., the cabinet-making company his grandfather had started in 1865. In addition to being an astute businessman, Charles was an avid outdoorsman and fostered an early interest for the outdoors and nature in his only son. He owned a camp on the South Branch Oromocto River, where the family spent many pleasant weekends. The river flowed about 180 metres from the door, and the young boy and his father spent idyllic hours on the water together, sometimes fly fishing, sometimes canoeing, sometimes just watching birds and wildlife. David caught his first trout at age five, and then later he purchased a guidebook so he could identify the other fish he observed in the shallows and deep pools of the river.

By grade two, his fascination flowed to bugs and butterflies. From the age of ten, he kept journals, carefully recording everything he observed: fish, frogs, toads, snails, insects, and birds. Besides his dog, he kept turtles, goldfish, and a rabbit for pets, learning much through the relationships he shared with them and the observations he made about animal and fish behaviours.

When he was only twelve, David chanced to meet Dr. W. Austin Squires, the curator of the natural science department of the New Brunswick Museum in Saint John. Just two years earlier, in 1952, Dr. Squires had published *The Birds of New Brunswick*. Curiously enough, some fifty years later, David would contribute to another book by the same name.[26] While the older man may not have remembered that initial meeting, he left an impression on the young boy, who bought a copy of Squires's 221-page book. When David began calling Dr. Squires to tell him of a particular sighting, the older gentleman took time to question him or suggest additional information he might gather.

By age fifteen, David could recognize and identify by sight and song an impressive variety of birds common to the area. He was so keenly interested in birdwatching that as a teenager he happily invested in his first set of binoculars, a set of Baker 8x40s, made in England. His mother drove him to Thorne's Hardware in Saint John, where he purchased the glasses for fifty-seven dollars — a wise choice that would still be in his possession fifty years later.

His mother, Mary Louise, was very close to her son, but David watched her struggle, time and time again, to gain sobriety. And helplessly, he watched her fail. Eventually, he saw his father fall into the same rut. Fearing he carried the addictive gene, David swore he would never drink. He was intensely loyal and carried his troubles silently, never speaking of them to friends. It was a large and painful responsibility for a young boy to shoulder.

Although there were shadows in his life, David's mother supported and encouraged his interest in wildlife, driving him to museums and birdwatching sites. She bought him a series of Frank Ashbrook's bird identification books, but it was his Aunt Florence Christie — his father's sister from Ontario and a dedicated birdwatcher — who gave him his first real field guide, Roger Tory Peterson's *A Field Guide to the Birds*.

Charles Christie was proud of his son's achievements at Rothesay Collegiate School and Camp Aldershot, a summer military training camp near Kentville, Nova Scotia. By age seventeen, David had advanced to cadet major. Such experiences conditioned him to receiving and responding to the orders of his superiors and gave him an appreciation for strict methodology and process.

After David graduated from high school, his father encouraged him to enrol in a forestry program at the University of New Brunswick in Fredericton, hoping he would take an interest in the family business. David willingly indulged his hopes for a while. He spent two summers working for his father's business; two more for Dr. Squires at the New Brunswick Museum; and then another for what is now the Canadian Forestry Service doing botanical work on forest plots and documenting the relationships between forest bird populations and spruce budworm, which had become the foremost economical and environmental issue in the province at that time.

Meanwhile, at university he had joined the Fredericton Field Naturalists' Club, which Peter Pearce and a few friends had started in January 1960, the first in the province. He and Peter watched birds together, reporting their findings to Dr. Squires, who maintained official records on sightings. David and a friend had then started the Saint John Naturalists' Club in May 1962, shortly after the Majkas started the Moncton club. During one of the first outings with the three clubs, David met Moncton members Alan Madden and Peter Candido. Alan remembers David offering to buy him a lens for his new Pentax 35 mm camera. "We had never even chummed together," says Alan. "David was simply very generous."

In mid-November 1963, as David was preparing for morning classes at university, he received a call from his father to say that his mother had died in the night of complications arising from pneumonia. Less than a year later, in August 1964, his father succumbed to cirrhosis of the liver. Suddenly, at twenty-two, David was an orphan and the heir to a business he never wanted. With help from his Aunt Florence, David sold the company and its assets, allowing him to pursue his own interests. While his university studies helped take his mind off of his losses, he still felt uprooted and unsettled.

Alan Madden remembers him calling to say, "My father passed away and I inherited his wealth. I've decided I'm going to be a bum and go birding." Despite this joking declaration, following his completion of the forestry program in the spring of 1965, David accepted a position as the first full-time park naturalist at Fundy National Park. In addition to managing an interpretive program, he was also a park biologist. He needed a summer assistant, so he called Peter Candido. Peter was now in Montreal, putting in time until university started in the fall and working at various small jobs to make some money. He was picking night crawlers for pay when David called to offer him a naturalist position at Fundy. He jumped at the opportunity.

Peter enjoyed being around David and was impressed with the depth of his knowledge. "David is modest. You don't realize how much he knows unless you ask him something specific. Then out comes all this data. He doesn't initiate information, but if you mention a subject, he will have something interesting to say about it. He's also very young at heart; a lot of naturalists are like that. The learning may get more sophisticated, but the basic curiosity is still there. Maybe that's what keeps a person young."

Peter recalled a girl whom David visited. Sometimes both of them spent the evening with her, sitting on her porch and talking. "Like a lot of guys, he doesn't like to show emotions, but he's more reserved than most. He never said anything to me, but it was obvious he liked her." Unfortunately, the girl wanted out of the small village where she had grown up. "He was sad when she left," noted Peter, adding that to his knowledge, David never had another girlfriend after that.

On occasion, they drove to Caledonia Mountain together to see the Majka family. Both enjoyed the camaraderie and casual atmosphere. "Mary would be baking her bread in the kitchen and talking at the same time," recalls Peter, who is now a molecular biologist. "She'd be busy with the kids but would also have some other idea cooking. In the evening, I'd borrow their car and go out on some of the rugged trails on the mountain or talk to Mike about his interests in astronomy. He always had really good Scotch."

David also enjoyed the sense of inclusion he felt when he was with them, even spending the night after getting his car stuck in their muddy driveway following that April field trip when they first met. On one occasion, Mary watched the young man as she prepared supper. He stood in front of the living room window, hands in his pockets, staring at the view across the valley. She recalls the moment, "Usually young men don't stand and gaze and contemplate things for very long, but he stood and stood and looked."

When he turned around, she asked him, "Do you like that view?"

"I wish I could look at a view like this all my life," he sighed, later commenting how wonderful it would be to live there.

After the boarding house where he was staying in Alma shut down in late autumn 1965, David moved temporarily into the park bunkhouse. One night, as an early winter storm brought snow flying about the wooden building, the solitude weighed heavy and he made the snowy drive to the Majkas' on Caledonia Mountain. As he nosed his car into the deep drifts of the Majkas' driveway, the tires began to spin. He abandoned the vehicle and trudged up the long drive to the house. Mary answered the unexpected knock at her door to a snow-blanketed David. "I'm stuck again," he grinned sheepishly.

By then, the Majkas had already decided that he should live with them. On November 23, 1965, David Christie arrived, suitcase in hand. He never left.

At the time he moved in, David was twenty-three and Mary was forty-two. They came from different cultures, but their ways of living meshed. They both retained a childlike curiosity that stoked an intense interest in the natural world and both had spent many hours observing nature's inner workings. Mary sensed what David needed most was family and security; what Mary needed most was to nurture.

"I can see how Mary's organizational skills would come into play and give Dave the direction he may have needed at that time to keep on track," says Reverend Roland Hutchinson, the young student minister who had befriended Mrs. Gamble. "It must be terrible all of a sudden not to have a family."

Mary understands precisely how David came to fit in. "There are many people in my life who influenced me, but David is the most important. I wouldn't be the person I am if he wasn't around. He is a part of me — a core that is very strong and never going to be touched — and I can't think, outside of him, that I could live. I know he feels the same way."

While their family circle expanded in the early to mid-1960s, Mike was becoming widely respected for his work ethic and his skill at mentoring others. His colleagues appreciated his quick wit and quiet manner. He kept a cot in his office and spent the night when the weather looked nasty, rather than miss a day of work. He was utterly committed to pathology. He loved a difficult case and undertook the challenges of his work with Hercule Poirot determination, digging, searching, and researching until he found the answers. As time passed, his increasing knowledge and expertise became highly appreciated among the physicians. If there was any question or uncertainty about a pathology report, Mike was the one to consult.

"He was the senior esteemed pathologist," says former colleague and friend Dr. Hank Taylor. "But he also had an intellectual honesty. If he didn't know, he didn't try to pretend he knew. He had no ego or self-importance."

Another colleague, Dr. Mike Antle, recalls how Mike always sat in a back corner of the doctor's coffee room. "I remember asking him one day why he always sat in that same spot. He told me, 'The surgeons are always waiting for phone calls from the operating room, so it's important they have the space by the phone. The family doctors must rush to see their patients so they need the space by the door. My patients are in no rush for me.'"

Mike counteracted the intensity of his work with leisure hours spent engrossed in solitary, meditative tasks. While he took great pleasure in birding expeditions and many of the weekend family activities, Mike also happily indulged his quiet, reserved nature by picking mountains of berries and mushrooms and marsh greens, chopping stacks of wood, fishing, and feeding the birds. One year he picked enough pea-sized wild strawberries for Mary to make fifty-two jars of jam. He especially enjoyed the colourful flocks of blue jays. He once conducted an experiment to see how much bread the blue jays could eat in a day. Bringing home an armload of old loaves from the bakery, he set out loaf after loaf and watched it disappear.

He never forgot how Mary supported him in Ontario as he followed his choice of career and he wanted her to be happy. "He used to tell us with what Mary had to go through in the war, that anything she wanted to do, she could do it," says friend Larry McLaughlin. "He has spent his life making it up to her...the things that happened in her life."

To many friends, Mike and Mary may have seemed as different as darkness and light, but their shared interest and respect for natural things rooted them together, as did their acceptance of each other's individuality.

"One of Mary's great dreams and visions was to immerse herself in things of nature, to continue that great love and respect she had for her father," says Roland Hutchinson. "She spoke several times of nature and her father in the same breath. I think it would be fair to say they were inseparable. This also is seen in the strong bond that Mary and Mike had with David. His love for nature would have been very early on identified as a uniting factor. The whole family was nature-oriented and they found a great deal of enjoyment and identity in that. Because of David's family circumstances, the Majkas saw this as an opportunity not just to be friends and colleagues, but to be family."

David, for his own part, slid seamlessly into the fabric of the Majka life, save for one minor complication. He wasn't sure what to call Mike. Somehow Mike seemed disrespectful, but Dr. Majka was too formal and Dr. Mike felt a little odd. In the end, he settled on "The Boss" (a nickname given by an Ontario colleague) to the great enjoyment of all, as everyone knew who the real boss was. For their part, Mike and Mary affectionately called David their "third son." He became so inseparably ingrained into their family life that some of their closest friends would swear he had been formally adopted.

David was like a big brother to Chris and Marc. He recognized the same passion for exploration and knowledge in Chris that he'd felt himself at that age. Chris, especially, enjoyed the time with David and sometimes helped him with interpretive talks, campfires, and singsongs at Fundy Park during the summer months.

Mary remembers an argument she had with Chris. Upset over his rude retorts, she sent David to talk to him while she headed to the woods to calm herself. "I could hear them talking loud upstairs. David was saying, 'You don't know what it's like to not have a mother. You need to value your mother.' It was a great help coming from David."

Chris's curiosity for nature and his desire to document everything he discovered gave him maturity far beyond his years. Albert Einstein was his hero. He had a small menagerie consisting of snakes, turtles, and an iguana, which he acquired from an animal trainer at the local rural exhibition. The trainer walked away with eight little brown bats and Chris went home with the lizard — both considered it a good trade.

His collection of insects started out in a shoebox but grew to standard-sized storage cases. His bedroom housed mounted collections of insects, moths, and

Chris, the budding biologist (age fifteen),
in his room at Aquila, 1969.

butterflies, as well as stuffed birds and a variety of aquatic life preserved in formaldehyde — salamanders, clam worms, a small turtle. Chris was always on the lookout for specimens that might supplement the collections of the New Brunswick Museum. He stowed dead birds and animals in airtight plastic bags in the freezer until they could be transported to the museum.

Once, when a repairman came to fix the freezer, he turned to Mary. "This is none of my business," he said, "but why are there dead mice, squirrels, and birds in the freezer? You don't eat them, do you?"

By the age of fourteen, Chris was working on a revised list of New Brunswick's butterflies, having been astounded to realize the last list was done in 1899. He kept detailed typed notes on a card file system. As a member of the Lepidopterists' Society in the United States, he corresponded frequently with professionals and scientists who, no doubt, hadn't a clue of his age. One time Mary received a phone call from a Mr. Madden from California. He wanted to come to meet Christopher Majka. Mary told him that Chris was at school.

"Oh, is he a teacher?" asked Mr. Madden.

"No," replied Mary, "He's a grade nine student."

Mr. Madden was perplexed. "You mean that Christopher Majka, member of the Lepidopterists' Society, is in grade nine?"

This must have intrigued the gentleman because, while on a collecting trip, he made it a point to visit the young man. After arriving on Caledonia Mountain and engaging in a weighty conversation with Chris about butterflies, he sat down with a glass of wine in hand to admire the view. Presently, Mary noticed with some concern that the elderly gentleman's hands were shaking. Speechless, he pointed outside. A cow moose followed by twin calves passed in front of the house, pausing to stare curiously in the window. "If I hadn't seen it, I would never believe it," Mr.

Madden repeated afterwards. No doubt he left for California with more than a tale or two about his trip and the people he met on Caledonia Mountain.

High school principal Harry Doyle remembers one year when Chris took a month off school to do spring surveys on pelagic birds on an oceanographic research vessel with the Bedford Institute of Oceanography in Halifax, Nova Scotia. Harry reminded Chris that when he returned, he'd have to write a one-hundred-question multiple-choice final exam. Chris thought that would be no problem. He went on his survey, and then returned and wrote the exam.

"That son of a gun made a hundred. I couldn't have made a hundred on that test," Harry said, shaking his head, still amazed decades later.

If Chris was clear in his ambitions, his younger brother had a harder time sorting out his own identity. Mary says Marc ran the gamut of emotion, flipping from happiness to anger, laughter to tears, excitement to complaint. His big brother cast such a large shadow that Marc determined he would not waste any energy competing but would cast his own. He was the more physical of the two, even from a very young age. Sometimes people would ask, "And what grade are you in, dear?" Mary, amused, would explain he was only three.

While he shared his family's love of the outdoors, he chose a different path. Marc grew his hair long to Chris's short, played guitar and French horn while his brother collected insects, and in a brief period of defiance shunned his mother's cooking for store-bought bread and Kraft Dinner. As he grew older, he continued to tinker with electrical things and bought himself a Citizens' Band radio — handle "Mad Man of the Mountain" — later qualifying as a licensed amateur radio operator.

Marc (age eleven), Aquila, 1969.

He possessed the ancestral fibre of adventure and exploration. Determined to achieve his own independence, he thrived on self-sufficiency challenges. When he was only fourteen, he had an opportunity to work as an interpreter at Kejimkujik National Park in Nova Scotia for the summer. He told his mother he wanted to go alone. "Off you go," she said. He got a drive to Saint John, where he took a ferry across the Bay of Fundy to Digby, and then biked the remaining eighty kilometres to the park. A year later, he hitchhiked to Halifax by himself.

But he remembers his first real taste of freedom came when the Majkas bought snowmobiles. He'd careen through the old woods roads with their Samoyed sprinting in hot pursuit. Inevitably, a tree would get in the way or he'd get the machine stuck and be unable to work it free. At such times, he tied his scarf around the dog and sent him home for help.

In fact, Marc sometimes drove his snowmobile the twenty kilometres cross-country to school. Harry Doyle called to express his concerns over safety to Mary.

"This is no problem," she assured him. "This is just the way we are."

"It was my first experience with free-range kids," he said later. "Now we have research that says we've ruined our kids by structuring and protecting them."

Just as the Majkas were making a life for themselves on the mountain, Mary received word that her brother, Heniek, was coming for a visit. She had not seen him since the end of the war. Travel outside the Iron Curtain was difficult to arrange. It had taken him years to receive a passport and longer to get the appropriate approvals and documentation for travel. Mary counted the days until his visit.

She picked him up at the airport and on the way home filled him in on the family's activities. She mentioned that Chris was spending a few weeks in Saint Andrews, assisting a resident naturalist at the Sunbury Shores Arts and Nature Centre. To her surprise, Heniek, who was the chief librarian at a biological institute in Warsaw, said he had heard of the small Bay of Fundy village. "I know exactly where that is. I've had lively correspondence with the librarian at the Fisheries Research Board's biological station there. We exchange publications with them."

Mary immediately made arrangements to visit Saint Andrews, where Heniek was able to spend some time with his correspondent. Before they left to drive home, he had received an offer of employment with the Fisheries Research Board. The salary was generous and included a rental house. Heniek, honoured by the offer, said he would consider it overnight.

Mary was elated. "I was very happy because, having only one brother, I had not been able to enjoy him as much as I wanted to. I was full of hope and convinced he would accept, especially because Poland was economically very poor. I felt a kingdom had been offered to him."

She was crushed when Heniek refused, explaining that he was a patriot and could not leave Poland. He told Mary, "It's different for you. You were forced to leave Poland. If I left it now, I would feel like I was betraying my country."

Having lived most of her life separated from the family she loved, there was great pain in her goodbyes as she put him on the plane to return to Poland, a country she had left far behind.

෴

Pioneering

*I always felt I had been given a mission, and while I never felt
a distinct vocation, the great theme in my life has been to love
and to serve. These are the two things that dominate my life.*

David is outside taking pictures of a dragonfly. It had been wedged in the grill
of his truck, frantically beating its iridescent wings, but he managed to pry it off
uninjured. His rescue mission complete and documented, he walks to the house
with me.

Mary meets us at the door. "David Christie, have you been outside doing
gymnastics? Look at that stuff on your sweater!" She plucks bits of fluff and grass off
his back and arms. "And look at your wet shoes! Why don't you put on dry ones?"

"Because they'll just get wet too." David grins at me.

"What about your duck boots...you're too lazy, that's why. Too lazy to look
for them. Ahhh..." She waves her hand in dismissal and moves to her customary
chair on the Bridge.

"He can be a tidy person, but his office and his bedroom are a source of
amusement to me. He has letters forty years old." She rolls her eyes. The stacked
bookshelves, boxes, and impossibly high mounds of papers support her assessment.
He keeps an inventory in his head. If he cannot recall a decades-old detail or date
immediately, he knows where to find it.

"In his closet you never know what is there. He still has national park uniforms, his red-and-black UNB jacket, feathers from a hen that died twenty years ago, animal teeth, flying squirrel tails."

"One is fresh, the other is old," David defends himself, grinning. "One of them has dried louse eggs."

As he turns to leave, Mary looks at me, eyebrows raised...see what I mean?

"Enough," she says. "I have pictures to show you." She turns her attention to a photo box on her lap, slides open the cover, and takes out a packet of photos. "Ah, look! That's where that went...Dave, come see this!" She holds up a dry, shrivelled leaf with what looks like a woven sack of silk attached. "It's a lambkill leaf with some sort of gall insect on it. I brought it with me last summer from..."

When I begin to laugh, she chides me. "You laugh, but to us this is something to learn about. You never want to stop learning. This is how you love life."

○३

New Brunswick is small enough that Mary could drive her Volkswagen from one end of the province to the other in a little under six hours. In such a place, the degrees of separation are slim and people talked widely about the Polish doctor's family who, instead of choosing the comforts of city life, elected to live in a wild setting on top of Caledonia Mountain. In the 1960s, immigrant families were uncommon in the area, so the Majkas' European customs afforded them a certain degree of notoriety. Mary was the subject of several magazine and newspaper articles. In 1965, a *Chatelaine* magazine journalist visited Caledonia Mountain to interview Mary for a series on Canadian women. The subsequent article portrayed her as a hunter and a gatherer who lived off the resources of her wilderness mountain but also implied she had a wide social circle by noting she had once taken a bear roast to a New York party.

"I really felt until now like a drifting piece of wood," Mary told her. "Now I have roots." She called Caledonia her "dream mountain" and said her neighbours were "so generous and open-hearted, I have never seen such hospitality."

This rootedness and acceptance into the community gave her a jumping-off point. Serendipity gave her a push.

A newspaper article featuring Mary's technique for colouring and etching traditional Polish Easter eggs prompted the hostess of a locally produced TV show, *At Home with Helen Crocker*, to invite her as a guest. Mary appeared several times, demonstrating how she cooked her Polish specialities — cabbage rolls, perogi, and borscht — as well as a few non-traditional edibles, such as cattail stalks and wild mushrooms. After filling in for the hostess during a dental emergency, an idea began to take shape. She had already been giving casual nature talks in area schools for several years, a practice begun after Chris asked her to speak to his class about migrating birds. Soon, other organizations were asking for her help with YMCA day camps, outdoor retreats, and field trips for children.

"When I saw Canadian people had little interest in nature, then I intentionally went and approached the schools to do a program. But my main reason was because I want to share. I want to tell them how wonderful and interesting and fascinating the natural world is."

Volunteerism was a relatively new approach for the school system in the 1960s, notes Harry Doyle. "But she set up a rapport that made it easy for us to begin getting involved with volunteers."

Mary approached the superintendent of schools, asking him to consider offering formal outdoor education and field trips so children could experience nature first-hand. The superintendent thought the idea had merit but was not practical, as teachers had no training in controlling the children outside the classroom setting. He told her, "We are more concerned with teaching children the basics. Outdoor education is a frill."

Since it appeared that an outdoor education program would take more time to formalize, it dawned on Mary that she could reach more children via television than she could in person. When she proposed a new nature show for children, with herself as hostess, the program director suggested a taped audition. Using a stuffed robin, a nest, and robin eggs as props, she talked about what the birds eat and where they build their nests. Within a few days, Mary received a call from the studio, "Turn on the TV. You're on in ten minutes."

The fifteen-minute segment, *Have You Seen?*, soon became a half-hour show. Each week, a short film clip of Mary toting a butterfly net and leading a pack of skipping children preceded the live broadcast. Her set was designed as the interior of a log cabin. Chris and Marc were regular recruits on her show. She never rehearsed or used a script and rarely pre-planned beyond selecting a general theme that might include stuffed and mounted wildlife and, on occasion, live animals.

Margie McLaughlin remembers Mary showing up at their home one morning, blowing in like a gale, announcing she needed Barbara, her five-year-old daughter, to help with a show on lambs. Mary had taken the backseat out of her Volkswagen and Margie could see a lamb's head bobbing up and down through the car window. "I haven't a clue where she got it, but she just told me to get Barbara dressed and have her at the studio on time," says Margie. It never occurred to her to say no.

Mary interviewed Barbara on live television, asking questions and using the child's answers to share information. All was going well, Margie thought, pleased that Barbara was completely at ease, but she noted the lamb was not so content. It wouldn't stop bleating, so Mary asked her friend to take it outside. Margie still laughs about the incident. "There I was, standing outside the television studio on Halifax Street in downtown Moncton, holding this lamb on a tether and thinking, 'I hope no one I know drives by!'"

Mary's ideas for turning life into a valuable lesson seemed endless. Once, she brought in a live bat. As she took it from the box to show how harmless it really was, the bat took advantage of the opportunity and flew straight at the camera, landing spread-eagled on the lens. On another occasion, she showed up at the studio with a dead mouse in her purse. She had caught it that morning in her kitchen. Thinking it would make a good prop and a topic for the show, she dropped it into her purse before leaving the house.

"On her way to Moncton her gas line froze and she called a taxi to bring her here," relates Jack Christie, the show's producer. "When she opened her purse to pay, the cabbie saw the dead mouse. She came in the studio laughing and saying, 'I wonder what kind of person he thought I was to be carrying a dead mouse in my purse.'"

Jack remembers a woman who was never flustered. "She was always happy and pleasant, never upset when things did not go well," he says. "She would either laugh it off or use it to her advantage. And she had a way with children. She could relate to them well and didn't talk over their heads."

Jack says her strong Polish accent was an asset rather than a hindrance. "You had to really listen to understand her. She was very excitable about things, and because that excitement made her talk faster, people would have to listen closer."

Mary always ended her show with, "Go out, enjoy yourself, have fun!" It might have been a mantra for her life. *Have You Seen?* ran on CKCW-TV from 1967 to 1974 throughout New Brunswick and also in parts of Prince Edward Island and Nova Scotia, bringing important exposure to Mary and helping establish her reputation as an expert in the natural world. Mary Majka's name and face became familiar to an entire generation of children and parents.

Mary encouraged many children not only through her television show but also through the naturalist clubs. At fourteen years of age, Brian Dalzell was a "closet birder," his interest sparked when, flipping through a bird book in a store, he spotted a bird he recognized. "When I drew the connection between the bird in the book and the bird in the wild, something clicked." His mother bought him the book for Christmas and he spent hours trying to memorize each bird depicted on the pages. He began watching *Have You Seen?*

One day, his mother met Mary. She mentioned her son's interest and Mary told her about an upcoming Moncton Naturalists' Club meeting. When the teenager arrived at the meeting and saw all the adults he almost didn't go in, but Mary spied him and drew him inside. "She was like a mother hen, taking people under her wing. She made it known that an interest in nature wasn't anything to be ashamed of. Mary helped me find and define my passion, just by recognizing my potential," says Brian. He went on to build a career of birdwatching.

"I can't tell you the jobs I've had since then. If it wasn't for my birdwatching skills, I'd be in the league of the unemployed," Brian says, looking back on his thirty-year career as a naturalist. "Mary lifted people up to her level. Everyone needs mentors and she certainly excelled in that regard. She not only inspired people to reach their potential, but she enabled them to pass it on to others. She gave a gift that keeps on giving."

While participating in a bird-banding program on Grand Manan Island, Brian made it a point to involve children. "During that ten-year period, I worked with about twenty-five hundred children. I always made sure everyone had a chance to see and touch the birds. I think I imagined myself as Mary Majka. I wanted to pass on the love of nature that she encouraged in me. It may not take root in all of them, but maybe one in a thousand will turn out to be exceptionally gifted. So I treat everyone the same and hope her influence will spread far and wide. Like ripples."

For all of these different projects Mary was involved with or initiated, she was never paid a salary. She saw her work as a service she provided for the education of children. The TV studio forwarded her all the letters sent in by parents and children commenting on her show. She answered each one personally.

Because she spoke in terms and language that helped people to understand more about their environment and how to protect it, she began to receive more requests to appear at schools and clubs as a speaker. She also appeared on, or guest-hosted, other locally produced children's shows, such as *Small Talk* and *Romper Room*, and an adult talk show called *Supper Club*. Sometimes she was stopped on the street or in stores because people recognized her. In fact, decades after her earliest education endeavours and into her eighties, people would stop her in grocery stores or shopping malls to comment that they had watched her when they were young, or they had taken one of her school excursions or field trips that had changed their attitude toward nature.

Mary's involvement in outdoor education and her television show fostered more confidence about her ability to influence others. She still carried the weight of regret from that small, seemingly insignificant, incident in Salzburg when she watched

Mary as a guest of *Small Talk* with Miss Beth, CKCW-TV, circa 1971-72.
(Courtesy of Jack Christie)

the women running for the bus with their suitcases and had done nothing to help them. "I can still see those women running. When there is something you know you have to do and you don't do it, you suffer for the rest of your life."

The television show marked a shift in Mary's life. She was beginning to understand how to make things happen. And she already knew what she wanted to happen next.

Mary believed that organizing the three established naturalist clubs in the province under one umbrella organization would create a more effective voice for conservation. The three groups were already corresponding and taking field trips together. Mary envisioned a combined federation that would use the New Brunswick Museum as a headquarters for the collection and compilation of data from the individual groups.

From the onset, David had identified the goals of his own Saint John Naturalists' Club to be actively working to preserve unique natural areas and to "apply our aims provincially by the formation of a provincial organization of naturalists." But he noted the club was not yet strong enough to work on the former, and more study was needed to determine whether a provincial organization would best serve the needs of the area's naturalists.

Mary saw no point in waiting. "I am a woman of action. When I do something, I want it done right now. I deal with things immediately. Because of that, I am very dictatorial."

Now that David was living under their roof, she convinced him it was time. In 1967, to celebrate Canada's Centennial year, the Moncton Naturalists' Club took on the establishment of a provincial organization as a project, and she and David presented the idea to the other two clubs. The Saint John club showed interest, but Fredericton members worried it would detract from their own initiatives. Moreover, some of their founders feared that belonging to a federation would bring them into a more activist stance, something they were reluctant to consider.

Mary believed action was imperative with respect to the protection of wildlife, the environment, and sensitive areas and that those concerned about the future should join voices and gain strength through cohesion. She also realized the clubs needed a unified front with a clear direction and a spokesperson to represent them. Failing to gain the unanimous support of all three clubs, she had to set the initiative aside; she was not, however, giving up.

Her commitment to action also prompted Mary to revisit an issue she had taken up just after they had acquired Aquila in 1961, when she, Mike, and the boys had been exploring a backcountry road in their car. The road had started high on Caledonia Mountain and then dropped to the narrow valley floor of a gorge. Steep ridges rose on both sides, leaving barely enough room for the road and a creek alongside. This was a most enchanted place, aptly named Crooked Creek. It was a wild area visited mostly by hunters and anglers or by local teens in need of a cooling swim in summer. The creek itself was not wide, but Mike speculated it must have an abundance of rainbow and speckled trout. Branches had brushed against the side of the car as they passed a few clearings and then rattled across a covered bridge.

Mike had stopped the car suddenly, astounded to see all manner of garbage and junk tumbling over the embankment close to the creek. This was a municipal dump. It didn't take any imagination to see that when the water ran high during spring or heavy rain, it would wash the garbage downstream, over waterfalls, and into the swimming holes used by the village youth. Beyond the obvious impact on the fish and wildlife, such waste would pollute the very waterway that provided so much enjoyment from fishing and swimming, not to mention what might be leaching into the creek.

At that time, the Majkas were still new to the area. Mary didn't know how government worked, but she had appeared at a county council meeting in hopes that, presented with the Crooked Creek dump problem, council members would understand the critical situation and agree to relocate the dump. It wasn't quite that easy. The council felt the location was both convenient and unobtrusive. Her appeal was dismissed.

Several years later, now knowing more about the procedures such matters required, she called and wrote letters to politicians, even making several trips to present her case directly to the provincial government offices in Fredericton, but without success. Most of her appeals were met with the promise, "We are working on it." Eventually, when the chief engineer with the provincial Department of Health became involved due to the health issues, she thought her fight was over. But rather than relocate the dump, a decision was made to divert the river.

Her discouragement was evident in a letter she wrote to the chief engineer a few days later:

> For a very long while now, it seemed as if my wish would come true, but I realize it was just a wish and so it fell literally into the water of the Crooked Creek, together with all the garbage that will fall there henceforth. After all, the authorities are much stronger than one woman who does not have any idea about these things — the way they always have been and will be run.[27]

The letter must have made an impact because the diversion work was stopped and a new dumpsite was designated some distance from the river, but still within the Crooked Creek gorge. She was asked if she were satisfied with the outcome. "Of course not!" she responded. "This beautiful valley does not deserve a garbage dump, period."

Then, just like a bad mystery movie, came an anonymous phone call. "Mrs. Majka, if you are interested in the garbage dump in Crooked Creek, you'd best go and see what is happening." She and Mike drove to a small look-off with a view of the valley. In plain sight, she could see a large area cleared of trees, and bulldozers and excavators were busy clearing more brush and digging trenches for a new dump. She began to cry. Mike consoled her, but she felt that her intervention had made the situation worse. After she returned home she called Brenda Robertson, a newly elected MLA for her district, and asked her to come down to see the excavation work. Brenda complied and was immediately on side.

"Mary was passionate about the environment," recalls Brenda, "and there weren't too many people in those days who were passionate about the environment."

Brenda worked with the proper authorities and the municipality to halt the excavation, replant trees, clean up the former site, and establish a new dump in a more appropriate location. Later, when Mary suggested the province stop roadside spraying because it was harmful to wildlife and people, pointing out it cost less to cut roadside bushes mechanically, Brenda again saw the logic. She phoned Mary a week later. "It's done," she said.

"From my knowledge and working with her," says Brenda, "and listening to her dreams about the environment, I believe she awakened the sleeping environmentalists that were around, shall we say, and the general population, especially in the southern area of Albert County, learned from her."

This passionate Polish woman intrigued Brenda. As their friendship developed, Brenda offered guidance from a political standpoint in how to best approach a project by ensuring research was provided and the proper authorities contacted.

"When a project was simmering in the back of Mary's mind, we'd get together and talk about it to try to figure out the best avenue for development. She'd listen. You could say to Mary, 'I wouldn't go that avenue.' You can't jump over local people with responsibility. She doesn't do that anymore."

Mary had had a number of mentors and teachers in her life, but perhaps David was the most significant. During their many hours spent together, Mary questioning, David answering, they played guessing games. Mary would ask David to describe a bird and she would have to figure out what it was. Other times, he would mimic a birdsong and she would guess which bird it belonged to. Mary would bring home a bouquet of plants and flowers, and David supplied the names. In kind, she taught him what she knew about mushrooms and edible plants. Occasionally, Mary and David travelled the trails of Fundy National Park together as he worked and she plied him with questions on unfamiliar birds or trees or insects that they encountered. She came to love the park, its hills, river valleys, colourful history, and its creatures.

Shortly after her TV show had begun, the park superintendent asked her if she would create a nature centre for children at the park; she leapt at the chance. Mary's own intuitive understanding of nature had grown through daily observations. Encouraged as a child, she sought new experiences that enriched and built on this foundation. She believed that children were born with a special sense passed down through the millennia. If not recognized, nurtured, and encouraged, this innate sense of wonder and curiosity might be lost. Such a loss to a child, she felt, was a loss to the future.

"Today that ability to simply enjoy nature is more than just a romantic, sentimental feeling," she wrote. "We have to realize that the next generation is the last one to have a reasonable chance of straightening out all the trespasses against nature that mankind has allowed itself."[28]

The opportunity to mentor and educate the children who had been previously overlooked excited Mary, but for a project like this, she felt she needed training. So during the summer of 1967, she joined Chris as a volunteer at the Sunbury Shores Arts and Nature Centre in Saint Andrews. The centre, then in its third year of operation, focused on delivering programs that encouraged the integration of art and nature.

Mary made friends with the centre's founder, Dorothy Meigs Eidlitz, an American who summered in Saint Andrews. The two women spent some time together, and the elder lady must have taken a liking to Mary, as she offered her a scholarship to attend the 134-hectare Audubon Camp on beautiful Hog Island in Maine's Muscongus Bay the following summer. Since 1936, the Hog Island camp had been offering nature study programs with some of the most respected naturalists and educators in the nation, including Rachel Carson, who had visited the island in 1960 and mentioned it in her book, *Silent Spring*. The lessons Mary learned while on Hog Island contributed to her understanding of the sea and coastal landscape of the Gulf of Maine and, by extension, the adjoining Bay of Fundy.

At home, she had been the subject of good-natured ribbing from David and Chris. "They would tease me because I wasn't as smart as them. They always made me feel like I didn't know anything, but when I went to the camp in Maine I was the star. I thought, Gee, I shouldn't listen to those guys."

After Hog Island, she returned to Sunbury Shores Arts and Nature Centre to assist staff naturalist Stephen Kress (now a well-known ornithologist) with interpretive programs. It was a chance to get more practice and to fine-tune the two-week pilot program she would be delivering at Fundy National Park later in August.

While at Sunbury Shores, she chanced to meet Carl Buchheister, the president of the National Audubon Society. After observing her easy rapport with the children during a field trip, he offered her enrolment in a four-month naturalist course beginning in March 1969 at the Sharon Audubon Center in Connecticut. The nature centre provided a place where children could discover a love for nature and adults could be trained to teach effectively. Mary was delighted to be given such an opportunity.

From the beginning, it appeared 1969 would be an eventful year. David had left Fundy Park the previous year, after he'd been transferred to a desk job he did not want. In March, he was working at the Université de Moncton as a research assistant

Mary babysitting a baby harp seal, Aquila, March 1969. (Courtesy of G. Vienne and J.P. Varin)

when they received an odd request. A French film crew from Paris, documenting the seal hunt on the ice floes between Newfoundland and Prince Edward Island, bought two downy white seal pups from the hunters and needed a safe place for the animals until the filming was complete. Someone from the university put them in touch with Mary and David.

The two pups, nicknamed Majka and Christie, were flown by helicopter from the ice floes to Caledonia Mountain. Mary and David lined the walls and floor of a small guesthouse on the property with cardboard, then shovelled snow inside so the seals would have a quiet, secure place. They need not have worried, as even outside, the pups did not wander far. Whenever someone approached, they would wobble toward that person, crying like a baby. Using powdered egg yolk, vitamins, cod liver oil, and high-fat cream, Mary mixed up a formula the consistency of thick pancake batter, but it was no easy chore to feed the unwilling pups. Afterwards, her clothing reeked of fish oil, but she didn't mind. The pups remained at Aquila under their care for four days before being picked up by helicopter and then flown via commercial airline to France. The brief but unusual experience was a forerunner of things to come.

Later the same month, Mary left for the Sharon Audubon Center. She discovered the facility was also a gathering place for environmentalists and naturalists. While there, she met a number of prominent people involved in the Audubon Society who would remain friends and valuable contacts. In the coming years, bird photographer Russ C. Hansen and Les Line, then editor of *Audubon* magazine, made several visits to the Majka home.

During her stay at the centre, she missed her family terribly, making several emotional phone calls home. But despite her loneliness, she revelled in the beauty of the location. One day as she walked she sensed she was not alone. She turned, seeing nothing but a large, mature oak tree, its branches spread wide and in bud.

> I felt as though a hand grabbed me and said sit right down here. I did sit, right beneath the tree, then eventually I lay down and pressed my cheeks against the exposed roots of the oak. I could feel the rough texture on my face and the life within. It was one of those moments when I felt I was one with the tree, part of the roots, part of all that which surrounded me. I dissolved into that tree.

Years later, she would write, "Have you ever tried to get acquainted with a tree? First, you touch its bark, then you shake a branch, as you would shake a hand, and when you look up into its crown you see its nodding head and hear a whisper of welcome. Don't just stroll on! Now it's time for the tree to get to know you."[29]

More and more often, Mary was experiencing a deep spiritual and physical kinship with her surroundings, describing it as "a flight that takes you beyond the borders of tasks and thoughts, in which your individuality dissolves and you become one with something much bigger, where feelings and thoughts no longer belong to anyone or anything, and you are part of something ever present, never ending."[30]

Mary had been influenced and touched by nature's beauty and healing interaction, but now she was learning how to intuitively express what she knew and felt in terms others could also comprehend and appreciate. She felt a calling to become a conduit for the voice of nature, to become nature's storyteller.

> What Audubon gave me was not so much knowledge of nature —
> I had that instinct already — but they taught me to organize things
> in such a way as to help people learn. It also was an assurance that
> what I was doing, I was doing properly. It taught me how to handle
> children and groups, and it gave me confidence in myself.

The training gave Mary grounding in interpretive work that was largely responsible for the projects she would soon undertake. Upon completion of her course, she returned to New Brunswick and then, based on the recommendations from her previous pilot program, threw herself into developing the very first nature centre for children within Canada's national park system.

She made miniature habitats in saltwater and freshwater aquariums, terrariums, and cages for the fish, insects, and small creatures gathered from within the park environment. Behind a window in the centre, she installed a large frame holding a beehive so that the children could study the bees at work through the glass. A hollow pipe leading from outdoors into the glass-sided hive allowed the bees freedom to travel. As Mary and the children explored the forest, seashore, pond, field, and brook habitats, they brought some of their discoveries back to the centre to be kept in a suitable habitat. Because a true naturalist is not a collector of living things but a person who loves and respects nature, she had the children return all living specimens to their natural habitat at the end of the day.

Mary recognized children who were predisposed to intuitive nature awareness and encouraged them. She didn't stress the formal identification of creatures or plants but rather the enjoyment of observing. She allowed the children to make their own discoveries, to experience and enjoy nature, as she answered questions and explained what they had found.

"You can become a naturalist by studying and watching nature, but a true naturalist at heart is something different," she says. "Some children are born with this ability. They see the world in a way that other people don't observe or are not sensitive or perceptive enough to capture. It's a gift."

She recognized that parents had lessons to learn as well, and in a handout she suggested they could best teach by example and begged them to "refrain from stepping on spiders, killing snakes or frogs, breaking eggs in birds nests, just because they happen to be in your path. Instil in your children the idea that life is as precious to these creatures as yours is to you and it does not make you a hero when you kill something innocent and small."[31]

Sometimes her hikes attracted up to eighty participants at a time, so she was fortunate to have Marc as a helper. She drafted a proposal to expand the nature centre concept to other national parks, with herself as a trainer for the program. She travelled to Ottawa to present it in person, but at that time parks officials did not share her vision that educating children should be part of a nationwide national park mandate. Disappointed, she returned home. She knew nature had much to gain from the education of young people.

Blair Stevens was one of the student interpreters who worked at the park with Mary. He first met her when he was a grade ten student on a field trip. At that time, she urged him to pursue the study of nature and ecology. "My father was a hunter and had fostered my interest in the outdoors, but Mary was a naturalist. She switched my interest more to preservation and studying the intricacies of nature. She encouraged me in a way that said this is a good and reasonable thing to do and you could make a living at it. Before this, it was a passing interest, a hobby."

Blair says her encouragement helped him choose a career path. From his summer employment at Fundy, he would go on to earn a bachelor of science in ecology and remain within the national park system as a biologist for another eleven years. Blair recalls, "She challenged people to do things better for nature or for the preservation of history. She saw it in terms of causes, events, projects, more so than humanistic." He pauses, his voice full of emotion. "There are people who influence you at key times in your life and they have a major impact. Mary was certainly one of those people for me."

It could be said that by the end of the 1960s, Mary had taught some valuable lessons and she had learned some valuable lessons — certainly about bureaucracy and dealing with people but also about the power of an inner passion and how sharing that passion ignites and influences others.

While her nature programs at Fundy National Park were well received, sometimes her outspoken observations about park policy and practices were not. "We had tried to influence the way the park did things, but Mary was a thorn in their side," says David. "After I left the park, it seemed she was always running into things that needed change. Not that she was looking for them, but she would find them."

When Mary pointed out that work crews repairing a dam on the Point Wolfe River had drained the pond, exposing the entrance to the beaver dam and disrupting the beaver colony, the superintendent told her the engineers had advised him it was the best time of year for repairs. "You are listening to the needs of the engineers?" Mary was shocked. She had watched a mother beaver laboriously dragging branches across the muddy river bottom to feed her young. "In a national park you should be listening to the needs of the wildlife!"

She also discovered that a storm sewer close to a restaurant and gas station was draining into a nearby pond and the septic overflow from the campground was draining into the nearby marsh. Mary's "snooping around," as it was sometimes referred to, was not always welcomed, but such comments did not discourage her.

"It was rather a strained relationship," recalls Blair Stevens. "They [the superintendents] were glad to have someone standing up for the natural part of the park, but on the other hand, she sometimes made life difficult for them. There were some superintendents who didn't want to see her coming because she stood up for what she believed in. If she thought they were doing something that shouldn't be done, she told them directly, had good arguments. She did her homework thoroughly. She was a force to be reckoned with, but in a very good way."

Mary says, "When I was younger, if something didn't go my way, I got angry and didn't accept it. But David had a way of excusing everything — people, things, happenings — whereas I was not like that. If someone was angry, I would think he was angry because of me, but David would say, 'Maybe he just had a bad day.' This is something I learned from him and it benefited me tremendously."

In the barest of terms, Mary was a fixer and a doer. When she saw something that needed fixing, she was the one to make it happen. "If I didn't do it, I wouldn't be myself," she says.

However, in July 1971, one of Mary's interventions had unexpected results. In an attempt to resolve a developing conflict between the student interpreters and their supervisor before it became nasty, Mary received the blame for inciting the incident. In reality, Mary had stepped in to defuse a situation in which she had no direct involvement. She paid for it when she was painted as the leader of a student revolt. Stunned and hurt by the accusation, she collected her things from her office and left.

When Mike came home from work that evening, he found her crying inconsolably. The next morning, as she slept, he called the superintendent and told him that Mary would not be returning. He may not have cited the real reason for Mary's resignation, as in a subsequent letter the superintendent writes, "We realized you had heavy and continuing commitments on your time but took it for granted that your apparently inexhaustible energy would continue undiminished. I believe 'indestructible' was how I described you to Dr. Majka." A month later, Mary wrote back, "It was not my energy that was being destroyed, but my morale and personal dignity."[32]

Following the incident at Fundy, Mary needed to get away. She drove to Green Lake, Maine, to visit her friend Phyllis Jordan. The hiatus seemed to restore her spirit. Phyllis recalls that Mary would get up early in the morning and slip into the lake for a swim, then return to the cottage, her arms filled with ferns, flowers, and mosses to make a bouquet.

"Green Lake was where Mary made a contribution that enriched my life and gave me years of pleasure that continue to this day, whenever I can commune with nature," writes Phyllis. "Can you imagine having your own private naturalist? Mary and I walked through the woods and she taught. Her enthusiasm was catching and her laughter was wonderful."

Her respite wouldn't last long; there was more loss to come. Before the end of 1971, her dear friend Frieda Gamble passed away. Mary was her executrix. Roland Hutchinson performed the funeral service. As difficult as it was for him, he knew her death was also hard on Mary. "Theirs was a very dear friendship. Mrs. Gamble was a homeland figure, an icon of Poland, a mother figure, I am sure. Having to deal with these things would have been traumatic for Mary, in spite of her being a person who has dealt with all kinds of trauma in her life."

Emotionally, it had been a tough year for Mary, but on the rebound, she seemed to throw herself into her education projects with even greater energy. It was something that came naturally to her; it had certainly been one of her father's great passions. She knew the key to exposing more children to nature was to ensure that teachers had a better understanding themselves, and she turned more attention to making this happen.

The previous year, she had planned and organized a series of one-day outdoor education workshops for teachers held at area high schools and collaborated on a quarterly outdoor education publication designed to give teachers ideas on how they could engage the students in nature and outdoor activities. During the summer of 1972, she stayed with David's Aunt Florence in Saint John while she taught a summer extension course on outdoor education techniques for teachers at the University of New Brunswick's Saint John campus. This was the first course of its kind. It was becoming more apparent that environmental education should be part of school curriculum.

Then, in 1973, the City of Moncton introduced a new winter outdoor education program as part of a wider initiative encouraging outdoor activity. Bob Cameron, the parks and recreation manager, had worked with Mary on several youth excursions in the early 1960s so he wanted her involved. "She was a natural at getting their attention and keeping it," he recalls. "She provided a hands-on experience and had the children getting down and getting dirty. I remember her rinsing them off in the river so we could send them home clean."

Mary, assisted by two university students, led half-day field trips with grades five and six students, showing them how a typical classroom topic such as geography, history, art, mathematics, language, social studies, or science might directly relate to the world around them. "They not only learned about meteorology or trees or nature, but they learned the concepts that went with that. They touched the earth and its realities," recalls Bob.

One group wrote in a letter to the editor: "We learned about different kinds of trees and were shocked to see how they had been destroyed in the park. We collected mosses and observed birds and evidence of garbage and water pollution . . . may this program continue for many years."[33]

Although the program was short-lived, Bob Cameron developed huge respect for Mary. "There is a spirit there, and that spirit comes out whenever she takes on a task. She also has an ability to make you feel good about what you've contributed."

In tandem with her educational projects, no issue was too obscure for Mary if it concerned wildlife or habitat preservation. For example, when the City of Moncton had been developing a regional plan in 1971, she submitted recommendations on behalf of the Moncton Naturalists' Club that were endorsed by schools and hiking and forestry associations for the protection of the areas around two city reservoirs as natural green space for hiking and study. In the proposal, she wrote, "Just as any live organism, so a city has to breathe, drink, eat and deposit its waste, and as any living thing, a city needs its quiet places for enjoyment and recreation, repass [sic] and solitude."[34]

Doug Koch, who was working for the consulting firm hired by the city at that time, remembers her well. "We perceived Mary as a very well-informed and articulate activist, an effective advocate for conservation and certainly a special character. I think for me, Mary's draw was her unique enthusiasm for nature and her absolute conviction that it should be protected."

All her workshops and programs, coupled with her television show and a developing relationship with the media, established Mary as an expert on the front lines of a growing environmental movement. As well, her own desire for knowledge and her concern for the environment led her into membership with a number of organizations, including the Conservation Council of New Brunswick (of which she was a founding member), Atlantic Society of Fish and Wildlife Biologists, National and Provincial Parks Association of Canada (now CPAWS), and the Canadian Forestry Association, which invited her to be a member of the board because they wished to introduce natural resource conservation programs in schools.

Her increasing involvement in these associations enabled her to attend lectures and information sessions, provide input into pressing environmental issues, increase her circle of acquaintances, travel across the country, and advance her own education. Mary began building a network of colleagues, friends, acquaintances, and resources that would serve her well in the coming years.

Elsewhere in Canada, other environmental organizations were coming into their own. Also in 1971, the Audubon Society of Canada continued its evolutionary process and became the Canadian Nature Federation (CNF).[35] Mary encouraged friend and university researcher Eric Tull to take an active role in the new federation after he suggested New Brunswick needed representation. Eric had met the Majkas when he started a post-doctoral fellowship on seabirds at the Université de Moncton. He had called to inquire about an upcoming Moncton Naturalists' Club field trip to Mary's Point, and Chris offered to drive into the city to pick him up. The field trip turned into supper and an overnight stay, which evolved into a lifetime friendship.

"I was basically adopted by the family and started spending weekends with them," says Eric. "Mike would drive me out and take me back Monday morning. I had come from Toronto, where birders to some extent would do that, but the Majkas went the extra step and created a home for naturalists. People would just drop in. There was always something going on — birding, fellowship, friendship — she was always planning field trips. They made it a home away from home."

At Mary's urging, Eric became the New Brunswick representative to the CNF and, along with Mary, attended their founding meeting in the spring of 1971.[36] At that meeting, the CNF encouraged the formation of a provincial body, thus paving the way for preliminary discussions as the clubs decided whether to form a federation.[37] Mary had never given up on her desire to bring the naturalist clubs together under one organization, and the seeds she had planted back in 1967, when she and David first brought the idea to the clubs, were about to sprout. Her tenacity had paid off.

"Mary can be quite domineering; a very forceful personality," notes Eric, "often not the most patient of people. If she doesn't happen to agree with what is going on, she will push in and push her point of view. You either accept or push back. This can be off-putting at times, but she is also extremely warm, friendly, welcoming, so that as you get to know her, it compensates for some of these features and you get a great relationship."

On a cloudy Saturday, November 18, 1972, eighteen naturalists from around the province finally met at the Fairway Motel in Sussex to form the New Brunswick Federation of Naturalists (NBFN), with David Christie as its first president.[38] In his first published address to the members, David wrote, "For years, we looked at the organizations of some neighbouring states and provinces, envying the things they were doing, but with a small population of naturalists, never having enough support for a group of our own."[39]

The founding directors of the New Brunswick Federation of Naturalists (left to right): Al Smith, Mary Majka, Peter Pearce, David Christie, Eric Tull, and Beverley Schneider.

While he knew Mary from previous outings, Peter Pearce, a founding member of the Fredericton club, remembers the meeting as his "introduction to Mary's dominant personality. Mary has always had a lot of good ideas and is not shy about promoting them," he says. "Over the course of many meetings I went to, especially when I served as president of the [NB] Federation, I felt she came on strong at times, seemingly to David's discomfiture. He's such a nice guy. I thought Mary would put him down a little every now and then. She is a forceful character.

If she believes strongly enough in a cause, she promotes it and let the chips fall where they may."

David was by then working as curator of the New Brunswick Museum's Natural Science Department, having assumed the position in August 1969 after his childhood mentor, Austin Squires, retired. The role allowed him to study and share his knowledge and expand his network. It also raised his profile as a biologist and naturalist within the region. He was quickly becoming one of the province's foremost authorities on bird populations.

The museum was a natural hub for the collection and dissemination of information, and soon after assuming the new job, David had begun publishing a regular newsletter, *N.B. Naturalist*, with articles on natural history. After the formation of the NBFN, the *N.B. Naturalist* became the Federation's magazine and David continued on as its editor, assisted by Mary and by Peter Pearce, then later by other members. The magazine had already been a valuable tool for collecting and distributing information on birds, mammals, insects, weather, and miscellaneous nature news, but it then became the main communications link between the executive and the membership of the NBFN. By gathering sightings and observations from around the province, reporting on rare or unusual animal, bird, and plant sightings and trends, it also became a detailed testimony of the province's natural history, which may have otherwise gone unrecorded.

In April 1973, the NBFN boasted 248 members.[40] As a direct result of the newly formed Federation, Sackville resident and Canadian Wildlife Service employee Al Smith started the Chignecto Naturalists' Club. Following that, Mary, David, and Eric travelled to the Miramichi area to promote the Federation, leading to the creation of the Miramichi Naturalists' Club, followed by the Kennebecasis Naturalists' Society. With the existing clubs in Moncton, Saint John, and Fredericton, this spread of enthusiasm boded well for the fledgling organization.

Just as Mary began to wade deeper into the role of an environmental advocate, she was needed back in Europe in her role as a daughter. In 1973, her mother, as a result of severe osteoporosis, suffered damage to her vertebrae in a fall and would not walk again. Mary immediately flew to Austria. Since Mary had left Europe in 1951, she had seen her mother fairly regularly, in both Canada and Europe. When old age prevented Maria from travelling, her daughter paid her extended visits in Austria.

Mary stayed with Maria for six weeks, during which time the two women grew much closer. Mary learned that her mother had been an unofficial social organizer at the manor. She had conducted skits and plays, wrote and recited poetry, organized concerts. When others were sick, she brought them violets that she dug from the forest and potted. She helped in the kitchen and made batches of jam. Perhaps sensing they had few visits left, Mary asked her mother about her father. As Maria recalled details of his family history, Mary took notes. And, finally, after decades of silence, they talked about Henryk's death.

In the aftermath of her husband's death, Maria had learned that a sum of money disappeared from his school. With his upcoming move to the Chełm school, the financial records would be reviewed and the missing money would have to be accounted for. Maria never learned the details concerning the missing funds but suspected an influential home and school association, comprised of estate owners whose sons attended the school, might have funnelled money from the school's budget into the association coffers for some purpose. She knew there had been scandals surrounding the association's activities in the past. Whether Henryk was involved or simply discovered the missing money when he reviewed the accounting is unknown. Dishonest dealings seem to be at odds with the character he exhibited — his actions portray a man of honour and compassion. One thing was certain: regardless of where the criminal fault lay, Henryk knew he would be held accountable and the resulting scandal would ruin both his career and his family's reputation.

Before he took his own life, Henryk sent letters to both his sister Kazimiera, and his wife, Maria. Kazimiera received her letter first, prompting her to travel to Grodno. In the letter, Henryk stated his regrets for the effect his death would have on his family, especially on his daughter, and that he felt terrible leaving her, so the two women took Mary to Warsaw, hoping she might influence her father, should they find him. They published an ad in several local papers begging him to come home.

Kazimiera and Maria tracked Henryk's movements as he travelled by train to Warsaw and Częstochowa, hoping to borrow money from friends. Unsuccessful, he continued to Sulejów, a small village on the main rail line between the two cities. There, he disembarked and walked to a small park, where he sat on a bench and consumed an overdose of pills. Polish people place enormous value on dignity and honour. For a Polish patriot, death was preferable to dishonour.

When his body was discovered, Maria and her sister-in-law travelled to Sulejów to make the identification. Because Henryk's pension would be withheld in the event of a suicide, Kazimiera urged the coroner to list the cause of death as heart failure. She wanted to ensure that Maria, with her two small children, would not lose her widow's pension. The deception would also protect the family from more public scandal. She must have made a convincing argument. They buried him there and returned home.

"I never shed a tear," Maria told her daughter. "Not a single tear. What he did was cruel." As Mary and Maria shared the experience that had shaped both their lives, Mary also came to know and understand her mother on a deeper level. During her childhood she had witnessed warm displays of affection between other children and parents and wondered why her mother never held her close. She finally realized the coolness was just her mother's nature. Maria endured many hard years following her husband's death, and she did the best she could for her children. Mary admired her strength, which she only came to appreciate long after her childhood was over.

Mary, who continues to keep a photograph of her father on her night table, still senses there was more to the story. Once, she contacted her brother and her cousin Maja, Kazimiera's daughter, seeking information. Heniek had no new insights. Maja provided some background on the family history, writing that her mother had told her about the incident many years ago, but she made her promise never to reveal what she said. Maja refused to break her promise. So, Henryk Adler's death persists as somewhat of a mystery, and he remains a man Mary would never really know or understand.

Back on home soil again, there was much work to be done. The first NBFN annual general meeting was held in Odell Park, Fredericton, in September 1973. By then, the membership had grown to almost four hundred and the Federation was working to address three key issues: public education and improvement of laws protecting birds of prey, protection of Machias Seal Island, and the establishment of nature reserves in the province.[41]

All three issues were close to Mary's heart. Within the organization's first year, the committee on birds of prey expanded on what Mary had started years earlier and was successful in having the hawks and owls protected under the Fish and Wildlife Act. They also successfully lobbied federal and provincial governments to discontinue issuing permits that allowed farmers to shoot birds, mainly robins, that were causing damage to blueberry crops.

That same year, members of the Fredericton Field Naturalists' Club were dismayed to learn a study had not been done to assess the ecological effects of a proposed provincial park surrounding New Brunswick's highest peak, Mount Carleton.[42] Mary quickly reviewed the province's inch-thick conceptual plan and prepared a five-page brief with recommendations. She and Eric Tull presented it on behalf of the NBFN at two public meetings held in northern New Brunswick. The brief supported the plans for the creation of provincial parks but urged an ecological assessment of the development, suggested a protected primitive zone, questioned the continued logging in the area, suggested restrictions on motorized use, and endorsed a proposed interpretive and nature program, among others.[43]

They hoped the park would maintain its wild nature. Following a multi-day foray into the northern New Brunswick wilderness around Mount Carleton, David warned that immediate action was needed to preserve forest wilderness before it was too late. "Looking back, one thought dominates: Just how threatened are the remaining wilderness areas of New Brunswick? Forestry roads push closer and closer to each other — roads that don't appear on the provincial highway map, but nevertheless are often bigger than many numbered highways. If an adequate wilderness is to remain, the time to act and protect it is soon, the sooner the better."[44]

With its members on the front lines of nature, the Federation was reporting on trends and populations, observing and monitoring changes in the environment, then presenting a voice for nature to public and government agencies. In the spring of 1974, the NBFN hosted an Atlantic naturalists' policy session in Moncton. National and provincial environmental organizations gathered to share ideas, projects, and aspirations. It was an important move, a strengthening of ties between scattered organizations with common desires. They identified establishment of natural area reserves as a high priority and tasked each provincial organization with creating their own wish list of protected areas that then would be communicated to the Nature Conservancy of Canada, a grassroots organization tasked with acquiring and protecting ecologically significant lands for future generations.[45]

The New Brunswick Department of Natural Resources, in anticipation of future legislation allowing for the creation of ecological reserves, had already solicited recommendations from the NBFN for potential Crown land sites that might serve for scientific research, preservation, education, living museums, and benchmark habitats.[46] They agreed, as a group, to establish their own lists of rare and endangered species and to build relationships with governments by complimenting and supporting all positive progress.

The Federation continued to make resolutions and present briefs to government and in doing so gained momentum, credibility, and influence. It maintained its vibrancy, many of its members continuing to take on conservation projects, monitor bird populations, construct and maintain nature trails, participate in advisory councils, and speak publicly on behalf of nature. Not all members, though, were in favour of wading into the more controversial issues. Sometimes during Federation meetings, Peter Pearce felt the tension.

"I sensed there was uncomfortableness among some members that we shouldn't get too deeply into strident environmentalism, but stay with our mandate to promote natural history," said Peter. "[Mary] was so committed to the cause of environmental protection. She was going faster than anyone else. It's quite clear in my mind that David was the support behind the scenes, especially in the early days."

Even long-time friend Jim Wilson, who has great respect for her, says moving Mary off her course would be like trying to move the Rock of Gibraltar; you just have to work around it. "When you're involved in anything as a group, Mary's opinion weighs heavily in the room. She's un-ignorable. She hasn't got all the answers, but she is a visionary. She's a great person to lead but not the best to be part of a team because she has difficulty working with people. This can be frustrating for the rest of the group."

Mary had momentum by then and was not about to sit back on her laurels. She had petitioned the federal government before the Federation was even officially formed for more protection of seabirds on Machias Seal Island, a small nugget of rock several kilometres from Grand Manan Island, in the Gulf of Maine. Even today, the island's sovereignty is not entirely clear. Ambiguity in the delineation of boundaries between United States and Canada in the Gulf of Maine can be traced back to the vague and disputable wording of early land grants and treaties, although Canada could surely claim squatter's rights to the island. The British government erected a lighthouse there in 1832, which is one of the few still manned, and Canada has maintained a continual human presence on the island since that time. The island had been under the jurisdiction of the Canadian Wildlife Service since 1944 because it supported a significant population of Atlantic puffins and terns.

When the Majkas had first visited Machias Seal Island in 1968, two Canadian lighthouse keepers and their families were the only human occupants, but fishermen from coastal Maine regularly transported tourists to the island to view the birds. Although federal regulations later limited the number of people visiting the sanctuary to twenty-five per day, those visitors walked freely about the island without due care, stepping on eggs, disturbing the nesting birds. Even then, Mary worried that visitation would only increase in the future and continued human interaction would not bode well for the birds. Several years later, editor Les Line, from *Audubon* magazine, visited her home on Caledonia Mountain following a photographic expedition to Machias Seal Island and voiced similar concerns. The conversation prompted her to write to the newly formed Ministry of Environment, asking for protective measures to ensure the continued well-being of the nesting populations on the island.[47] But, because the island was in an area as grey as the mists of the Atlantic, it was not a problem easily solved.

In 1974, to raise public awareness, she wrote an article for *Nature Canada* about the problems facing Machias Seal Island and suggested solutions, one of which was creating an international bird sanctuary. "Throughout its recorded history," she wrote, "Machias Seal Island has been mishandled, mismanaged and for the most part, blatantly disregarded."[48]

She also sent letters to the Canadian Nature Federation, suggesting they employ a student warden on the island for the summer and help finance the construction of bird blinds. The CNF complied, supplying funds for blinds, which NBFN members built and erected, and placing a student warden on the island for two summers. In 1975, the Canadian Wildlife Service would take over this function, ensuring continued safety for the birds.

Mary took on other international issues as well. After reading an article in *Nature Canada* about the overhunting of whales by the Japanese, Mary heard that the Japanese ambassador to Canada and a Japanese trade delegation were visiting Moncton. She presented the ambassador with a copy of the article and a brief in which she reminded the ambassador of Canada's moratorium on commercial whaling.[49] She encouraged other conservation organizations across Canada to add their voices to the NBFN's with similar presentations as the delegation worked its way across the country.[50]

As other opportunities arose for the protection of habitats, people would alert Mary for action. When a friend noticed logging on Crown land close to a great blue heron rookery, he contacted Mary. She immediately called the Department of Natural Resources, pointing out the land surrounding the heron colony had been designated as a proposed ecological reserve. "They stopped cutting. And I had never even been there to see what was happening," she said. "People would just call me up because they knew I would act." A decade later, Phillipstown Blue Heron Nesting Site would be officially designated as an ecological reserve.[51]

In 1978, while leading an NBFN field trip to view ancient hemlock stands at Shea Lake near Plaster Rock, naturalist Erwin Landauer discovered several specimens of uncommon orchids growing in the silt and sandstone soil at the outer fringes of a bog. Lady's slippers stood waist high with flowers reportedly as big as a fist. Few could imagine such plants growing wild in New Brunswick. Landauer returned to the area a number of times, discovering seventeen different wild orchid species, among them Venus' slipper-orchid and a very rare small round-leaved orchid, and the first New Brunswick discovery of the Lapland buttercup. Such a rich variety of orchids and other rare plants growing within a small area made this a valuable piece of property. The land had already been identified as a potential ecological reserve, but the presence of the rare orchids made immediate protection crucial.

To accommodate the orchids' habitat, the proposed protected area would have to be enlarged. Landauer, also a member of the NBFN, spoke to Mary about his concerns because he felt assured she would know how to proceed.

Mary ably took up the cause. As a member of the Environmental Council, which was a group of citizens who met every two months and served as advisers to the provincial ministers of environment and natural resources, she was invited to attend a meeting hosted by Fraser Inc. of Edmundston, New Brunswick, the pulp and paper company that owned large tracts of land surrounding Shea Lake. Fraser had begun a program of replanting cut-over areas, and they wanted to show the Environmental Council how they were contributing to environmental sustainability. For two days, as the council members toured the lumbering operations and nurseries, Mary bided her time. Then, when the entire group gathered for a wrap-up meeting with the president of the company, she was prepared. She was gambling the president would want to end the tour on a positive note.

"Are there any questions?" he asked the assembled group.

Mary spoke up. "I have a request. I would like you to protect a portion of swamp that you own in the Shea Lake area." She brought out a photo album filled with photographs of the orchids. She carefully and clearly explained the value of the plants, why it was necessary to protect them, and what would be lost if they were destroyed.

Mary remembers the president laughing as he said, "Well, you are quite a flower girl. And I am a businessman. However, since you have asked, I can promise you, we will save this place."

He proved good to his word, taking immediate steps to protect the area from disturbance. A decade later, in 1988, Fraser Inc. would lease thirty-six hectares of Shea Lake bog and fen to the Nature Trust of New Brunswick, the first in a network of protected preserves established by the trust.[52] This event would further serve to illustrate how Mary could convince business and government to invest in the environment. She did her homework. She thoroughly prepared her material and then presented her case effectively with logic and respect. She had no hidden or personal agendas and served to gain nothing for herself. By then, she was learning when and with whom she could apply pressure. She was shrewd and wise enough to know when to push and when to fold her cards. She believed in making personal contact, preferring to meet the people she was dealing with face to face. She did not demand; she asked reasonably and politely.

On occasion, Mary's efforts on behalf of wildlife and sensitive habitats laid the groundwork for others to finish. In the mid-1970s, a tiny amphibian making its home on the outskirts of Fredericton had gained the attention of local naturalists and biologists. The only known New Brunswick population of the gray treefrog was in a garbage-strewn gravel pit near the confluence of the Nashwaak and Saint John rivers, making both the creature and its habitat subjects of great interest for the NBFN.

"For a naturalist, it is a real joy to go out and see something they haven't seen before in their life, but mainstream people don't understand this," says Dr. Jim Goltz, a provincial veterinary pathologist and naturalist. "The more rare and exotic it is, the more you desire to see it and the more thrill when you do. It incites real joy and wonder."

A time would come in 1981 when the location was proposed as a new dumpsite, and it appeared the frogs' habitat might be seriously threatened. Mary, who was serving as president of the NBFN at the time, prepared letters of concern for the Minister of Natural Resources and the Fredericton City Council.[53] The minister referred the matter to the Environmental Council. Since Mary was also a member of the council, she frequently (but unsuccessfully) brought up the subject of protecting the gravel pit for the little gray treefrog — so often that it became an ongoing joke among the members.

"She planted the seeds of awareness that there was something special," said Jim, "so later, when the time was right, a bunch of us were able to meet with the officials and protect the site. Without her intervention, it would have made our job harder."[54] In 1995, the Nature Trust of New Brunswick would enter into a lease agreement with the city, allowing them to create the Hyla Park Nature Preserve, Canada's first amphibian park.

Mary had learned to use both the organization and the media to best advantage. Newspaper photos of her as early as the 1970s show a lone woman among men, confident and earnest, her hands in motion. The strength of her influence came from her motivation. Mary was pioneering a deeper awareness of environment. She was nature's champion, pure and simple.

The fact that she was an uncommon player in an uncommon role did not escape the attention of her son Chris, who by that time had begun pursuing his own career in biology. "She played an educator, activist, naturalist. My mother was very committed to pursuing her interests and having a career. She came from an environment in the 1950s when women were housewives, nurses, teachers, but she had the notion of doing television shows and outdoor education. She was bucking the trend and as a consequence of that, put a lot of her energies into it."

Newspaper journalists found themselves drawn in by her passion. Former *Times & Transcript* editor Edith Robb remembers the first time she travelled with her future husband/photographer, Bill Robb, to Caledonia Mountain to interview Mary about a story about living on the land. Mary took them on a search for mushrooms. "It's hard to say what most impressed me about Mary, but the list would include her incredible stamina as she hiked through the forest, her oneness with the natural world around her, hearing sounds where all was hushed, seeing sights where all was shadowed, and appreciating and delighting in her mountain with a spirit that was as big as the outdoors around her.

"When we returned to her cozy home, tired and chilled, she put on a roaring fire, fried up the mushrooms, and served them on toast. In all my travels all over the world since that day, I swear I have never tasted a more succulent feast.

"Something else was noticeable that evening. Mary was younger then, but even at that point, it would be fair to say her countenance was not the glamour girl image of the magazines. But as she perched in front of the fireplace, talking at length about mushrooms, both Bill and I watched the transformation of a rather plain face into a truly beautiful one. In the soft glow of the fire, for the first time I understood the term 'inner beauty' and I saw how an inner fire can ignite the world around it."

ℰℭ

CHAPTER NINE

Calidris

When you observe nature, you are constantly watching, not necessarily just the birds or animals, but it is the whole picture you see. You walk on a trail and you see a feather, a leaf, or a track. You are constantly observing these things and putting them together into the story that is being told to you.

Mary is busily gathering papers, photographs, letters, and file folders in the basket of her wheeled walker when I arrive. She seems agitated and instructs me to wait for her at the Majka cottage. David will drive her there later.

It's just a short walk through the woods from the "Big House" on the hill overlooking the Bay of Fundy to the Majkas' cottage beside the shore. I continue to the beach, where the tide is creeping in silently, fingers of froth scratching the beach. At this moment, it seems unlikely this is the bay of giant tides. At Alma, to the west, the incoming tide hefts boats from the floor of the bay to the top of the five-metre-high wharf. At the Hopewell Rocks, to the east, tourists photograph the famous Lover's Arch sandstone formation as it fills with water. But here at Mary's Point, the water slides in, inch by inch, like an advancing line of cloud, slowly covering acres of glistening intertidal mud.

Presently, Mary's voice drifts over the treetops, sounding distressed. I soon learn the cause of her agitation. Mike, who is now eighty-four, fell a week ago. He lay on the floor in his room below the Bridge all night, unable to rise. He was uninjured but clearly needed closer attention and physical assistance. They moved him up into Mary's room on the main floor, so she has been sleeping on a sofa, as stairs are difficult for her to navigate. She is also trying to manage a large project, arrange housekeeping and prepare meals. The incident has upset her routine.

"I have discovered although I have a very flexible nature and am quite resilient, I still need to have order in my life," she laments as she prepares a platter of crusty bread, sliced meats, fresh vegetables, and cheeses for lunch. "I get upset because I cannot straighten things out. I am like a gypsy with no place to call my own."

"In other words," says David, "she is a DP again."

"Yes, when I was displaced the first time, I was much younger and it wasn't much fun. Now I am older and it is less fun. I live under some kind of cloud of tension and so often I break down and cry. David is suffering too. I know I am demanding too much and he is tired. He has his own things he wants to do, and when I talk to him, he doesn't take it in. Then I start repeating things. It drives him nuts, and then I think maybe I am an old ratchet for needing it done right away. So we have to straighten out our life."

She sat up late last night and wrote him a letter, emptying her feelings of despair onto the page.

"I would say I am still sane and still in one piece because of this cottage. I try to stay here as much as possible. The other thing is in the evening we go for a drive to the marshes. They are soothing, like a balm on my soul."

More than the Big House, even more than Aquila, this cottage at Mary's Point is truly her sanctuary. She "discovered" it quite by accident.

∞

Mary first became acquainted with Mary's Point just after the Majkas acquired Aquila, when a friend, knowing her interest in birdwatching, extended an invitation to their cottage on the point. There were hundreds of thousands of birds on the beach, she said. At that time, Mary assumed the comment was an exaggeration, but if there were even a hundred birds, it was worth a drive.

When she arrived, the tide was high and chocolate brown water covered much of the crescent-shaped beach. As Mary walked onto the arc of sand, thousands upon thousands of birds lifted into the air in startled flight. She stood in stunned amazement.

Nearby, a dog ran and barked while children chased and cheered. As the birds returned, streaming onto the beach like iron filings toward a magnet, one of the children picked up a rock and threw it. The dog chased after it. The birds again rose in the air. With a sound like wind in birches, they swept outward over the water. Mary was torn between amazement at the beauty of the birds in flight and

Semi-palmated sandpipers take flight at Mary's Point. (Courtesy of David Christie)

distress over the obvious disruption. She knew the children didn't mean any harm. They were just having fun.

Then, as she watched, a merlin appeared on the hunt, pointed wings silhouetted against the sky. Again the flocks rose in alarm; the rustle of each feather magnified thousand-fold. Watching the drama, she could feel the fear of their flight in her heart as tens of thousands flew like a tidal wave over the surface of the water, then banked, flowing upward, the flash of their white underbellies catching the sun in a glittering exposé of light and shadow.

The merlin manoeuvred swiftly, swooping back and forth, to isolate a single bird from the flock. When successful, the chase was on, one small sandpiper fleeing for its life. The two soared and twisted in a dance of horrific beauty and precision until in a sharp, quick turn the merlin snatched the tired creature from the air and disappeared into the trees along the shore to enjoy its hard-won meal.

The rest continued to flow thickly through the air like a swarm of bees, one moment a dark smudge, then, as they banked, a flickering white like a mirage materializing in the sky. When they returned, the chatter of their landing was like the rush of surf. Soon again, they were intently about their business, the common drama of life and death an event of the past.

Later, when her friend took her for a drive in his dune buggy, she saw something else that disturbed her. The deep gouges and arcs in the soil and sand told her the beach and marsh was also a popular playground for motorized vehicles. She stayed at the beach until the tide emptied the bay and the flocks disappeared, leaving behind a vision of gleaming mudflats against emerald marsh grass and red sandstone against blue sky. She didn't yet know exactly where these huge flocks came from, or where they were headed, but she sensed this place was as integral to their journey as it would become to hers.

Back home on Caledonia Mountain, she told Mike about her experiences with the birds, the children, and the dune buggy. "Something has to be done to protect them," she said. Mike was doubtful. The land was privately owned. How could she do anything to protect birds on a private beach? Mary knew he was right, but the idea lingered in the back of her mind. She knew only too well how survival depended on sanctuary. She also felt that sanctuary depended on her.

The Majkas began making regular visits to Mary's Point to observe the shorebirds, sometimes bringing friends and other birders. Sometimes Mary guided groups of children to the point for field trips and they explored the various habitats. She and David studied the area extensively, not only to discover more about the shorebirds but also to document the life of the dunes, salt marshes, and creeks. They observed creatures inhabiting the mudflats and tidal pools, followed the action of the giant tides, and noted their influence on the land. They noticed the greatest concentration of birds arrived in late July and gradually began to disappear in mid-August. They soon identified more than fifteen species of shorebirds, including sandpipers, plovers, yellowlegs, and dowitchers.

Mary photographing marine life, mid-1970s. (Courtesy of Brian Townsend)

In the fall of 1974, they had the opportunity to buy one of the two cottages located at Mary's Point, a small A-frame set back from the shore. It was tucked into the forest for protection but opened in front to provide a view of the beach and bay. Perhaps more importantly, the property included the narrow dirt road that provided the only vehicle access to the shore. They named it Calidris, the Latin name for the genus that includes the semi-palmated sandpiper, the most common species of shorebird at Mary's Point. The purchase of the cottage on the shore was to mark a subtle shift in Mary's life. A new chapter was about to open to her future, one that was deeply connected to her past.

The following spring of 1975, just after returning from a visit to British Columbia, Mary's Uncle Leopold called. "Your mother is very sick. Come immediately if you wish to see her alive." With great apprehension, Mary flew to Austria. Her mother was asleep when she arrived, so Mary woke her. She opened her eyes, looked into her daughter's eyes, and said, "I'm glad you are here. You know what to do." These were her last words.

"I stayed a long time, took over the care for her. I became sort of motherly toward her. I was thinking the roles had reversed. I told her how much I loved her, how nice she looked. I could see her expression relax."

Mary rubbed her thin arms and called her by the name she'd known since childhood. "Good Mizzi, brave Mizzi," she murmured. She recalled words Maria had sobbed several years earlier, "I don't want to live much longer. I want to be with my mother again."

As the days passed, she received a letter from David; a chit-chatty note telling her what was happening at home, intending to give her cheery news and lift her spirits, but his tone irritated her. She wrote back angrily, "I'm not interested. My mother is dying. Have compassion. Say that you are sorry or that you feel for me!"

She apologized later, "I just wanted to know they understood the situation I was in, but they were writing to me about porcupines." When she recognized the end was very near, she called home. "I need someone to help me. I cannot manage this alone." The next day, David was on a flight to Salzburg. David's presence brought comfort. They took long walks and talked about her mother. They sat with her and looked through photos, talking about her life, hoping she could hear their voices. Three days later — on April 18, 1975 — Maria's breathing changed.

Mary, needing some rest, found an empty room near her mother. She fell asleep but awoke from a dream that her mother was shaking her, saying, "Wake up, wake up!" She crossed the hallway and opened the door. "I could see she was gone. There was nobody there." Over the next few days, friends and relatives arrived for goodbyes, services, and prayers. Maria's ashes were buried beside her beloved mother at the family plot in Schärding.

After the ceremony, Mary and David decided to extend their travel. It was spring and the birds were migrating. They visited a shallow saltwater lake in Austria where storks were building nests and spoonbills, avocets, and egrets patrolled the ponds and puddles. Again, nature provided necessary healing. They continued to Vienna, Salzburg, and Innsbruck, visiting the places where Mary had lived and worked during and after the war. They saw museums, churches, and castles, stopped at roadsides to study plants and scan for birds. In Switzerland, they spent a few days in the Alps in a cottage belonging to friends.

While there, Mary spied a cluster of crocus bulbs that had washed down the mountain in the spring runoff. She tucked them in her pocket, thinking she would plant them back at the alpine cottage but forgot and took them home to Canada. She planted them at Calidris, a springtime reminder of her past. Where once they bloomed high in an alpine meadow, the transplanted immigrants now thrive by the sea, a continent and an ocean away, showing the strong and resilient can adapt to even the greatest changes, finding their roots in new landscapes.

Later that year, in a letter to friends, Mary would write of her mother's death:

> All her life she was a calm and composed person; her wish was to die peacefully without undue medical interference and artificial sustenance. Following her directions for three long weeks, we all watched her life ebbing slowly away into unconsciousness and death. In a way, it was a time in which I was dying a little too but yet there was nothing sad or depressing about it. In the most crucial point of our lives, we became once again very close through my accepting her death and her submitting to it. If my mother has taught me anything, this was her finest lesson and her most precious gift to me.[55]

Upon her arrival home from Austria, Mary spent little time grieving. Within weeks, she began working as a staff naturalist with nationally recognized photographer Freeman Patterson during week-long photography workshops he and a partner were conducting in his home at Shampers Bluff, New Brunswick. Freeman and Mary had met while she was conducting a mushroom walk at the first annual general meeting of the New Brunswick Federation of Naturalists in 1973. Impressed with her expertise and engagement of her audience, he invited her to assist him with his workshops by introducing his photography students to nature.

Participants stayed at local farmhouses and used his home for the workshop.

"At that time, we were teaching in the basement, eating at the table, working outside," recalls Freeman. "In that casual atmosphere, Mary functioned extremely well. She would come trotting in with some discovery — 'See what I have!' She was always bringing a different perspective, a different kind of examination of the world. On discovery, they learned the exotic is not more important than what is right under your feet."

While Freeman taught students how to see and capture their surroundings on film, Mary taught them the significance of what they were viewing. Sometimes Freeman told them to leave their cameras behind and to follow Mary, to see the river, trees, and wildflowers through her eyes.

"She was high impact. I think even more so than she is now. She is more laid back now," says Freeman. "Talk! You would be gasping for breath. Often when she talked, she would be so consumed with what she wanted to say that any other subject was more or less out. Although I think all that enthusiasm for most people is extremely refreshing, sometimes people get tired... but they never get cross."

She bent coat hangers into hoops, then asked each participant to toss the hanger and show her what they found within the circle, perhaps grass or moss, flowers or insects. She explained the significance of their discoveries and anticipated other plants or insects they might find within the circle.

"She has this very holistic approach to things," says Freeman. "She can pull out the details that make the vast web and show how totally everything is connected. This is what she did with the hoops."

Or Mary might disappear into the forest, emerging with a surprise for each participant — a palm-sized terrarium in a plastic container, planted with a colourful array of mosses, grasses, violets, and lichens. The parting gifts were her way of reminding them that even the small and inconspicuous could be a thing of beauty, worthy of the photographer's attention.

"I can see her collecting those flowers and making those baskets. They were tiny little things," says Freeman. "And they were more precious than if she had gone out and bought something. She made a gift that to her had value — it was beautiful in its own right. What better gift than a tiny little bit of New Brunswick?"

Mary assisted with Freeman's workshops for a number of years. During that time, she heightened her photographic skills, but she acquired something else as well. "I learned from him to take in beauty in a very different way than I did before ... not only beauty of nature or pictures, but a beauty of everything, the soul, the spirit... even the beauty of your own ideas."

But perhaps the most valuable gift was that of friendship. Over time, Freeman and Mary became closer than many others she called friends. When she visited, she brought him hampers of food, cakes, and preserves. "Enough for herself, David, me, and the entire Canadian Army," jokes Freeman. "She is always very dynamic and she tends to set the tone for every situation she's in. I could be having a quiet day and all of a sudden Mary arrives and the whole day changes. She is an event in itself."

Mary considered him one with whom she could relate in an artistic, expressive sense. She gave advice on some of his photography books, and later the two of them flew to Africa, travelling through the nature preserves and desert dunes in a four-wheel drive, photographing Namaqualand's famous fields of spring flowers. "There is a pace [*sic*] and stillness in these mountain meadows, filled with colour and fragrance, that very much approaches a heavenly image," she wrote in a letter home. The trip suited her nomadic streak and her need for movement and discovery. She made many friends along the way. They picked up fellow photographer Colla Swart and the three travelled to the edge of the ocean together.

Colla shares this memory: "Mary ran to the edge of the rocks, as far as she could, and threw both her arms heavenwards as if to embrace Canada in the distance on the other side of the Atlantic, and also to embrace life. I will never forget her tears of joy and excitement."

This was Mary: salt in her face, leaping waves at her feet, arms flung wide, embracing the wind.

Throughout her life, Mary had acquired considerable personal strength from the stories of Poland's cultural history. She realized there was great importance in having tangible touch with the past. She had been dismayed to see what little regard Canadians had for historic structures, as evidenced by the vanishing covered bridges that had so charmed her when they first arrived in New Brunswick. Certainly a number of them fell victim to midnight marauders, floods, or battering by oversized vehicles, but when the Crooked Creek bridge, which she regularly travelled through on her way to Fundy National Park, was replaced with concrete and steel in 1972 to reduce maintenance costs and accommodate lumber trucks, she questioned the misplaced wisdom. How could you put a price on the preservation of history?

Later, the Department of Highways announced a new section of highway would bypass the last covered bridge on the main road between Moncton and Fundy National Park. This bridge would also be dismantled and replaced by a concrete and steel structure. Mary decided she had to do something before they all disappeared.

Over tea, she and a friend, Mary Harmer, decided to call Brigadier Milton F.

Gregg, a retired federal cabinet minister and former president of the University of New Brunswick who was well known for his involvement in heritage conservation, to ask his advice about how they might save the remaining covered bridges. Gregg advised them to form a non-profit association to give order and focus to their mission. On July 9, 1975, the Albert County Heritage Trust (ACHT) was incorporated, with Mary Harmer as its first president.[56]

"When I persuaded her to become the first president, she said, 'I don't know how to do that,' but she was a tremendous organizer," recalls Mary. The trust's aims were to acquire and restore treasured landmarks, which might otherwise disappear, then give them back to the community. "I wanted people to know why they are here and to understand their role in the scheme of things. I am always trying to invoke in other people the ability to see what I see and enjoy it."

Under the auspices of the ACHT, they convinced the Department of Highways to allow the Sawmill Creek covered bridge to remain as a picnic site, parallel to the new highway. The trust initially assumed the responsibility for its maintenance and its security. On more than one occasion, Mary spent Halloween night sleeping in her Volkswagen inside the bridge to discourage vandalism, much to the amusement of the local community. But it also became a story related with an undercurrent of admiration and respect for the unusual come-from-away who would go to such lengths to protect a bridge.

The two Marys also used the ACHT to apply for and receive funding to hire four students who worked through sticky summer heat and clouds of black flies to clear brush from an overgrown pioneer cemetery on Caledonia Mountain. The boys unearthed, repaired, and reset tombstones, delineated the cemetery's original boundary, uncovered the stone foundation where the church once stood, and built a fence around the property, thus respecting the memory of the mountain's early inhabitants.

While not the first organization she'd had a hand in founding, the creation of the ACHT was a significant milestone as Mary branched out in yet another direction. While serving as a trustee with the National and Provincial Parks Association of Canada from 1970 to 1976, she had been commissioned to write a book about Fundy National Park, the first in a proposed series on Canada's national parks. She hired a secretary and incorporated the drawings of two local artists and apparently enjoyed the process immensely. She quipped in a letter to friends:

> If anyone wants to write a book, please contact me and I will tell you what to do. Have an intelligent, vivacious secretary. Buy yourself a comfortable lounge chair. Have a cottage on the seashore with no blackflies or mosquitoes to torment you. Sit outside all day long

preferably with binoculars at your hand so as to observe hundreds of thousands of migrating shorebirds. Have a garden with lots of juicy tomatoes, young carrots and radishes to make delicious salads to refresh your spirit. And Write your Book![57]

The reason for the secretary was that although Mary spoke several languages, she had problems with spelling. She had been labelled lazy all through school, so

Mary and Buffy, watching the tide on Mary's Point beach, 1976. (Courtesy of Brian Townsend)

it was actually a relief to her when high-school tests had revealed the diagnosis of dyslexia. When she began petitioning government and industry, she enlisted Mike's help typing letters and briefs. For a time after David moved in, he and Mike shared the job of typing her correspondence, emails, and articles from longhand notes or dictation, but eventually this became solely David's métier.

In the book, she wrote about the park's geology, natural and cultural history (exploring both legend and fact), and shared some of her experiences within the park habitats. With characteristic humour, she tucked in a few recipes, such as Moose Nose and Baked Skunk. It showed her appreciation of history and the role it played in the identity of the community. By the fall of 1976, she had finished her manuscript and sent it to the board of the National and Provincial Parks Association for review, "after having had innumerable battles with Dave who continuously criticized, corrected, and improved my writing."[58]

Mary was unhappy with the subsequent editing as she felt key elements and chapters were deleted. She refused to allow her name to be associated with the work in its revised state. When the original manuscript was returned to her, she took it to Brunswick Press in Fredericton, which agreed to publish the book. *Fundy National Park* was released in 1977.[59] By then, she had resigned from her position on the board, saying she'd had enough of cliques and feelings of exclusion in the past and did not need these same feelings resurrected.

Mary spent all her spare hours at the cottage. While Mike joined her for suppers, he slept at Aquila midweek as it was a shorter drive to the hospital. David, who was still working at the New Brunswick Museum in Saint John, stayed with his Aunt Florence during the week. The boys were there as time allowed, but Chris had been pursuing his interests in biology at Mount Allison University since 1971 and Marc would leave for the University of New Brunswick that fall to begin a degree in computer science. She had raised them with independent spirits, and both would forge their own lives away from Caledonia Mountain and Mary's Point, Chris following his interests in biology and the arts in Halifax, Marc pursuing a career in electronics and computer science in British Columbia, then later California.

Most days, she had the cottage to herself. The climate at Mary's Point was more temperate than on Caledonia Mountain, the soil rich, well drained, and workable. Mary built a large vegetable garden and occupied her days tending her garden, preparing meals, exploring the coastline, swimming, and watching the birds.

One afternoon she sat on a grassy knoll overlooking the sand beach, watching the flocks of shorebirds roosting at high tide. Occasionally, the birds jostled each other, sometimes smaller groups fluttered above their neighbours and shuffled into another position. Their subtle peeps lifted in a single collective murmur. For the most part, the birds rested quietly; so still, in fact, that at first glance the flock might be mistaken for a great pebbly sweep of smooth rocks on the beach. Mary estimated there were fifty thousand to sixty thousand birds spread out along the shore.

To her right, the western shoreline of gritty burnt sienna sandstone wrapped around the waters of Ha Ha Bay. To her left, the hook of Mary's Point, a two-and-a-half-kilometre-long peninsula jutting into the bay and shaped somewhat like the head of a goose. The point was a haven to all manner of wildlife — raccoon, red fox, coyote, deer, even bear, certainly to the great flocks of birds already resting on its shores — and especially so to the woman sitting alone with her thoughts and binoculars.

Suddenly, a shadow raced across the calm water and she looked up to see an immense shimmering cloud obscuring the sun. A single rippling organism filled the space between sea and sky, weaving back and forth. She dropped her binoculars and watched, wide-eyed and stunned, as the massive flock gyrated, swirled, and swept across the surface of the bay as if a single life force. She could feel agitation and energy pulsing through the air. In her own chest, her heart pounded in response.

> When I saw this, I burst into tears. I cried a deep, sobbing cry because I was so moved and upset that there was no one to share this with. Right then I decided we had to share it, we had to tell other people about it; we had to invite other birdwatchers and naturalists. I was watching a phenomenon, something so awesome and such a wonder of nature that it needed to be shared.

Mary later estimated the flock to contain a million birds, and David surmised that Hurricane Blanche, which had rolled up the eastern seaboard several days previous, had held up or redistributed several waves of birds, which then congregated, arriving at Mary's Point en masse.[60]

Just as Caledonia Mountain had invited Mary to explore and discover unfamiliar paths, this unusual hook of land was slowly revealing itself to her.

On another day, Mary was gardening at the cottage when Harold Brewster, an elderly neighbour and amateur historian, came visiting. He brought her a story he had written about a young French/Mi'kmaq girl who had once lived, died, and been buried on the point. His great-aunts had told him the romantic tale many times, repeating what had been told to them by their mother. It was for this woman that Mary's Point was named.

According to Harold, Marie Bidoque had been conceived from a brief liaison between a young Acadian man and a Mi'kmaq woman during the era of the Acadian deportation of 1755 and before the arrival of the English settlers along the Fundy shores in 1783. Popular legend states that when she was a child, her father disappeared during the deportation and her mother drowned. The young orphan grew up under the care of her Mi'kmaq grandfather. After he died she had to fend for herself. The English Loyalists came to settle the land, and Marie's life presumably took a turn for the worse. What followed were unsubstantiated tales of unrequited love, heartbreak, and betrayal between Marie and the Englishmen. Eventually, it is known that she built a cabin and made her home on Mary's Point. She fished, hunted, collected mushrooms and marsh greens, and probably grew her own garden. It seems she lived a solitary existence, belonging with neither English nor Aboriginal cultures, and so remained on the point until she was an old woman. One night, the legend states, Marie fell victim to the Fundy tides. Whether by accident or intent, no one knew. Her body was buried near the cabin where she had lived, on the tip of Mary's Point, with a circle of stones to mark the spot. A local historian, Ray Steeves, wrote that as late as 1961, Mi'kmaq Mary's grave could still be seen.[61]

As a child, Harold and his friends had sometimes put berries and other food on the grave so her spirit wouldn't go hungry, but when he and Mary were unable to locate the old burial site, they deduced the shoreline must have eroded and the grave lost to the tide. Nevertheless, Harold's story of love and loss captured Mary's imagination. Although what he had written was clearly romanticized, Mary believed it was grounded in fact. Her research turned up several references to support the existence of Marie.[62]

Mary had no doubts that she was a real woman, not myth or legend, but part of her destiny. "Sometimes I talk to Mary. I feel part of me is Mary. She was a Native and I have a Native soul. I always feel this in my heart; I live very free...an almost nomadic life. I don't, inside of me, have any rules or regulations of any kind. I am very free-spirited and I think she was too. She was part Native and part French, and she was a bit of an outcast as well. I somehow have this feeling that there was a special hand that led me to this place to do what I had to do, to make that Mary known again and to make nature known better and to protect this place."

The legend of Mary helped create almost a spiritual bond between Mary and the point of land bearing her name. In years to come, when people would mistakenly assume that the point was named for her, Mary would tell the story of Marie Bidoque, keeping alive the woman who may have faded into obscurity had Mary not become the keeper and protector of her story.

Mary at Mary's Point, "arms flung wide, embracing the wind."

Like Mi'kmaq Mary, Mary Majka possessed a very private side. Despite the fact that she was an adept hostess and a gregarious and sociable individual, continually inviting both friends and perfect strangers into her home as well as offering her cottage for meetings of the naturalist associations, she could not function without regular hours of solitude. The mountain had given her its strength and instilled in her a sense of purpose and adventure and exploration. Calidris became a symbol of rest and respite and of rejuvenation. She matched her own rhythm to that of the bay, working, travelling, and gardening during low tide hours; swimming, canoeing, or birdwatching during high water.

She swam regularly with the flocks flying just above her head. Sometimes they skimmed the surface of the bay, swift flowing around her, like river around a stone. They were so near, she felt the wind from their wings on her face.

The beauty of the landscape and her intimate interactions with the birds invoked profoundly altered states of being. She felt as if, for a heartbeat, the lines of separation between her and her surroundings vanished and she was granted a glimpse into another realm of existence. She considered it a gift but sometimes felt ill-prepared to receive it. "I feel inadequate; like it's a secret I have accidentally touched upon, and I think to myself, this is something that is not for me to know yet. It is an overwhelming experience of beauty that shakes you."

Jim Goltz vividly remembers his first visit to Mary's Point. As he sat on the

Semi-palmated sandpipers, Mary's Point. (Courtesy of David Christie)

beach, quietly watching the birds, two people emerged from the forest behind him. "Down came this woman in a one-piece black bathing suit and a fellow wearing glasses. They ran into the water and proceeded to swim. They did this in a ceremonial way, with appreciation for the landscape and the unique qualities of the Bay of Fundy. I felt they were performing a ritual for their daily swim. The shorebirds seemed to know them."

David and Mary's exploration and research continued to deepen their knowledge of and appreciation for the unique land characteristics and the flora and fauna inhabiting the point and its history of human habitation. They documented the birds, canoed along the shoreline, swam in the bay, walked the marshes, explored the forests. Now that they owned the cottage, they were one step closer to protecting that crucial segment of coastline.

Under the direction of Dr. Guy Morrison, the Canadian Wildlife Service (CWS) had started compiling data on the maritime shorebird migration in 1974, and Mary, Dave, and a small band of volunteers conducted regular shorebird counts at various migration sites on both sides of the upper Bay of Fundy as part of this research.

The next year, CWS began a banding operation in James Bay, Ontario, another area with known large gatherings of shorebirds. They knew the west coast of James Bay was a major migration pathway for a number of species between northern breeding grounds and wintering areas in South America. Scientists had a sense that the two locations were important links in a chain, but all the pieces had not yet fallen into place. They were unravelling the layers of the point, but there were still mysteries left to solve.

Volunteers regularly inspected the flocks, monitoring their numbers, checking bands, and reporting their findings to CWS. At the height of the season, single flocks might number between one hundred thousand and two hundred thousand sandpipers. Some of the birds arrived with splotches of bright yellow, blue, green, and magenta dyes that would disappear when the birds moulted in the South American summers. These markings helped identify specific individuals within the large flocks and monitor their movements. The banding program also revealed a sense of community within the flocks; often the same birds were observed arriving together over consecutive years. They know each other.

As they gathered and compared the data, scientists gained a clearer picture of the birds' migratory routes of travel. It appeared that the birds left their barren breeding grounds in the eastern arctic from late June through July; first the females, followed by males, and finally the newly fledged offspring. After a refuelling stop on the west coast of James Bay, they began arriving in waves on the muddy intertidal flats and marshes of the upper Bay of Fundy in mid-July. Here, they lingered, foraging for food until almost doubling in size. Clearly, the upper Bay of Fundy was the

Mary Majka with visiting birdwatchers watching migrating shorebirds at Mary's Point beach, 1977.
(Courtesy of Brian Townsend)

primary stop for what appeared to be millions of the hardy little birds, making it, particularly Mary's Point, an area of great scientific and conservation interest.[63]

At that time, federal and provincial governments had approved the second stage of planning for a tidal power development in the upper Bay of Fundy. One of several options identified was construction of a tidal dam across Shepody Bay that would possibly be anchored at Mary's Point. No one had yet invested time or energy into assessing the environmental and ecological impacts of such a major tidal development, and environmentalists worried that pursuing this route without due caution and research could have dire environmental repercussions.[64] The data gathered from the shorebird surveys was essential in determining the potential impact of the proposed tidal power project.

But for many, it is not the science of migration but the complexity of their flight that captivates. No single bird appears to lead; instead, they fly as a single, collective body, billowing like a silk scarf on the wind. Scientists believe the manoeuvres are evasive techniques intended to elude predators such as peregrine falcons and merlins, which can swoop into the flocks, knocking out a single prey, but beyond this survival technique, the birds seem to take particular joy in the exhilaration of flight. The aerial displays often mimic the wash of waves on the shore.

Meanwhile, across the bay, Acadia University student Peter Hicklin began looking for clues to what drew the birds to the area as part of the research for his masters in biology. "Like Mary, I had seen the great numbers of sandpipers, and whenever I asked the questions — what are they doing here, where did they come from, where do they go — nobody could answer. Hence, my feeling was that we could not protect them without knowing the answers to these questions." His curiosity led him into his life's work with the birds.

Wading into what appeared to be barren Fundy mudflats, he found a rich environment supporting sandworms, small clams, and a dense concentration of *Corophium volutator*, a tiny invertebrate commonly called "mud shrimp." The one-centimetre-long, lipid-rich crustacean, which tunnels into the intertidal mud, reproduced at an impressive rate. Hicklin discovered the shorebirds' arrival coincided with the breeding cycle of the mud shrimp. Based on his fieldwork, he observed that a single shorebird might consume up to fourteen thousand *Corophium* in a single tidal cycle, supplying each bird with the necessary fat stores to fuel its final migration leg, a seventy-two-hour non-stop flight over the Atlantic Ocean to South America. It was a critical relationship. Without the birds, the mud shrimp might overpopulate, literally eating themselves out of house and home. And without the mud shrimp, the birds would not have the fat stores enabling them to reach their destination.

It appeared that the Bay of Fundy intertidal zones provided an ideal refuelling stopover with a rich and available food resource for the birds. Protecting the intertidal shorebird foraging habitats from coastal development became a top priority. Al Smith, who was by then acting regional director for CWS's Atlantic region, placed newcomer Peter Barkhouse in charge of gathering material for a proposal to acquire key properties for protection.

Barkhouse recalls an enthusiastic reception. "Mary knew I was a biologist and was involved in the process of acquiring the site, so she was quite happy to show me the shorebirds. A big driftwood log was the spot where people used to go down and sit and view the birds. Mary made pretty sure people didn't go too much beyond that, but this time, someone started to walk down the beach. She took off after them in a flurry, her arms waving. She had a very shrill voice. She wasn't rude about it, but she got her point across. Most people reacted positively. There probably were some disgruntled along the way, but I think most respected that they shouldn't disturb the birds."

Mary's tendency toward impulsive responses sometimes got in the way of progress as CWS navigated through the tricky process of acquiring and managing the site. Hicklin remembers her being dismissive of government protocol and timetables. "She has a lack of appreciation for process," he notes. "And process is very important in government."

Mary functions better as a leader and grand schemer. She finds details tedious and would become frustrated when government procedures and policies got in the way of something she wanted to do. For this reason, while much mutual respect existed between them, the relationship between Mary and CWS was not always smooth. Her obvious impatience did not mesh well with the scientific minds of federal employees who, while recognizing and respecting Mary's passionate responses, preferred to deal with David's practical appreciation for proper procedure.

In fact, Al Smith doesn't remember much about Mary's involvement in the early process of acquiring the land. "We tended to deal more closely with David. David is really the unsung hero of it all. He is the biological brain behind the operation, but he never gets credit for a lot of things because Mary is the vocal PR person."

As crucial as David's contribution was, his forte and first love was scientific study, not publicity or project management. He was comfortable in the background, supplying the glue that kept Mary's projects on track. Working together, they made an indomitable pair, each one with a different approach but both motivated by an uncompromising concern for the environment.

In 1978, the Canadian Wildlife Service struck a deal with the private landowners and acquired the three upland islands and marshland of Mary's Point. Under the Canada Wildlife Act, the site was designated as part of the previously established

Shepody National Wildlife Area, which now encompassed approximately one thousand hectares at Mary's Point and the nearby Germantown Marsh. On paper, this provided federal protection, but the designation did little to actually prevent disturbance to the birds, as there was no federal money for enforcement. In fact, notes Al Smith, only one CWS enforcement officer covered the entire province at that time.

While Mary's Point had become a destination for dedicated birdwatchers and naturalists, locally there was little respect being shown the land and the flocks. Non-birding visitors sometimes disturbed the birds during times of rest with their activities close to roosting areas. There were scattered incidents of dogs and children chasing the flocks, hunters using the birds for target practice, teenagers having late-night parties, and people on dune buggies, motorcycles, and other vehicles riding roughshod over the beach, dunes, and delicate marshes and mudflats as they had always done. In Grande-Anse, across the bay, a vehicle plowed through a flock of sandpipers that were roosting on the dirt road because a high spring tide had covered the beach, killing or injuring more than twelve hundred shorebirds.[65]

Mary devoted much effort to educating visitors and discouraging disruptive activities on the beach. Daily, she explained where the birds came from, where they were going, why they needed to rest at high tide. She and David regularly walked the beach collecting broken glass, lobster shells, cans, and other refuse in a box. Herein lay the paradox of the situation: While she wanted to share the phenomenon of the birds with others and knew that protection of the area required publicity, drawing more people to the beach who had intentions other than birding in mind could only incur negative impacts on the birds.

David once spied a man, with his family, carrying a picnic basket and a firearm. When he asked what he was doing with the gun, the man told him, "Oh, I'm just going to shoot them snipes."

Jim Goltz had a similar experience when he stopped into a restaurant on his way to view the shorebirds. Some of the locals struck up a friendly conversation with him. When Jim said he was going birdwatching at Mary's Point, one fellow piped up, saying, "That Mary is always keen to protect the birds, but we like to shoot 'em and bake 'em in mud till the feathers come off. Then they're easier to eat."

"I wasn't sure if they were serious or if they were baiting me," recalls Jim, "but even so, it indicated some locals saw her as being eccentric but were also somewhat intimidated by her."

While she was doing her best to ensure that people understood the importance of allowing the birds to roost undisturbed, Mary felt they had to take a more active role in controlling beach access. Closing the existing gate across the cottage driveway occasionally slowed vehicle access but did not stop it completely, as most of the offenders considered the lane to be public property rather than a private right-of-way. Sometimes cars parking on the lane blocked the Majkas' access to or exit from the cottage.

"I felt that being the owner of the access and a portion of the beach, I had the right as a private owner to do whatever I felt like," says Mary. "For example, if my name wasn't Mary Majka, I could have closed the beach, not allowing anybody. I did a lot to protect and promote the birds and felt that CWS should respect that."

Mary once stood her ground in front of a young man on a dune buggy, trying to prevent him from driving on the beach. The youth might have struck her had Mary not leapt from his path. Another time, a large group of young people attending a noisy beach party blocked the road. Mary walked, in the dark, to a neighbour's home to call the RCMP. It resulted in an unpleasant confrontation between irate partygoers, law enforcement, and the Majkas.

Dune buggies and beach parties were not the only problem. For a number of years, the point had been a destination for organized overnight horseback trail rides from a nearby guest ranch. Once, Mary came home to discover two participants on a trail ride had left their group and broken into the cottage. The girl was drunk, lying on the sofa, and the cottage smelled like vomit. When Mary turned on a light, the girl opened her eyes and said, "Oh, I know you. You're Mary Majka. I've seen you on television." Not wanting them to remain in the cottage, Mary told them to get in her car so she could drive them back to the ranch. On the way, the drunken woman piped up from the backseat, "Have you a pen and paper?" While her companion rummaged for something to write with, she asked Mary, "Can I have your autograph?"

Meanwhile, her attempts at policing did not gain Mary popularity with some of her neighbours; all they saw was a shrill foreigner, waving her arms and ruining their fun. "Why doesn't she just go back where she came from?" one disgruntled neighbour commented. However, for every dissenter, there were many more who appreciated her efforts to protect the birds and safeguard their habitat.

Coming from Europe's patchwork culture, Mary was tolerant and accepting of opposing viewpoints, habits, and customs. She could understand her neighbours' point of view and reluctance to accept change, but ultimately it was what was best for nature that motivated her; people just needed to be better educated. In 1978, *Nature Canada* published an article she had written about the Bay of Fundy shorebirds, giving the site national exposure. In it, she painted a compelling portrait, both informative and inquiring. Her point was to show the value of what could be lost without adequate protection from disturbance and development.

She finished the piece with questions: "Sitting on a sandy beach amongst these delicate creatures I try to understand what motivates them to start their perilous journey. What guiding light sees them through?"[66]

Through her words, she brought out the unique qualities of the migration, took it beyond a scientific study, and awakened the imagination of the reading public — but the piece was also the impetus for members of the scientific community.

Peter Hicklin, already working on contract with CWS, read Mary's article. He saw that by bringing the reader into the shorebird experience, Mary created a deeper connection that would help encourage attitudes of conservation and protection. "Mary gets attention from around the globe," he says. "She is the character who popularized the issues. She showed that people can protect the environment; conservation would not be where it is without public support and education." This scientific writer then realized that there was great power and possibility in writing to improve public awareness and turned some of his energies to publishing, not only for the scientific community but also to reach a more general readership. The two needed to work hand in hand.

Between the publication of conservation articles and scientific reports, by the late 1970s, Mary's Point was gaining international recognition. Two American scientists contacted Hicklin, questioning how CWS had managed to acquire and protect Mary's Point. They were hoping to find solutions for Delaware Bay in New Jersey, another shorebird migration point where much of the coastal land was under private ownership.

Hicklin brought them to visit Mary. On the way, the three men stopped, spellbound, to watch as chimneys of shorebirds spiralled up, up, up, in the still afternoon air to catch the high level winds. They looked like a tornado of birds. It was a rare moment.

At the cottage, Mary prepared and served a meal, then spoke about her involvement at the shorebird reserve: how she wrote articles and talked to the press to gain public support and how government and private individuals can work together. Afterwards, she took one of the men to the beach for a walk.

The other two stayed at the cottage with Mike, who had remained quiet throughout the afternoon. Suddenly he began to talk. "He didn't speak with emotion, didn't ramble, but he spoke quietly with passion," says Hicklin. "Bless his heart, for that few minutes, in a time when conservation was just starting to happen, he spoke about why it was important to him, his children, and the Canadian people. It was a good two- or three-minute spiel that left us unable to respond. Then he excused himself and went to get us a cup of coffee."

It was a memorable visit for all three men. "They went back to Philadelphia and

New Jersey inspired by their trip north and began writing articles and meeting people and the next thing we heard, Delaware Bay had been declared a Hemispheric Shorebird Reserve," said Hicklin. "This is Mary's strength. She's an example for others."

During the years that Mary's Point was gaining international recognition as a significant shorebird migration site and Mary was getting involved in heritage conservation, she undertook another significant project on the home front. In 1976, two years after they bought Calidris, the Majkas had purchased an additional sixteen-hectare parcel of land surrounding the cottage. The property included a dilapidated old house originally built in the mid-1800s. Through the years, the house had been stripped by salvagers; the windows and doors, even floorboards and banisters disappeared; wind reached its fingers into the cracks and holes in the walls, gradually pulling, tearing, and tugging the frame. The collapse of the stone wall on the north side of the cellar caused part of the house to sag.

Swallows had built nests in every cranny, even in the old stone cellar, and raccoons set up housekeeping. Plaster hung in chunks and decades of graffiti adorned what was left. But even so, situated on a high, proud hillock overlooking the bay, the derelict structure was an object of character and beauty, for decades a favoured subject for landscape photographers and painters.

The Big House, as it was when the Majkas purchased the property, circa 1975.

Proud owners of the soon-to-be-restored Big House, circa 1976 (left to right):
David Christie, Chris Majka, dog Buffy, and Mary Majka. (Courtesy of Marion MacKinnon)

Since acquiring Calidris, Mary had been visiting the old house, as if she were visiting a friend. She often sat outside in the long grass and dreamed, or wandered through the structure, touching the old timbers, wondering why the house attracted her so.

One day, she walked to the house in the rain. Streams of water flowed through the holes in the roof and she realized if she did not do something soon, it would be lost. She made the decision to restore it. Despite opinions from others that she was crazy, she contracted a local handyman/carpenter, Gerry Jones, to begin restoring the house. His advice was to bulldoze it to the ground and start over; nonetheless, he agreed to take on the project.

The restoration work commenced in 1977 and took two years to finish. Mary learned much about old house construction during the process and even took a woodworking course so she could help out. The fieldstone foundation rested on bedrock, perhaps one of the reasons the house was still standing. Large hand-hewn beams formed the skeleton and birchbark insulated the walls. Plaster mixed with horse or cow hair covered the laths, then this was either painted or covered with wallpaper or newspaper. The wide cedar boards salvaged from the ceiling gave some indication of the grand size of trees cut from the virgin forests of centuries past. The house had never had electricity or plumbing.

"At first I felt badly when they started to tear off the plaster and remove the splitting clapboards," says Mary. "I thought, this house is so beautiful in this abandoned state and I am going to ruin it, so I was determined not to change its character, inside or outside."

When swallows returned to the upper floor of the house, she ordered the workers to cease construction around the nests until the young were fledged. "It would have bothered me for the rest of my life, had I knocked out a swallow's nest just because I needed a room renovated," she says.

Every morning Gerry and Mary shared a cup of tea and discussed the next phase of the work. Sometimes the discussions became heated. "He was trying to rein in my great imagination, but I wouldn't want to give in."

When an old sluiceway washed up on shore, neighbour Glen White identified it as part of the dyke spanning a nearby creek, which had been breeched in a storm five or six years previous. The sluiceway, some fifty years old, was held together with hand-carved treenails rather than metal spikes that would corrode in the saltwater. Incredibly, the structure remained intact through the battering of the tides and winter ice, a testament to the old construction techniques. Mary was delighted

The Big House at Mary's Point, 2004. (Courtesy of Deborah Carr)

the artefact had found its way back home and used the planks to build exposed beams inside the house.

Glen also filled her in on the history of the old house. An original house on the property had been stripped to the floors and the materials used to build the existing home. The remaining stone foundation was made into a tavern for the men working at a nearby quarry. It had been a rather raucous establishment that was the site of regular fist fights and skirmishes, and even a murder or two, if one was to turn an ear to popular legend. Knowing the story of the house made its occupants come alive for Mary.

"When I started living here, my thoughts often went to the people who built the house and lived here. I felt the ambiance and vibes. Now, it probably holds our personality."

Mary removed some walls, opening up the main floor of the home to the light, and "the plants just crawled in." They built a sunroom four steps up from the living room and called it the Bridge because it overlooked the bay, like a captain's bridge. Other seafaring names followed. The sunken room below the Bridge became the Hold and the living room, the Main Deck. The Swallow's Nest was upstairs. They furnished it with antiques inherited from David's grandmother and later from his Aunt Florence as well.

By the time they completed the restoration in 1979, Caledonia Mountain had begun to lose its allure. Hunting camps had sprung up like mushrooms, clear-cuts turned dense forestland into waste zones, and trucks kicked up dust as they sped up and down the road. The mountain had become a popular playground for snowmobilers and ATVers. Some days, Mike complained that they needed a traffic light. They sold Aquila back to the former owner and moved permanently into the Big House.

A new Mary had made her home at Mary's Point.

∞

CHAPTER TEN

Conservation

My legacy is that I have been able to make people realize that some things are worth saving and protecting and treasuring. The fact that people now understand there are things, like heritage, that need to be protected so they will be remembered; this, I think, is my achievement.

David is wearing a threadbare sweater with holes in the elbows and strings hanging from the bottom. Mary begins teasing him about it, plucking at the frayed threads and saying if he insists on wearing it, she needs to mend it. He playfully swipes at her hair. She giggles. Within moments, they are nattering at each other over some silly detail, a sequence of events that they cannot agree on. The argument begins to escalate and Mary's voice rises in annoyance. They argue like children.

I am uncomfortable and embarrassed to witness the tone and bite of their disagreement. David offers an explanation. "She says I contradict her and it makes her look stupid to other people. But sometimes she just doesn't feel well. Then she is more irritable. I recognize this and it doesn't bother me. It has to get really bad before I get angry and snap back."

"Excuse me, I want to say something," Mary interrupts. "People who watch us have a different perception of our relationship. They take it more serious than we do. All these funny squabbles and angry outbursts are completely outside the feelings we have for one another. There is a core that is very strong and never going to be touched. Outside are all these irritations, but they have nothing to do with what is between us. Our disputes are unimportant."

Mary told me once she would never speak to Mike in such a manner because it would upset him. She knows when she has pushed David too far. She then retreats. "His grandparents, aunts, parents doted on him. If they saw how I handle him...."

"I learned to fight you by fighting my father," David says with a grin. "He prepared me for you."

We talk for a time about their relationship. David says she is the most important person in his life. "She was there when I needed her. We'd get things off our chest just by talking about it, and that's been important. Even though she badgers and bullies me, this doesn't change. She is my family. She loves me, criticizes me, helps me, accepts my faults. We accept each other, even if we don't agree."

Tears fill Mary's eyes. "It is moving to hear how he feels. I wouldn't be the person I am if he wasn't around. People always think it is Mary, Mary, Mary. Sure, I am the leader, but without his support and assistance, I wouldn't even dream of starting anything. He is so much a part of me. It is difficult to express. Like he said, it is everything."

⚘

It had now been two decades since the Majkas arrived in New Brunswick, and Mary had mothered her own children and many others; she had moved to the front of a swelling environmental movement, becoming almost a poster child for nature. There were often injured or orphaned birds and animals under her care. She'd involved herself in so many different projects, organizations, and events that her life must have seemed almost frenzied at times. She was in constant motion. While she had dropped membership in several organizations, she was still actively involved in the Conservation Council, Environmental Council, the Moncton Naturalists' Club, and the activities of the NBFN, serving as president from 1980 to 1984. As soon as she took office, she launched into a campaign that saw New Brunswickers choose the black-capped chickadee as their provincial bird. Coincidentally, twenty-five years later, on October 27, 2005, Mary would stand proudly in Government House and receive the Order of New Brunswick from Lieutenant Governor Herménégilde Chiasson and Premier Bernard Lord. Prominently displayed on her invitation would be the black-capped chickadee.

As well as the hours she devoted to safeguarding the beach at Mary's Point, she also began leading whalewatching and birdwatching tours from Grand Manan Island. And, of course, there was always a variety of bird counts, surveys, and field trips throughout the province to participate in and Federation events to organize. At fifty-seven years of age, she showed no inclination for slowing down; if anything, some thought she had her fingers in too many projects. A journalist once told her, "You hold too many crows by the feet and each one wants to fly in another direction."

In 1980, after David quit working at the NB Museum, he was able to spend more time helping Mary with her various projects. This marked the beginning of a closer collaboration and working relationship between the two, and afterwards they were rarely seen apart.

"David is considered family," she told journalist Jill Little. "We're like two horses pulling a wagon — working every day, side by side."[67]

In the years since acquiring Calidris, Mary had become more actively involved in heritage conservation. Most certainly an appreciation for interpretation and preservation of history was something ingrained in her from a very young age. Her father not only read historical books to her, but he had a PhD in history. He regularly took her to watch the excavation and restoration of a series of fortifications along the Niemen River in Grodno. During these visits, surrounded by the smells of rock dust and dirt, Mary listened with such keen interest that one day when a group of teachers arrived to view the site, she was able to lead them around and interpret for them the work being carried out.

In 1981, the Bank of Nova Scotia announced that its future building plans would include a new bank in Riverside-Albert. Having served the villages of Riverside-Albert and Alma since 1903, the existing three-storey building with a gambrel roof had both great historical significance and aesthetic value. It was one of the remaining few built by the Bank of New Brunswick before the company merged with the Bank of Nova Scotia in 1913. Inside, the brickwork, oak-panelled walls, carved mantelpiece, and wooden columns were reminiscent of turn-of-the-century style. In 1928, the structure had been moved a mile on skids, inch by inch, using a horse and rotating capstan, to its present, more visible location at the intersection of two highways.

Disturbed that the old building would be destroyed, Mary contacted the bank's head office in Toronto, suggesting that they should consider adding an extension to the existing building; one that would preserve its facade and elegant lobby, which showed the bank's venerable status as an institution. "The bank answered that they were not interested in antiquity, only in a new modern-style bank," recalls Mary.

In March 1982, she received a request from the village office to attend a meeting with council members. Thinking that she would be warmly received and supported because she was trying to preserve the village's history, she went prepared to share her visions for saving the building. From the moment she walked in and saw grim faces, she knew this was not the case. The mayor got right to the point. "We've lost our bank because of you."

The village had received a letter from the Bank of Nova Scotia stating that their building plans had been halted. Mary was speechless. In her discussions with bank representatives, nothing had been said about cancelling the new development. Shattered by their accusation, she stood up and left.

Hoping to get to the truth, Mary drove to Saint John to speak with the general manager in person. He told her they had most certainly not cancelled plans for the new building. "As it turned out the bank's plan to build in Riverside-Albert was shelved because another bank had been damaged by fire and this was a higher priority project," says Mary.

He expressed regret for the misunderstanding and promised to clarify the bank's position. She then asked that she be notified when the time came for the building to be removed and was assured that would be done.

On July 11, 1984, two men entered the old bank and pulled off the biggest bank robbery in New Brunswick's history, stealing almost $180,000 in cash. This was major news for a village the size of Riverside-Albert. The two men were apprehended; however, the cash was never recovered. The robbery seemed to elevate community interest and support in saving the bank.

Despite the bank's earlier assurance, one evening in 1985, Mary received a call from a friend notifying her that a request for bids to demolish the building would close the following day. She lay awake long into the night, wondering how she

Old Bank Museum, 2004. (Courtesy of Deborah Carr)

might stop the process. The next morning, she called the bank president (twice), a contact at Heritage Canada, several friends, and politicians. She was grabbing at straws, looking for advice, trying to spread the word, gain support. By 7:00 p.m., all options spent, she was beginning to accept defeat when the vice-president and general manager for the Maritimes Region of the Bank of Nova Scotia called. "I understand you are interested in the bank in Albert," he said. He asked if she represented an incorporated organization, and she told him about the Albert County Heritage Trust. "In that case, I think we can help you."

In a single minute, she swung the arc from failure to success. The bank could offer the building as a donation. It was a winning proposition for both. Mary received a heritage building, and the bank saved the demolition costs, wrote off the building as a donation, and scored public relation points. All Mary had to do was move the structure.

Mary was thrilled with the coup but didn't have any money to move a building. Without skipping a beat, she boldly asked if they might give her the money budgeted for the demolition. They agreed.

Then came the problem of relocating it. Mary made a call to the media and a story appeared in the local newspaper. Shortly thereafter, the BNS began construction of the new facility directly behind the old building and Mary was given a deadline of May 21, 1985, to have it moved.

Mary envisioned the bank would house a museum, tourist information centre, and perhaps a small café. She estimated the entire relocation and restoration project would cost twenty-five thousand dollars. She knew how to stretch money — and how to solicit it. With the BNS money, grants, personal donations, corporate sponsorship, and fundraising efforts, she secured almost all her financing. David loaned four thousand dollars to make up the shortfall. With the clock ticking, just weeks to spare before the May deadline, she acquired a highly visible property diagonal from the present location at the junction of two scenic highways.

Moving day required a coordinated effort to ensure electrical and telephone wires were raised or disconnected and law enforcement and highway engineers were advised. The building would remain on the street overnight behind proper barricades. The crew was on site, preparing the building, and Mary was taking pictures to document the move when the village's deputy mayor approached. He told her the village would not permit her to leave the building on the street overnight. Mary was stunned.

A few phone calls later, the misunderstanding was sorted out, but as spunky as she appeared, the incident disturbed Mary. The previous few weeks had been stressful, and direct confrontation was not her strong point.

David had been at a meeting out of town and when he finally returned late that night, she was in bed, tearful and upset. "You weren't here," she cried. "I've had a terrible day. I'm going to sleep. Goodnight. You handle the situation!"

Fearing there might be attempts at vandalism, David took his sleeping bag and slept in the dislocated building overnight.

They completed the move the next day and Mary put the episode behind her. Through the Albert County Heritage Trust, she applied for a series of grants enabling her to hire employees and finance the repairs and modifications to the building. They rebuilt the vault, replaced cracked plaster, cleaned woodwork, reshingled the roof, painted and reinforced stairways. They modified the building for accessibility, added a bathroom, and landscaped the property.

The Old Bank Museum was finally ready to open two years later with a tourist information centre, museum, and manager's office on the first floor; a small café on the second floor; and a 1900s-style bank manager's quarters with parlour, kitchen, and bedroom on the upper floor. During the first summer of operation, costumed staff and waitresses welcomed thirty-five hundred visitors to the historic museum and café.

After successfully restoring her own home and the bank, rescuing a dilapidated lighthouse was a relatively easy chore for Mary. The Anderson Hollow Lighthouse was a small salt-shaker-style structure built in 1889 at the end of a long wharf that stretched over low-tide mudflats at nearby Waterside. It possessed a rather moving history. Exposed to the battering waves during gales, the lighthouse was relocated to a safer position on shore, then later to a private property, where it remained until falling into such disrepair that the property owner told Mary she could have it if she carted it away.

Mary brought in two movers to assess the viability of moving the structure to a new location beside the Old Bank Museum. One felt a lit match might do the trick. The other pointed out that the top and bottom of the structure seemed solid enough, but the middle was rotted. Although it might be tricky, he thought it could be done. That was good enough for Mary.

The men secured a rope around the upper part of the lighthouse and tied the other end to a truck to attempt to separate the top from the middle. As the truck began to move forward, the rope tightened and Mary held her breath. Suddenly the entire top of the lighthouse began to lift and separate. It flipped over and fell upside down to the soft ground. The metal chimney pipe took the brunt of the impact, wrinkling like an accordion, but little else was damaged. They transported

Aerial shot of the Big House at Mary's Point, showing the Bridge and greenhouse, 2008.
(Courtesy of Deborah Carr)

the top via pickup truck to the site of the Old Bank Museum, about twenty kilometres away.

A few days later, an odd procession made its way along the same route to Riverside-Albert: a highway patrol car with its lights flashing, a flatbed truck carrying the bottom portion of the lighthouse adorned with red balloons and streamers, and a lineup of traffic behind. The detached sections of the Anderson Hollow Lighthouse remained forlornly plunked on the damp spring ground beside the Old Bank Museum until workers repaired the midsection of the lighthouse. Within a couple of weeks, a boom truck placed the light room back on top.

The Anderson Hollow Lighthouse would still have another move to make, one that earned it the nickname "The Travelling Lighthouse," a moniker well deserved.

Whenever winter winds funnelled up the Bay of Fundy, Mary was glad she had decided to add an attached greenhouse and Jacuzzi to the Big House at Mary's Point. "It's a summer garden in the middle of winter," she wrote gaily in a Christmas letter to friends, "a place to sit in the sun, soak in the hot-tub, pluck ripe tomatoes from the vine, and have picnic lunches while the cold winds blow outdoors."

While she constructed it to serve as her own tropical paradise in winter, the glassed-in greenhouse unexpectedly proved useful accommodations for a surprise visitor — Timmy, the purple gallinule. Timmy blew into New Brunswick in a blizzard, landing in a snowbank in Memramcook in January 1987. When found, the bird was in shock and unable to fly. One frozen leg required amputation, so he was taken to Mary's Point for rehabilitation. All things considered, it could have been worse. Sharing his new humid space with tomato plants, impatiens, begonias, geraniums, and ivies, he no doubt felt quite at home. Because of his handicap, Timmy was not a candidate for travel or freedom and so remained a long-term resident of Mary's Point for eleven years. While he could no longer enjoy the freedom of flight, he did enjoy plenty of water for drinking and daily hygiene, and all the devilled eggs, hamburger, earthworms, and caterpillars he could eat, as well as any insects he could hunt down in his large enclosure.

During the first year, his caregivers witnessed, with delight, Timmy's metamorphosis from the dull camouflage plumage of an immature bird to the brilliant iridescent purple-blue and green feathers of an adult. Thereafter he remained purple-blue, but each year moulted heavily, and during those times he would hide himself behind foliage. As snowy white undertail feathers once again emerged beneath his new tropical suit, so did Timmy, proudly strutting his new raiment for all to see.

As rare as it was to find a purple gallinule in the Bay of Fundy region, Mary and David already had experience with two others. Jamie Boy and Tina had taken up residence with the Majkas after being blown off their southern migration route during a Christmas snowstorm in 1978. Both birds were successfully rescued from snowdrifts and subzero temperatures, but Tina, who was weak and suffering from frostbitten toes, needed time to recover. A well-meaning attempt to send Jamie Boy via commercial airline to a private bird sanctuary in the Bahamas was foiled by stubborn customs officials, who refused to accept the bird even with the proper certificate of health. So, after a full round-trip of air travel, instead of a steamy palm-shaded pond, Jamie Boy found himself sharing a heated sun-porch with the lovely Tina. Mary and David cared for the two birds through the winter and the following spring personally transported them to the Stanley Park Zoo aviary in British Columbia.

"Only those people who have a reverence for life and the knowledge of the marvels of these species can understand how a species can get so far out of its way and then to recognize the needs of the species," says Jim Goltz. "You have to have a tremendous range of knowledge, compassion, sensitivity to go to these lengths."

Through Mary and David's varied activities they became known as the "go to" people whenever someone had a question on wildlife or nature. Throughout the 1970s and 1980s, there were relatively few sources for information, help, or advice on sick or injured animals in New Brunswick — certainly none so visible in the

Mary and a baby ring-necked dove. (Courtesy of David Christie)

public eye as Mary or David. Even CWS and the Department of Natural Resources used their services, as their mandates did not include rehabilitation. They accommodated the needs of each creature that came their way with the same uncomplaining dedication, arranging air transportation to warmer climes when required, paying expenses from their own pockets, creating suitable habitats in and around their house and outbuildings, and welcoming the newcomer into the family routine without a thought to effort or inconvenience.

"I feel that I am part and parcel of life and not just separated from it. I don't think of myself as a creation of God separate from all the other living things. We're all the same, all of us. When I see a living thing, I don't ask myself, 'Do I like this, is it useful, is it cute?' To me, it is here just as I am here and its life is just as precious as my own," says Mary.

Summer brought one of their most celebrated and energetic creatures.

Peppy was a baby squirrel, a survivor of a felled tree during a logging operation. Mary fed the baby milk and distilled water with an eyedropper for a few weeks, holding him in a soft cloth and rubbing his belly to encourage elimination. As the weeks passed, Peppy graduated to Pablum and egg yolks before accepting solid food such as grapes, rolled oats, and nuts.

He was given the run of the house and so built an enormous nest out of cheesecloth, tissues, and other scraps in Mary's bedroom. An open flap over a window vent allowed him his freedom, but he always returned to the nest at night. He fought with wild squirrels, harassed the dog, and almost drowned in the toilet. Come winter, he began gathering and hiding nuts.

When they travelled, Mary took Peppy with her, tucked inside her bra for warmth and safety. He even accompanied them while they conducted a whalewatching tour from Grand Manan Island, much to the delight of the tour participants. Over time, he became very attached to Mary, fiercely protecting her and his territory from known enemies, such as David and Mike. He would sometimes throw himself at visitors, chattering, scratching, and sometimes biting. David erected a sign outside the house: "Caution. Aggressive Squirrel." Even then, Mary defended him. In a letter to a friend, she wrote, "Peppy is doing what Mother Nature programmed him to do, and it is not his fault that he has no fear of humans and equates them as squirrels."

Peppy remained a house guest for a year, until he found a mate. When five young ones appeared, they realized "he" was a "she." Shortly after, to everyone's relief, Peppy moved out on her own. A progression of others took her place through the years, including a flying squirrel and an albino squirrel.

Sensing more animals would be coming their way, some of them requiring extended care, Mary applied to the Canadian Wildlife Service for a licence to rehabilitate injured wild animals. From that point onward, the house began taking on the characteristics of an animal refuge. The recovering animals and birds made Mary's Point that much more interesting as a place to visit, bringing the attention of filmmakers, journalists, and the curious public.

"They were the premier wildlife rehabilitators in the province," says Jim Goltz. "They encouraged other people to do it too." He says that while a vet would understand medical treatment, caring for a wild species requires understanding of their particular wild nature, habitat, food requirements, and stress threshold. This is where David and Mary excelled. They innately understood the creature's needs, or had a network of resources to consult if they didn't.

"Each of these creatures teaches us a lot about its species and reveals its own personality and special ways of showing us what it wants and how it feels about us," Mary wrote in a Christmas letter to friends.

Mary caring for one of her charges, a baby rabbit (kit). (Courtesy of Brian Townsend)

"Looking after this zoo takes a bit of work and time, but the rewards are far greater. We wouldn't want to miss it for anything."

In 1987, Mary's Point and Shepody Bay were declared Canada's first Western Hemisphere Shorebird Reserve.[68] This followed its official designation on May 24, 1982, as a Ramsar site, a Wetland of International Importance, due to its role in the migratory cycle of the shorebirds.[69] These designations sealed its protected status and the government's obligation to ensure the ecological integrity of the site.

On August 8, 1987, the Mary's Point Western Hemisphere Shorebird Reserve officially opened with great fanfare. Mary hosted a group of 250 people, who squeezed into the small lawn at Calidris and overflowed onto the beach, where a flock of

50,000 birds captivated the dignitaries and onlookers with their aerial acrobatics. For both Mary and David, it was an emotional day, the culmination of many years of physical and emotional effort toward educating visitors and protecting the birds. It had been twenty-five years since Mary first dreamed the idea of a sanctuary.

At the same time Mary and David were being honoured by CWS for the role they played in helping make the reserve a reality, a restoration project was underway on the historic 1867 Dominion Building in downtown Halifax to prepare it for a new role as the Art Gallery of Nova Scotia. The building's carved exterior stonework had deteriorated, and when engineers began looking for replacement stone, they had difficulty determining where the uniquely coloured red sandstone originated. They examined more than forty quarry locations before historical research revealed the source of the material was a long-abandoned quarry at Mary's Point.

Several quarries had operated at Mary's Point in different periods throughout the 1800s, shipping great quantities of red and olive-coloured sandstone down the coast to Saint John and Nova Scotia and the New England states. Boarding houses, a store, and a post office supported the industry and the labourers, many of them Irish and Scottish stonecutters. A short rail line ran from one small quarry to a larger quarry and wharf, where scows could be loaded with rock and sent down the bay.

Once researchers discovered the source of the unusual red sandstone, the Nova Scotia government approached the Canadian Wildlife Service, requesting permission to quarry 24,000 cubic feet of replacement stone from the protected reserve. Approval for the project was required from CWS, the Teed family (the former landowners), who had placed a restrictive covenant on any Fundy tidal power or commercial development of the property as part of the land sale,[70] and Mary and David, as their driveway was needed to access the beach.

Mary knew that quarrying the stone would cause damage to the beach and landscape, but she weighed the impact with the historical significance of providing the original stonework for the building. She stated publicly, "I am for conservation, but that doesn't stop with conservation of nature. I am, as well, a conservationist of historical artefacts."

All three parties shared the viewpoint that historical conservation was important and could be done without significant harm to wildlife habitat, so the company hired to extract the stone was granted restricted access to the beach. They would travel only at low tide and only after the migration of the shorebirds was completely finished.

Some people didn't understand how she could stand by and allow the operation. In a letter to the editor, one woman criticized Mary as selling her morals out for

The monument designed by Mary and carved from Mary's Point
sandstone by a Canstone stonemason.

financial gain. The truth was that since leaving Fundy National Park in 1972, Mary
had never been paid for any of her work. Everything she did stemmed from a deep
conviction that her life mission was to advocate for nature and heritage. The only
money that changed hands in the arrangement was a donation to a scholarship at
the University of New Brunswick in memory of J.F.H. Teed, a former owner of
the point and patriarch of the family who had sold the property to CWS. As well,
Canstone, the company restoring the Dominion Building, provided a monument,
designed by Mary and made from Mary's Point sandstone, to commemorate a
shared spirit of conservation.

What could have been a conflict between historians and naturalists instead
turned into an example of mutual compromise and respect, and in a subsequent
newspaper editorial, both Mary and the Teed family were praised for their cooperative efforts to balance the need for preserving history as well as wildlife habitats.
For Mary, it was a decision made not lightly but with practicality. Had she withheld
her approval, she feared the company might have built a road across the marsh and
fields, destroying valuable natural habitat for decades.

Now that Mary's Point was a site of international significance, birdwatchers, media,
and curious visitors from around the world visited the area during peak migration.
Although most were appreciative and respectful of the birds, their presence had
negative effects. Delighted in watching the aerial show, they sometimes ventured

too close in their desire to take photographs or to encourage the flocks to take to the air. Both Mary and David spent hours on the beach, talking to the visitors, explaining the story of the shorebirds and importance of keeping their distance. As much as they enjoyed it, this casual interpretive work on the beach sometimes interfered with other activities.

A grant, secured through the NBFN in 1989, allowed Mary to hire two young people from the local area to act as interpreters and general labourers. She trained and educated them, cleaned out a shed at the cottage for a shelter, then set them to work maintaining the trail and parking lot, picking up debris, handing out pamphlets, and talking to visitors about the birds. It was the beginning of a multi-year evolution of a Mary's Point interpretive program that over the decade to come grew to include an interpretive centre with displays, trails, a parking area, composting toilets, and full-time summer staff.

When a field adjacent to the site came up for sale, Mary and David purchased it to keep it from commercial development. With grants obtained through the NBFN, they constructed trails and viewing areas through the marsh and forests that were furnished with interpretive panels because Mary wanted people to appreciate the complexity of the landscape as much as the shorebirds. They hoped that CWS would agree to annex the additional property. However, due to budget cuts, they were no longer in any position to purchase land. So Mary

Mary's Point Interpretive Centre.

and David sold the property to the Nature Conservancy of Canada, which then transferred it, via a landholding agreement, to CWS.

Much of Mary's Point fell under the jurisdictional protection of the Canadian Wildlife Service, which contributed by building an observation deck and supplying an old utility trailer and furnishings to get the interpretive centre started. CWS also helped by maintaining the parking area and trails that NBFN had previously built. Al Smith recognizes Mary for driving the creation and development of the interpretive component and the policing of the site. "Certainly that would not have happened without their incredible involvement; the regulation and management, on-site supervision, and quasi-enforcement they provide is an amazing contribution to the integrity of the site."

Mary remained involved through the coming years, volunteering time and resources by applying for grants, managing construction projects, and improving and expanding the interpretive facility. Under her close direction, workers landscaped, installed composting toilets, added picnic tables, and one summer operated experimental gardens on their field adjacent to the centre. There was no grand plan or scheme — just a gradual evolution over time, funded by federal and provincial sponsorship and other agencies. Mary interviewed, trained, and managed all the staff through the years, hiring local people whenever possible. She ensured that they understood the ecology of the area and the other regional points of interest and were knowledgeable enough to speak to the visitors.

Denise Roy is an interpreter who shifted career paths after her life intersected with Mary Majka's. In the summer of 1994, she was a biology student planning a future in wildlife management when Denise says she started attending the "University of Mary's Point." Hired by Mary as an interpreter for the shorebird reserve, she was immediately impressed with the dedication Mary showed for her work.

"Within a few hours of meeting her," says Denise, "I learned about passion and what it can lead you to." She watched Mary's eyes fill with tears over the beauty of the birds in flight, knowing the emotion came not just from appreciation of an aerial ballet but from understanding the birds and what they go through to survive.

The first summer she worked at Mary's Point, she was the only female staff member. "Mary was very old school. The girls did girls' work, the boys did boys' work." While the boys were engrossed in manual labour, Mary led Denise through the marshes, teaching her about the ecosystems and the ecology of the habitat. They watched birds, tasted marsh vegetation, inspected the ponds. "I've never learned so much as I did that summer," says Denise. "It was the best summer of my life. I learned more from her than from all my university courses."

Mary picking goosetongue greens, Mary's Point marsh.
(Courtesy of David Christie)

"By teaching local students, they engendered a sense of responsibility," notes Jim Goltz. "Each person nurtured becomes a steward as well. When you cultivate this interest at a young age, it is never forgotten. This is proactive conservation; you are leaving a legacy."

Returning in subsequent years, Denise realized her future wasn't in wildlife management but in habitat protection. She went to work for the Nature Conservancy of Canada and now, at thirty-five years of age, says, "I am a realtor for nature. I have secured land for conservation in the upper Bay of Fundy area and now when I drive down there, I feel a special ownership in that I have learned about the area, love the area, and am doing my part to save it for future generations."

One of the finest lessons she learned was during the final year she worked at Mary's Point. On her first day as the site manager, she stopped in to speak with

Mary about a few things before reporting to work. Mary urged her to go for a walk to the point, saying that she should not saturate herself with work all at once but get reacquainted with the site. "This was a life lesson for me. I thought, 'Yes, I shouldn't rush into things. Stop, take it all in, assess, and then move forward.'"

At the same time that Mary began developing the interpretive services at Mary's Point, she also undertook restoration of a deteriorating community hall in nearby Harvey, about four kilometres from her home. The magnificent old structure had once housed exhibits for the agricultural society and served temporarily as a school when the community's schoolhouse burned. But with time and neglect, its foundation of rocks and piers had sunk. Birds and bats nested in the tower and raccoons took up residence downstairs. A small group of neighbours gathered to discuss how they might rescue the building, and Mary stepped in to provide direction and help.

After encouraging the community members to revive a trustee group to look after the building project and arrange the ongoing maintenance, she helped them obtain a grant for twenty thousand dollars that was used to hire local workers to lift the building and replace the foundation with new concrete piers and install a new roof and a new electrical system. Every inch of the beautiful wooden ceiling and walls was cleaned by hand to remove dirt and water stains from the leaky roof. At one point in the multi-year restoration, workers donned rubber boots, gloves, and face masks and set about cleaning out raccoon dung that had collected more than thirty centimetres thick in places. In later projects, other improvements were added, such as a well, septic tank, bathrooms, and kitchen.

When complete, they discovered the hall's acoustics were astounding. The building's tall, churchlike windows, square white tower, and attractive wood detail made it a landmark in the community and a source of pride. By regularly hosting concerts, community suppers, and other fundraising events in the hall, the trustee group continues to raise enough money to cover the insurance, taxes, and maintenance expenses. Rather than an eyesore, the hall is, once more, as it was meant to be…a place where friends and neighbours gather, where community comes together.

The offshoot of Mary's initiatives was the summer employment generated for dozens of students, residents, and seniors from the area. She believes that by creating opportunities to work on worthwhile community projects, she made room for people to feel pride of place and improve their future employment prospects. She encouraged others to get involved with the history and nature of their community. As a result, many became more appreciative and cognizant of their own cultural heritage and landscape.

"A lot of people will say she's made a great contribution to environment, history, and culture, but this lady made a great contribution to people," says Harry Doyle, who was elected a Member of the Legislative Assembly for the area after retiring from education. "If I had people who needed a job, she found a way to work with everyone and remained positive. She had a lot of compassion for people who were not doing well, and to me that is her strength."

Although there may still be a few who harbour resentment for her sometimes overbearing methods, most in her community recognize her contributions and are quick to give Mary praise for raising awareness of the value of a heritage she doesn't even lay claim to. Her projects also helped increase tourism prospects for the region, opening opportunities for other businesses to prosper.

Her concern for the Fundy coastal area wasn't limited to Mary's Point, and during this time period, she became even more vocal about marine and coastal habitats, urging caution on commercial rockweed harvesting, organizing coastal cleanups, and advocating for a Bay of Fundy marine park. She and David purchased almost two hundred acres of Fundy coast to keep it from development, donating sixty-nine acres at Two Rivers to the Nature Conservancy.

Over time, Mary had developed a methodology for making things happen that worked well for her. She dreamed up her plans, often late at night, then discussed them with David. His pragmatic approach was an asset, as she had to argue all the problem areas with him in advance.

"It often spurs me on. If I feel he is against it, I will try to demonstrate to him that I am right. Sometimes I complain, but in my heart I'm glad he is difficult. It is good to have a second opinion, even if it is contrary."

Typically, this meant Mary was well prepared when she finally approached the decision-makers, and her reputation was such that they knew her projects were worthy of support.

Susan Collins, an employee of the federal government who helped Mary acquire funding for a number of her heritage projects, was also impressed with the friendship Mary offered beyond their professional work relationship. Whenever there was business to be discussed, Susan would travel to Mary's Point for meetings that included social time, tea, and desserts. Her co-workers would often ask what took so long. "Just come with me and you'll see," she'd counter.

She remembers, in particular, one meeting when a group of officials arrived at Mary's Point to discuss one of her projects. Mary was in the middle of a minor crisis. She had several varieties of tomatoes growing in a sheltered greenhouse and the plastic covering had torn free. There had been a frost the night before and she needed help harvesting.

"We had all these government officials in their suits and ties and Mary was wound up," says Susan. "Nothing would do, but we had to go out and harvest the tomatoes before they were ruined. 'No' was not a factor, nor was time. Mary doesn't give you options. Everyone went along with it. These guys took off their jackets, rolled up their sleeves, and good-naturedly picked tomatoes. That's just the way it was there."

Mary's persistence and tenacity were certainly well known and respected on all political fronts within her own province, but in Ottawa, despite the fact she had received a National Heritage Award three years earlier for her work in heritage protection and interpretation, she wasn't as widely known. However, there were a few uninitiated federal officials about to become well acquainted with her dedication to cause.

In December 1990, an engineering mistake caused a rockfall that destroyed the Point Wolfe Covered Bridge in Fundy National Park. The landmark bridge was one of only a handful of authentic heritage structures remaining from the pre-park era, so it was a shock when the Canadian Parks Service (CPS) decided to replace it with concrete and steel. Mary refused to let such a decision go unchallenged. She was told CPS had a policy that did not encourage reconstruction of lost resources. They would maintain authentic historical structures but not change, improve, or add to them in any way that would compromise their authenticity. [71]

But Mary knew the value of a good story. She called a press conference, invited the media to Mary's Point, and conducted interviews: a lone woman standing up for the long tradition of a covered bridge within one of Canada's national parks. The story and interviews were broadcast across Canada. She began to receive letters of support in the mail. Some sent words of encouragement, some sent money. An engineer from Nova Scotia volunteered his services to help rebuild the covered bridge. Soon, the unsolicited donations had reached more than twenty-five hundred dollars. [72]

"It was a drop in the bucket for the whole project but was still a substantial amount," Mary says. She wrote a letter to CPS, including copies of the support letters received.

When she was told again that Canada's national parks were not in the business of creating replicas, Mary pointed out that the Fortress of Louisbourg in Nova Scotia was a very large, very profitable replica operated by CPS. This was a point not easily argued.

In January 1991, CPS historian/engineer Robert Passfield threw in his support by writing his recommendation to the director of federal heritage policy. He noted this was "one instance where a reconstruction would be eminently practicable and probably the most economical approach. Leaving aside policy considerations, there are sound engineering arguments in favour of constructing timber truss bridges on secondary roads in remote areas."[73]

Not long after that, Mary received a telephone call from Ottawa. "Congratulations, you won," said a voice on the other end of the phone. On February 11, 1991, CPS officials announced their plans to rebuild the covered bridge. Environment Canada would be financing the $545,000 project.

The new bridge was wider and higher to accommodate heavier vehicles and was constructed using steel angle blocks rather than black spruce, but otherwise few modernizations were visible. Its official opening took place on July 2, 1992. As Mary and Fundy-Royal MP Robert Corbett were driven through the replica in a Model A Ford, the Point Wolfe Bridge gained a new place in history. It was the first covered bridge built in New Brunswick since 1954 and would remain a fine example of communities working with government.

Mary always made it a point to show her appreciation. On behalf of Albert County and the Albert County Heritage Trust, she presented Corbett with a painting of the bridge done by local artist Alan Bell and promised the twenty-five hundred dollars in public donations for the bridge would finance interpretive panels depicting the history and succession of the bridges spanning the river.

Mary's successes with saving covered bridges encouraged other communities to organize bridge restoration projects and press the provincial government to take a stronger stance on the protection and promotion of the province's few remaining covered bridges. Today, the historic bridges receive the recognition they deserve and are being repaired or bypassed rather than demolished.

The previous year, Mike had reluctantly retired from the job he loved after receiving treatment for cancer. He was approaching seventy at the time. He became depressed after leaving work, so Mary suggested a trip to Europe; it was his first since they had left in 1951. They travelled to many familiar countries, but he would not return to Poland. That summer, because of a shortage of pathologists at the hospital, his friend Dr. Hank Taylor asked him to return to work and he happily agreed, remaining for another two years.

Upon retirement on his own terms in 1993, Mike devoted himself to his photography, amassing thousands of slides. He had always been content in the background of life at Mary's Point, and now he quietly read books on astrophysics and debated the science of black holes, black energy, and obscure aspects of physics with like-minded friends. He spent long hours cutting wood, picking berries, or sitting on the Bridge, watching the birds and wildlife and calling out his observations, "Thirteen Canada geese...one bald eagle...fifteen black ducks...Oh! Here comes our cat with a mouse." He looked forward to the weekly calls from Marc, now a hobby pilot and scuba diver, working and living in California's Silicon Valley.

Although now also in her seventies, Mary was not ready to quit. She said her projects were her way of showing her gratitude toward the adopted country that had given her a home. In 1993, she heard the federal government had slated a derelict wharf located on the Shepody River in nearby Harvey for demolition. The Harvey wharf was all that remained of a prosperous shipyard, which in the 1800s had produced eighteen of the largest wooden sailing ships to come out of Albert County during the heyday of sail. Shipyard owner Gaius Turner had been one of the era's most colourful and successful entrepreneurs, yet few remembered his contribution. The government saw liability; Mary saw opportunity. New Brunswick had a rich shipbuilding history but, as yet, had no provincial sites to commemorate it. She contacted the federal Public Works department, offering to take over the wharf property to create an interpretive site.

The Public Works disposal program has a clause allowing for incorporated, non-profit groups to assume responsibility of sites, but only with demonstrated public support. They offered to arrange the community meeting, but advertised the event in the wrong communities. When Mary discovered the mistake, she had only hours to spread the word. Regardless, the meeting was still attended by more than sixty-five people supporting the idea.[74] Mary's multi-year proposal was to repair the wharf and build a lookout point, picnic area, and an interpretive centre shaped like a ship. The plans were approved by all present, and the government agreed to contribute the cost of the demolition, seventy thousand dollars, to ACHT for restoration.

This all seemed too easy to Mary, who was used to wrangling for funds. Soon, however, the complications set in. The federal government owned the wharf, but the provincial Department of Natural Resources owned the submerged land it sat upon and the Department of Agriculture, the surrounding land. It would take two years to sort through the spider's web of sticky ownership issues so that ACHT could lease the property, but Mary used the time to dream and research. She had plenty to keep her busy with the interpretive centre at Mary's Point, and with Mary, there was always a new house guest or project of some sort to be accommodated.

In 1994, provincial wildlife officers found an emaciated white raven in the Kingsclear area and brought the bird to Mary. The albino, apparently rejected from the nest, was nothing but feathers and bones but under expert care gradually gained weight and health. They built a large enclosure beside the barn for the bird, which they named Albie.

White ravens are extremely rare, often the subject of myth and legend. In fact, noted Mary, "in Poland, when you find a very rare book, maybe an antique, you say, 'I found a white raven.'" They managed to keep Albie's presence relatively low key for two years, because Mary did not want the bird to be the subject of scrutiny, but after she mentioned it during a *Morningside* interview with CBC Radio host Peter Gzowski, the white raven and Mary's Point were on the receiving end of a fair amount of press coverage. Earlier that year, a film crew from CBC had come to shoot a *Land and Sea* documentary on Mary and the shorebirds at Mary's Point; now they came back to do a segment on Albie.

The coverage also brought criticism from a group of schoolchildren on the Queen Charlotte Islands who read about the bird in a newspaper article and composed a collection of letters and mailed them to Mary. They felt Mary was wrong to keep Albie in a cage. They had a resident spirit raven on their island, but theirs was free to fly. "I'm hoping that in receiving this letter from our class that you would consider setting your White Raven free, free like all the wildlife should be. And also letting the rest of your community experiencing [*sic*] the beauty of this bird in its environment," one girl wrote.

Mary wrote back, commending them on their concern, but disturbed by their accusations that she was "selfish" and an "abuser of animals." She cited her reasons for keeping Albie, in that the bird was too young to fend for itself when it first arrived and that people on the east coast may not be as kind to birds as those on the Queen Charlottes. She had seen too many birds senselessly destroyed by gunshot to be comfortable releasing Albie.

The students' concerns illustrate a common debate: is intervention to save a wild creature ethical if it means captivity? Mary concedes it's a tricky question, but justifies her work.

> Over the years, David and I have looked after between 100 and 200 individual wildlife, from beavers and owls to flying squirrels and songbirds. Of those, we have been able to release about 60-70% back to the wild. A few we had to ship to warmer climes in order for them to survive. Those shipments were done under permit from the appropriate authorities. Why are we doing it? One is a simple concern for something that needs temporary or permanent care. The other — a very important one too — is that we are constantly learning from those animals. We are more than just simple bird-lovers. We

have been studying birds and the experience has given us insight into moult, feeding habits, behaviour, etc. as well as methods of care.[75]

Meanwhile, every spring for eight years, on a high shelf in her outdoor cage, Albie the white raven carefully constructed her nest with twigs and moss provided. Every spring for eight years, she laid a hopeful clutch of unfertilized eggs.

During that eighth spring, a black raven came courting. He returned day after day after day to call from the branches of a nearby tree or from the top of her cage, as Albie frantically beat the cage with her wings, trying to get out. When Mary could no longer bear to watch, she told David to let her go. She hoped that since Albie had already made a nest, she would mate with the black raven and then return to lay more eggs.

Reluctantly, David did as he was told. He opened the door to the cage and came in the house. They both stood, looking out the window as Albie flew away. She never returned.

Albie's biological need to reproduce touched a chord in Mary. Starting her own family had been her greatest desire, and she enjoyed every moment of the mothering experience, taking great pride in the accomplishments of her two sons. "Looking back at the years when my children were still in my care, I feel that those were the years of my most important mission in life," she says. "Biologically, this is what a woman is here for. Other accomplishments are just frills. To be able to mother other children is like a special blessing, a present from God."

Perhaps one of the most significant examples of Mary's concern for children began when her path crossed that of Agnieszka, a thirteen-year-old girl from Poland who came to be known as Nishka. The story's roots go back to Mrs. Gamble and Roland Hutchinson, the young student minister who so enjoyed Polish cooking.

Roland's intrigue with Mrs. Gamble's stories of how she and her late husband helped found the Polish Methodist Church before being blacklisted by the communist regime following World War II had prompted him to write his thesis on the Gambles. In 1971, he had enlisted Mrs. Gamble's guidance as he made arrangements to travel to Poland to conduct research and interviews. While in Katowice, his arranged translator and guide was Marian Gamrat, a young electrical student studying English. When they parted, they exchanged addresses so Marian could continue practising his English. Roland promised to write, knowing that for those behind the Iron Curtain, communication with outsiders was a cherished connection.

More than a decade later, by then a pastor on Prince Edward Island, Roland received word that the Gamrats had defected from Poland. He found himself arranging refugee sponsorship through the United Church for Marian and Elizabeth Gamrat and their daughters. Mary provided translation help and advice. The family arrived in a blinding snowstorm to start a new life in Canada. Although they eventually moved to Ottawa, they remained in close contact with the Hutchinsons and with the Majkas, whom they considered extended family.

In 1996, the Gamrats brought Elizabeth's niece Agnieszka Trzcionka (Nishka) from Poland on a visitor's visa to spend the summer in Canada. Nishka was born in Sosnowiec, an industrial city seventy kilometres south of Mary's birthplace of Częstochowa. Her mother was disabled and unable to offer adequate care so her children had been periodically shuffled from relative to relative. The family had endured much and had little by way of basic necessities. They all suffered from malnutrition, health problems, and inadequate medical care. Nishka often interrupted her schooling to care for her three younger siblings.

Hoping they might find someone to foster the young girl, the Gamrats took her on a trip east to visit their friends. They spent a few days with the Hutchinsons, then the Majkas, before travelling to Prince Edward Island to visit another niece of Elizabeth's.

At Mary's Point, Nishka discovered the biggest house she had ever seen, a curious place with birds in the greenhouse and a squirrel in residence, a place where she was allowed to run and play outdoors. When darkness fell, she saw stars and heard coyotes howl. During the visit, Mary watched the young girl carefully. Mary saw herself as a child in Mirów.

After meeting the tiny wisp of a girl with the sad brown eyes, and being told the details of Nishka's plight, Mary could not allow her to return to her home situation without trying to help. When she learned that Nishka's parents' names were Maria and Henryk, and that she and the child shared the same birth date, albeit sixty years apart, she felt the two were destined to be together. In her mind, she saw a chain through time, connecting Mrs. Gamble to Mary to Nishka.

She discussed the situation with Mike. She was willing to spend her monthly pension cheque to help the child, plus take on whatever other expenses would be required. He felt that they were too old to have a young girl to care for. She respected his position but could not bear to think about Nishka returning to her previous circumstances. So Mary called Elizabeth's niece in Prince Edward Island. Sylvia and Tadeusz Gumienny shared Mary's feelings about the child's welfare. After hours of telephone conversations, they reached a solution. Sylvia and Tadeusz would be named her legal guardians; however, Mary would assume all financial support for the girl as well as cover the added expense of a larger apartment for the Gumiennys.

Nishka remembers the phone call that changed her life. She was back in Ottawa with the Gamrats, thinking she would be returning to Poland in a few weeks, when Mary called and asked her how she would feel about staying in Canada. "My first thought was here I am in this amazing place; it is so much better than home. Then I got scared. Would I ever see my family again?" Her Aunt Elizabeth made the decision for her. "She told me that this was best for me."

Mary arranged air travel, and Nishka returned to Mary's Point while Mary negotiated the complicated corridors and paperwork to acquire legal guardianship, landed immigrant status for the child, and acceptance into the Prince Edward Island school system. "I couldn't sleep, there were so many emotions going through me that I cried because I was happy, but I also cried because I was scared of being without my family in Poland," writes Nishka.

Mary's friend Jean Wilson met Nishka shortly after she arrived in Canada. A poignant scene from that meeting remains in her mind. "Then, we didn't know her whole story, but Mary was so gentle with her. She talked to her softly and privately in Polish and was very comforting and motherly. I can still see her combing and brushing her hair. Mary never had a daughter of her own."

Through the coming years, Mary would financially and emotionally support Nishka, arranging for her education, swimming lessons, providing spending money, college tuition, and living expenses. She knew exactly how it felt to be transplanted from a familiar life, language, and landscape into a foreign environment, so offered encouragement and advice at every juncture. Once, when Nishka tried to thank her, Mary told her, "You have no idea what you are thanking me for. But someday you will understand what it means to be here."

In an email to Mary, sent later when she was eighteen, Nishka wrote, "Now I understand…you gave me strength, will, heart, love, and most of all friendship; the thing that every human needs. With friendship, life actually means something…. I will never forget what you did for me and what I have learned from you. It will stay with me forever…. I hope I will have a chance to help someone the way you did and to inspire them the way you have inspired me."

"We both felt that some divine hand guided our destinies toward each other," says Mary. "To this day, Nishka feels that because she emotionally lost her mother I became the mother figure in her life."

In 1999, she would accompany Mary, Mike, David, Chris, and his partner Sheilagh Hunt to visit Pier 21, the newly opened Immigration Museum in Halifax,

Mary and Nishka at Crooked Creek.

the site where Mary and Mike first stepped on Canadian soil. Another emotional moment would come when she became a Canadian citizen in 2003.

Today, Nishka works full-time in Ottawa, living a life she could never have imagined for herself back in Poland. "Now I have too many dreams to think of," she says.

Having lost everything during the war and survived, Mary thought nothing of taking on responsibility for another's extended welfare. She holds no interest in money — Mike often admonished her for her spontaneous contributions to whatever *cause du jour* that moved her.

> Happiness does not lie in acquiring or having things. In the war, I had nothing, not even a toothbrush or a watch. If you can survive that and be happy, what do you need money for? Nishka was worth the effort. For her, it was important that there were people who care for her and love her. People to take care of her needs.

Mary's spontaneous willingness to undertake anything she felt to be worthwhile — whether protecting habitat, heritage, wildlife, or children — was something that came from a deep well inside. To not act when her heart demanded she do so would be to deny what was essentially Mary. "I wouldn't be me if I didn't do these things," she said. While she never set out to achieve personal recognition, Mary's work was beginning to receive nationwide accolades. In June 1996, when she stood in Ottawa's House of Commons before receiving a Canadian Healthy Environment award for Lifetime Achievement, the entire House stood to applaud. Later that same year, she received the Gulf of Maine Visionary Award.

By 1997, the tangled ownership of the Harvey wharf was sorted out, and Mary was able to start what she later dubbed the "Shipyard Heritage Park" project.

She had an ambitious vision. Once the wharf was stabilized and repaired — a mighty job in itself — she would begin developing an interpretive site that would celebrate New Brunswick's shipbuilding era and craftsmanship. Mary had conceptual drawings made and an action plan in place. She hired a researcher, a project manager for the restoration of the wharf, and local labourers. She and David visited other historic shipbuilding sites and travelled to the Maritime Museum of the Atlantic in Halifax to do research.

But ambitious visions cost money, and some of her initial plans had to be modified. Despite Mary's get-it-done attitude, funding could not always be wrestled into place. The interpretive site became a long-term project, but Mary was never idle. She still had annual employment grants to apply for, seasonal employees to hire and manage, and maintenance of the ACHT sites to oversee. As well, the Big House at Mary's Point enjoyed a constant stream of visitors and wildlife.

In 1998, with the help of her son Chris, they organized a fundraiser for the shipyard project: two sold-out benefit concerts at the Harvey Hall featuring world-famous Viennese-born pianist and composer Anton Kuerti. The two men had known each other for several years. Upon hearing of the hall restoration, Kuerti, who had performed in grand concert venues across North America, Europe, and Asia, offered to play in the tiny Harvey Hall while on vacation in the area. Flowers in preserve jars decorated the interior and people came from all around to fill the 150-seat hall for two performances. Kuerti's finesse as he performed three Beethoven sonatas and one by Czerny in the intimate rural venue made for an extraordinary experience for concertgoers. It was a moving performance. Afterwards, Mary, never one to pass up a chance to speak the praises of her region, sent an email to CBC's Shelagh Rogers, providing the details she knew would appeal to the radio host:

> The fact that Harvey is situated in one of the most picturesque parts
> of the province, surrounded by great expanses of marshland only
> added to the charm. During the performance, through the open
> windows, not only could you hear robins singing, no doubt excited

by the beautiful music, but also hear cows mooing in the pasture below. The century old hall never was blessed and honoured in such a beautiful way.

Over the coming four years, besides trips to Europe and Alaska, there were family celebrations. Mike and Mary's fiftieth wedding anniversary and the fiftieth anniversary of their arrival in Canada; a fortieth anniversary for the Moncton Naturalists' Club; Mike's eightieth birthday; and Marc's wedding to his long-time girlfriend, Lynn Taylor. As well, Mary was awarded an honorary doctor of science degree from the University of New Brunswick and a Golden Jubilee Medal. When their dear friend naturalist Rob Walker died in a 2001 car accident, Mary and David volunteered to finish, in his memory, the interpretation project he had started for the Cape Jourimain Nature Centre at the Confederation Bridge to Prince Edward Island. And, of course, there were always birdwatching trips and bird surveys throughout the province to take part in.

Intertwined with these events arose several medical setbacks for Mary and Mike. She ended up in the cardiac unit due to atrial fibrillations just before Christmas in 1997; two weeks before Christmas in 2001, Mike was admitted to the hospital after falling on the back steps. He had just arrived home again when, on Christmas Eve the same year, Mary was rushed to the hospital with severe abdominal pains. After emergency surgery for a ruptured bowel, she awoke to a cheerful pronouncement from her surgeon. "Well, Mary, to tell it to you straight, you had poop in your belly. As a present for Christmas, I gave you a colostomy, but I can reconnect you five months from now, or whenever you wish after that."[76]

Coming home after her hospital stay, she wrote gratefully, "Dave drove me through the Caledonia Mountain forests and I felt as if every snow-covered tree was greeting me. Descending the mountain, I could see Mary's Point and the Bay of Fundy below." She was so glad to be home and within the embrace of family, friends, and her beloved Mary's Point.

But Mary had lost the body vigour of her younger days. Because of a bad knee, which she had injured in a skiing accident in Austria, she began using a walker, and David often had to hoist her out of low-slung chairs and sofas. Her physical limitations frustrated her, but still her mind was as energetic as ever and always filled with ideas and plans. Just as she had done in her childhood, she often awoke at 4:00 a.m. and, unable to sleep, would arise, put on her bathrobe, and work on her projects, write letters, read, or knit until daybreak. Then she would return to bed for a few more hours of sleep. David, as well, was most productive after dark and could sometimes be found working at his computer at three in the morning.

Jim Wilson recalls collaborating with David on the *Birds of New Brunswick: An Annotated List*. Their committee struggled for several years compiling and verifying information for the book, and in the final throes of editing, Jim and David worked closely together. "It became a battle between Mary and me for David's attention," claims Jim. "In the end we were in contact daily and Mary was determined she would have just as much of his time. She chided me one day, saying, 'He worked all night on this for you.' At one point, I had the impression she was hardly speaking to me."

Their friends noticed that the roles were shifting. For many years, Mary had been David's caregiver, a mother figure to him. "When he first came here, what he needed most was family," she says. "A place he knew he belonged. He had problems, and I tried to work them out for him."

Now that Mary was less mobile, he became her legs, running errands, maintaining the house, feeding the animals, handling the background chores. But as much as David preferred to stand back from the limelight, no one has been deeper in the shadows than Mike.

Steady and strong and stalwart, Mike Majka was a man of simple pleasures and modest pursuits. While most visitors to Mary's Point found Mike to be quiet and reserved, given the chance he could be an eloquent conversationalist. Friends described him as warm, gentle, and caring, a true gentleman. "He was real companionable at times when we were together and not in Mary's presence, but virtually silent when Mary was carrying on," says colleague Dr. Hank Taylor. "He was chatty at work and held his own in the doctor's lounge, carrying on about local politics. In the end, when his hearing deteriorated, he was happy to chat and just get a nod from me that I understood."

It takes a confident man to be the husband of a very public and controversial woman. While they shared the same interests, their temperaments were direct opposites. And their love of nature manifested in different ways, leading them to pursue largely separate lives. But throughout their marriage, Mike always supported Mary's activities and was proud of her accomplishments and honours.

"Mike's love for me is such that he relishes seeing me happy, enjoying something that really matters to me," says Mary. "I have done many things that other husbands would have criticized, but I don't think he ever said, 'Why did you do that?'"

By the end of 2002, Mary's plans for the shipyard park were only partially complete. The wharf had been repaired and restored, the Anderson Hollow Lighthouse had been moved from its location at the Old Bank Museum, and a gazebo had been built for interpretive panels. There was still much to accomplish.

Just as the project seemed to be languishing, serendipity arrived from cyberspace in the form of an email from John Kernaghan, a *Hamilton Spectator* journalist

The Anderson Hollow Lighthouse makes its final move from the Old Bank Museum
to its present location at Shipyard Heritage Park.

from Ontario. John, while documenting a fourteen-day cross-Canada journey, had interviewed Mary and written about the shipyard project during the summer of 2002. In response to the article posted briefly on the *Hamilton Spectator* website, he received an email from a retired Dutch mariner in Texel, Holland, who had a connection to Gaius Turner's shipyard.

Ed Eelman's century-old farmhouse, built by his great-grandfather in 1903, had been constructed from massive timbers washed ashore following a shipwreck on the island of Texel, in the Netherlands. Ed's research into the origins of the timbers led him to a ship called the *Revolving Light*. A Dutch newspaper article described how the ship had gone aground off the coast of Texel during a sudden storm on the night of December 18, 1902. It had been en route from Buenos Aires to Hamburg and was being towed by tugboat through shallow channels when waves ripped it from the tow cable. Unable to re-establish the line, the crew abandoned the ship for the tugboat. Wedged helplessly on the sandbar, the ship succumbed to the waves.

Land and Sea crew filming the meeting of Ed Eelman and Mary Majka, Texel, Holland, 2003.
(Courtesy of David Christie)

That night, as the first remnants of the vessel washed up on a Texel beach, rescuers ventured out in open boats to search for survivors or bodies. Finding none, they gratefully salvaged the sturdy beams and planks washing up on their island of dunes, dykes, and salt marsh, an island sadly bereft of decent timber. Several months later, Jakob Eelman purchased a number of the ship's beams to build his son a home.

With a little more digging, Ed learned the ship had been constructed in the Turner Shipyard in New Brunswick. In an attempt to find information online, he stumbled upon the *Hamilton Spectator* article mentioning Mary's project, and he contacted the journalist. Once Ed and Mary connected, the emails flew across the Atlantic and the two discovered they shared interests in birds, nature, travel, and photography, not to mention a vested interest in the very first ship launched from the Turner Shipyard in 1875.

The numinous nature of the story was not lost on Mary, and she was tremendously excited at this turn of events. Just as the sluiceway that had washed up on the Mary's Point beach was reincarnated as decorative beams in Mary's house, so the *Revolving*

Light's beams came to support an historic home on the other side of the ocean. Her imagination followed the life of those great tall Canadian trees, trees that grew from a tiny seedling rooted in a forest overlooking a salty bay, trees that sheltered all manner of wildlife and birds for a hundred years. Those same trees were then felled and stripped and sawed into timber, perfectly pieced together by design into a magnificent sailing ship.

Mary knew she had to meet Ed and see the beams for herself. In October 2003, a *Land and Sea* film crew from the CBC accompanied her to Holland to document the meeting. Meeting Ed and seeing the beams in his house was an emotional moment for her; she recognized unseen threads at work, weaving their story through time and place. She came prepared for a ceremony to mark the moment and acknowledge the ship that drew the two landscapes and the two people together.

And so it was, that a century after the remnants of the *Revolving Light* washed ashore, Ed Eelman stood shin-deep in the surf of an October ocean, eyes squinted against the sea. In his hand, he held a single red maple leaf brought from a distant forest. Released, it settled on the froth to ride the rhythm of the tide. From the hard-packed sweep of fine sand, Mary watched with tears in her eighty-year-old eyes.

"For me, it was not just a physical journey. It was much more a spiritual experience of a magnitude I did not foresee when I started," she wrote to Ed later. "I took with me a small maple leaf, already in its red autumn colours, a symbol of our flag. To hand it over to you was a greeting from my country. To lay it on the waters of the North Sea was a salute from us to the *Revolving Light*, another linkage across the sea."

By the time Mary came back home from Texel, she had changed her plans for Shipyard Heritage Park. A replica of the *Revolving Light* would grace the wharf and provide the backdrop for this extraordinary tale of circumstance, of destiny, and of history repeating itself. All things considered, it had been a phenomenal year for Mary.

She was able to announce more good news that autumn. The Community Foundation of Greater Moncton — one of many such independent community foundations across the country that accepts donations from individuals and companies to create endowment funds used to support community initiatives and organizations — announced the Mary Majka Heritage Endowment Fund. Within five years, they expected to endow the ACHT and the Mary's Point Interpretive Centre with $1.5 million dollars in assets.[77] They anticipated the invested money would generate enough interest annually to cover the maintenance costs for the Albert County Heritage Trust heritage sites.

"This is something I have always dreamed about," Mary said when she heard the news. "This is an answer to my prayers. I know I cannot do this too much longer. All the things I developed and started need financial support. I have been a volunteer, but not everyone can do this. I need to have someone to take over for me, and they have to be paid."

To celebrate, the foundation commissioned six watercolour paintings of Mary's heritage sites by artist and friend Elizabeth Tener: Mary's Point Shorebird Reserve, Anderson Hollow Lighthouse, the Old Bank Museum, the *Revolving Light*, the Sawmill Creek Covered Bridge, and the Harvey Community Hall.

"What I've created are my children, so precious to me," she told the crowd gathered for the ceremony announcing the fund. "I'm so happy that my children will survive and still be important to the community."

However, six years later, the assets had not accumulated as expected. ACHT had received less than three thousand dollars. Mary's workload and the passage of time were taking a toll. Mary felt that she and David had to slow down. Neither could maintain the pace for much longer without repercussions. Sure enough, following a family get-together in August 2004, she was rushed to the emergency room with severe abdominal pain. David stayed with her, feeling helpless, holding her hand while she screamed in pain.

"The pain was so extreme. Everyone could hear her, and the nurses were struggling to get an IV in to administer painkillers. It was frustrating. They were poking and jabbing and you could see it hurt her," David relates the event. Finally, successful with the IV, the powerful painkillers began to work. David breathed a sigh of relief as her screams turned to a whimper. But suddenly, the heart monitor began to beep irregularly and Mary began to shake. Then her heart stopped beating. The medical staff rushed her off and David was left standing alone, tears in his eyes.

The medical team started Mary's heart again, but an X-ray showed her bowel caught in a hernia. Doctors were able to provide some relief, but it proved only temporary; two weeks later, she returned for abdominal surgery. It was a frightening experience for David, a reflective one for Mary. "I had never feared death much, and being faced with it, I didn't feel any sadness or regret. But later, after the operation, I felt that I should live. Not for myself, but because I could see how it shocked David and my husband. There were people for whom I wanted to live, not for myself."

A second hernia repair surgery followed in November, during which the surgeon also reversed her colostomy. She now felt a renewed, albeit diminished, vigour to finish Shipyard Heritage Park. On her birthday in 2005, she received the word that the Atlantic Canada Opportunities Agency would provide ACHT with the $102,000 she needed to complete the project. She hired a project foreman and

The family gathers at Calidris, summer 2004, just before Mary's surgery (left to right): Chris and Sheilagh, Marc and Lynn, David, Nishka and friend; (seated): Mike and Mary.

workers to upgrade the landscaping and a craftsman to build the replica of the *Revolving Light*.

Mike, too, was growing older and more feeble. Alone in his room one night that summer, he suffered the fall that forced them to rearrange their living conditions. Mike then required increased care and monitoring, while the shipyard project required much decision-making. At times, Mary felt overwhelmed.

Regardless, the project finally reached completion. She set the grandiose official opening date as August 12, 2006, Gaius Turner's birthday. The day dawned bright and clear as a crowd of about 150 people gathered, some in heritage costume. Mary had arranged for a reception tent, sailor dancers, bagpipes, a procession of kayaks flying the flags of various countries, floral wreaths to toss in the sea, and the Red Ensign to hoist on the ship's mast.

In addition to the dignitaries, there were three very special guests in the crowd: John Kernaghan came to write the final chapter of the saga he had started; Dr. Sam Turner, an American descendant of shipyard owner Gaius Turner; and Ed Eelman, who had crossed the Atlantic carrying a piece of the *Revolving Light* for Mary. It was carved to commemorate their shared history.

As Ed stood on the bow of the *Revolving Light* to christen the replica ship — not with customary champagne but with local blueberry wine — destiny had one last card to play. A sudden squall swept over the mountains, then whistled across the marsh, obliterating the bright sunshine. Bruised clouds, bulging with rain, darkened the sky and wind snapped the ship's pennants. Sudden rain and hail pelted down on the crowd and everyone dashed for cover, gathering in the reception tent, laughing and wiping themselves dry. Then, as suddenly as it came, the rain vanished and the sun emerged from behind the clouds. It seemed somehow apropos: a salute from nature, a reminder of the unforeseen storm that swamped the *Revolving Light* that fateful night in 1902.

It was an exhausting day for Mary — the whole project had taken a toll. She spoke very briefly to the audience during the ceremony, leaving others to carry the day. But she did tell the crowd it would be her last great project. This was her swan song. No one really believed her.

Opening ceremonies for Shipyard Heritage Park, August 12, 2006 (left to right): Kathryn Chrysostom, Marcia Babineau (wife of Lt.-Gov.), Mary, Lt.-Gov. Herménégilde Chiasson, MLA Wayne Steeves, MP Rob Moore, Olivia Chrysostom. (Courtesy of Deborah Carr)

From left to right:
Ed Eelman, Mary,
and Sam Turner
in front of the
Revolving Light replica,
August 2006.
(Courtesy of Deborah Carr)

With this major project behind her, the time had come to attend to more personal matters. Mike's health and hearing began to slide, the razor-sharp mind that had earned him so much respect at work began to soften. His hearing loss made it hard to communicate. He became more sensitive. When Mary raised her voice to make him hear, he'd say, "Why are you yelling?" Such misunderstandings upset her and sometimes, after he went to bed in a huff, she would stay awake long into the night, writing him a letter of explanation and apology, then leave it on the table so he would read it when he awoke in the morning.

"When he can read it, then I think he understands. He has time to contemplate it," says Mary.

Mike gradually required more personal care, and Mary responded gladly, even proudly, and without complaint. Although it often drained her energy, she would never consider a nursing home. She replaced her old black rotary dial phone with multiple portable units so she could more easily talk to him in another room. She bathed him, dressed him, and prepared special meals for him. When she and David went out, they arranged for someone to sit with him.

On November 11, 2007, Mike's heart stopped beating. David's attempts to resuscitate were unsuccessful and he died in David's arms. Preferring to grieve their loss privately, without ceremony, Mary waited until the following autumn

Mary and Mike Majka on the Bridge, Mary's Point (Mother's Day, 2003).
(Courtesy of David Christie)

to celebrate his life. On September 28, 2008, more than one hundred family and friends braved Hurricane Kyle to attend a memorial service and meal at the Harvey Hall, followed by a wine and cheese social.

When the hurricane had passed and the seas calmed, a small party journeyed by boat from Alma past the headlands and cliffs of the Fundy coast until reaching Mary's Point. There, idling in the bay with the Big House visible on the hill, they sprinkled some of Mike's ashes at sea, setting them adrift with a flower wreath made by a friend.

Two days later, Marc and Lynn, Chris and Sheilagh, Mary, David, and Nishka gathered at Mary's Point with Reverend Roland Hutchinson. In the field below the Big House, overlooking the Bay of Fundy he adored, they planted a red oak and a Canadian sugar maple. And beside the trees, they interred Mike's remaining ashes beneath a simple, unmarked stone.

The season had come for letting go. Five years previous (2003), Canadian Wildlife Service and the New Brunswick Federation of Naturalists had agreed to jointly take over the responsibilities for the management of Mary's Point, as Mary and David felt they no longer could devote as much time or energy. But organizations lack the passion of individuals. They hired university students, but they were not from the local area and did not perform heavy manual labour. Whereas Mary staffed the site according to the tide schedule, the students appeared only during regular daytime hours, so when visitors arrived to view the birds at an early morning or evening high tide, sometimes there was no one to greet them. More financial cutbacks followed and maintenance dwindled until staff appeared for only a few short weeks during the peak migration. For most of the 2008 season, the interpretive centre displayed a CLOSED sign and the site Mary had devoted so much time to create began to look dejected.

In the spring of 2009, their old friend Jim Wilson, who served on the board of directors for the NBFN, brought bad news. The funding for the Mary's Point Interpretive Centre had disintegrated. "I gave her a hug and said it's just this year. We're not abandoning Mary's Point. She was a little weepy, but then she got up and made us a lunch with wonderful soup and fresh bread."

That summer, Mary organized a group of local volunteers to provide inter-pretation, but the interpretive centre she had put so much energy into creating remained closed.

In the past decade, observers have noticed fewer shorebirds at Mary's Point, but Peter Hicklin says they've noted a decline in shorebird populations across many parts of Canada and east coast North America. Field studies in the upper Bay of Fundy show changes in the distribution and abundances of mud shrimp in the mudflats.[78] Is the nature of the mud changing, thus affecting the ability of the mud shrimp to create and maintain its burrows? Perhaps. Mary suspects an increase in the populations of the predatory peregrine falcons in the vicinity of Mary's Point may be a contributing factor by chasing the sandpipers to other roosting and feeding sites where they can rest and feed free from disturbance.

While Mary was managing the interpretive site, there were upwards of fifteen thousand visitors at Mary's Point each summer. Now, there is no one to monitor this, but with fewer shorebirds, one might expect fewer visitors. Many summer days, the beach is almost deserted. The birds rest quietly, undisturbed.

Just like the perpetual ebb and flow of the Fundy tide, nature's cycles are at work.

∞

Postlude

Closeness to nature has nothing to do with hiking through the countryside. It's not just when you are in the woods or fields or looking at a sunset that you are close to nature. You are close to nature all the time because you are part of it.

It is three days before Christmas, and as I make my way to Mary's Point, the sun gleams on the crusty snow; the fields are swirls of boiled icing. Sprigs of bowed marsh grass protrude here and there like arm hair. As I walk up the path to the house, I can hear the wash of the incoming tide. Black-capped chickadees flutter to birdfeeders and squirrels scamper along the ground collecting the fallen seeds.

Inside, Mary's home is warm and smells faintly of nutmeg and fir. A freshly cut Christmas tree stands ready. It won't be decorated until Christmas Eve, though. I join Mary in the kitchen just as the back door opens and cool air rushes in.

David enters, having just taken kitchen scraps to the yard. As I peer out the window, a family of seven finely feathered chukars emerges like comic book characters from their hiding place in the buckthorn and forsythia bushes. We watch them rooting through the vegetable scraps for a few moments, laughing at their antics while Mary prepares her workspace. The parents are escapees from a nearby hunting preserve. A Middle Eastern species of partridge, the chukars are bred for bird hunting. They had few parental instincts, but with Mary and David's help, they've successfully raised their brood and now roost on the roof at night. Mary can watch them through the skylight in her new two-metre by two-metre office that she calls the "Cubby-hole."

Mary decorating her famous hazelnut torte, Mary's Point, 2008. (Courtesy of Deborah Carr)

This afternoon, Mary is decorating a nut torte made solely from ground hazelnuts, sugar, and eggs. It was her mother's favourite recipe. The cake is sitting on the counter, having been baked this morning; it is already cool and ready for decorating. The secret to making the cake, she tells me, is in the speedy mixing of the ingredients. "In the olden times we did this by hand. I remember as a child, sitting and beating and beating the egg whites until, as my grandmother said, 'They are stiff enough that you can sit on them.'"

This is a cake for special occasions, a cake that carries many fine memories. "My grandmother and my mother used to bake it together," Mary says, pouring a carton of whipping cream into a bowl, then tapping the sides to get every last drop out. "When I was about five or six I was allowed to help them in the kitchen. I never actually made it myself until I was thirty or so because during the war you didn't have sugar or eggs or nuts."

Holding the mixing bowl in her lap, she rotates the electric beater in circles, whipped cream splashing. "When I was little we whipped this by hand. The pleasure was when you could lick the pots or spoons afterwards. There was always a reward for the hard work. It took a lot of elbow grease, but when you are young you are glad to do those things. For me, it was the process that was fun. Anything that had to do with cooking was always exciting for me." When the cream is whipped to perfection, she licks the beaters before putting them in the sink.

Mary sets the whipped cream aside and sorts through a bowl of kiwis and fresh strawberries, picking out the ripest ones, hulling the berries and setting the stems aside for the chukars. She peels the kiwi and cuts a fresh orange. She finishes and wipes her hands on a paper towel, "Okey-dokey, now comes the actual work."

She shaves slivers off the rim of the cake, then carefully slices it into three very thin layers. Each layer is sandwiched with whipped cream, fruit, and jam. She squeezes fresh orange juice into a bowl, then rubs the juice on the top of the cake, lifting the bowl to her lips to drink what remains.

David stands by, hands on hips, watching over her shoulder. "So what is the theme this year?" he asks.

"I usually have no plan, but as I start to make the cake, I begin to think about what I will put on it. Just now I am thinking perhaps it will be a lighthouse with Christmas lights on it." Mary hands David the dirty dishes. Grinning, he licks off the knives before placing them in the sink.

Mary has made this same cake hundreds of times through the years, but each one is uniquely decorated. Its fame has spread far and wide, having moved beyond the family's knowledge back in 1976, when the tradition of the nut torte merged with the 300 Club. At that time, Peter Pearce and David were neck and neck during a race to reach the three hundredth bird on their list of New Brunswick bird sightings. It had taken them years to reach this landmark, and David won by a very slim margin.

At the time, Mary hosted a small celebration, baking him a cake with "300" on top, and Marc prepared a Bristol board sign that read, "Happy 300th Bird Day!" Peter sent a telegram, joking about him being the first member of the 300 Club. When Peter saw his three hundredth — a yellow-throated vireo — they repeated the celebration and so began the tradition of a special "300th Bird Day" nut torte, presented to each person attaining the highly enviable landmark.

In the kitchen, the only sound is a squirrel digging out seeds from a window feeder, David turning the page of a magazine in the living room, and the metallic swish of the knife on the cutting board as Mary cuts out a silhouette of the Anderson Hollow lighthouse. With steady hands, she slides the lighthouse on the top of the cake and begins to decorate, cutting tiny slivers of fruit, then moving them carefully into place with a toothpick.

It takes a full two hours to finish, and I can't help but wonder if those who receive her gift can conceive of the time and patience involved in creating it. During our many afternoons together, I have witnessed displays of impatience and frustration, yet with this labour of love, she is as precise and deliberate as a surgeon.

"It is a pleasure for me," she says. "I think about the people who will enjoy it later. When I make this for someone, I know they appreciate the fact I went to all this trouble to portray their accomplishment. This is one of my creative outlets."

After the cake is complete — an edible work of art — I gather my things to leave. Storing them in my car, I decide on a beach walk to quiet my mind.

Fabius, their Bernese mountain dog, is under his customary tree, licking his recent travels from his paws. I think this is how animals taste their world, how they become so familiar with their place in it. Mary and Mike and David have also tasted their world in a profound and meaningful way, and taught others to do the same.

I wonder how I can ever reduce such a large and colourful life to mere words on the page. Even now, at the age of eighty-seven, she is lending her support to another noteworthy project in Alma to preserve the childhood home of Molly Kool, one of the first registered female sea captains in the world. The small, deserted home had been falling to ruin in a field before a concerned group of people made plans to move it to Fundy National Park, restoring it as a museum commemorating Molly's life. I hope that this is a good sign, that her work has inspired others to take up where Mary leaves off, caring for the sites she worked hard to create and each in their own way striving to preserve nature and history for the generations to come.

How do we comprehend the myriad ways each of us touches and influences other lives and how our words and actions can reverberate through time and space?

I follow David's well-worn path through the woods to the beach.

Each morning, David walks this path with Fabius and Kitty pulling up the rear, an unusual trio. Some evenings, he walks in search of the chukar family, gently herding them home to their roost like a shepherd. One night, it took him forty-five minutes to cover fifteen metres, as the birds unhurriedly browsed as they waddled. He waited, infinitely patient, until they were done.

David is ageless and unchanging. His wiry, boyish frame never developed the bulk of middle age, somewhat of a miracle, considering Mary's cooking. Such excess would only encumber him. Staying lean and nimble suits his needs, enabling him to wade through marsh reeds to spy on a sora rail or wriggle past the raspberries and goldenrod in search of an elusive black-horned tree-cricket. He swears one of the most exciting moments of his life was spotting a European redwing during a New Year's Day bird count. He has one wish...that man would live more in harmony with nature. Beyond that, he tells me, he has a happy and fulfilling life so has no need for dreams.

Years ago, we walked through the interior — the spine — of the point and he showed me different varieties of mushrooms and plants in the forest. We listened to a Swainson's thrush, a Parula warbler, a white-throated sparrow. He kept the songs of about 250 species in his head, he told me. "Is that all?" I asked.

"Well, maybe a thousand vocalizations then, if you count the variations of songs and callnotes," he conceded with a smile. That was just the birds. Then there are the hundreds of insects he can identify on sight or sound.

As we crouched in the low undergrowth of the forest, I remember thinking he was a master at unravelling the complex layers of life. I remember wondering how much of life I've been missing, living here on the surface of things.

I pass a small clearing with the nameless gravestones the Majkas had dug from the earth with reverence and repositioned with care, gravestones that would disappear a year later, stolen perhaps to adorn a doorstep or patio. Piles of droppings tell me a healthy rabbit population lives here. I notice ragged edges of branches where the deer have been nibbling. I pass Calidris. The A-frame cottage is sleeping now, closed up for winter, the window boxes empty and the apple tree bare, save for a scattering of soft soggy apples clinging to the branches. Over the years, wasps have peeled slivers from the wood, collecting shavings to build their nests. Lichen grows on the deck, moss on the shingles.

I think of the buildings I have known and how they take on the persona of their inhabitants. How they respond to the love and care and how, when that care is withheld, nature begins pulling them back into the landscape. I think of Aquila, transformed from a livestock pen into a warm and welcoming home filled with memories of decadent meals, laughter, and tea with lemon in front of a river-rock fireplace. Without its humans, it now slowly sinks back into the earth's embrace, a home for raccoons and other creatures. There is something both honest and apropos about this. I wonder what will happen to Mary's projects, once she is gone.

I know how Mary's life has shifted mine, how I have become more open to the broader drama taking place around me. I am grateful that she had the financial stability to volunteer for the difficult roles she undertook, to show others how to participate in earth stories, in heritage stories — not just observe them dispassionately but to embrace them as our own. This then, I believe, is her legacy. Through the example of her life, she has shown that by simply following our true nature, the nugget of passion that resides in each heart, we change our world. It doesn't have to be large or grandiose; it just needs to be true.

A park warden once explained how ancient stands of trees along the rain-forest rivers of British Columbia carry the story of the salmon, their ebb and flow through the years. As the salmon die and decompose within the river system, they leave behind nutrients. The tree roots at the water's edge absorb nitrogen isotopes from the decayed salmon, allowing scientists to graph the yearly populations of fish by analyzing chemical composition within the rings of the tree. The tree gains life and growth from what dies and is buried at its roots.

> A tree will get to know you with its own senses. There might be a time when, troubled, you come to see your friend; the tree will take you in its cool, green realm, calm you and refresh you, and you will leave consoled.[79]

As I follow the path to the beach, I look for the trees growing just before the forest gives way to the shore. One — a silent white spruce — has certainly withstood the storms of many seasons but somehow was afforded enough protection to grow sturdy and tall, its trunk pillar straight, its boughs stretching to shade, shelter, and protect all that surrounds it.

From the base of this mighty spruce, surely springing from the very same place, grows a white birch, its bark clean and pure. Its trunk branches into two arms, spreading wide and brilliant, reaching ever outward. It is stunning in size, simplicity, and beauty. Together, these trees have grown, one supporting the other, their very roots sprawling wide, intertwined and knotted below the surface. So supported by the spruce's silent strength, the birch has spread its limbs much wider and higher and farther than it could have alone.

I found this odd pairing of trees a year earlier after a beach walk with a friend. The two of us circled the entwined pair, almost in reverence, touching the bark, tracing the lines and grooves in wonder. We each caught the other's eyes, knowing we shared a single, identical thought. Tucked away in this quiet place, these trees lived almost in tandem with the lives on the bluff above. We saw and understood, without a word, there was deep meaning and miracle in this.

∞

Acknowledgments

First and foremost I want to thank Mary Majka for having the courage to embark on this journey with me and for maintaining faith and trust in my abilities to tell her story. In the very beginning, she told me she wanted an honest, forthright book. I am sure when she first agreed to this project, she had no idea how painful the process would become as we tread together into shadowed areas of the past. There were moments when I thought we may never finish, but she soldiered on, even when her heart was not in it.

I am also grateful to David Christie, who spoke openly and honestly with me, and who suffered countless interruptions in his own work to rummage for dates, facts, documents, and photographs. I appreciate his understanding and patience.

I am eternally indebted to my dear friend and colleague Gwen Martin, who played a major supporting role through this process. She patiently listened as I trekked through this story, asking all the right questions as I struggled to find clarity and vision for this book. I could not have completed this without her honest observations, sage advice, keen perception, and finally for the gentle manner in which she edited my wordy and sometimes muddled drafts as the manuscript took shape.

I also must thank friend and colleague Lynda MacGibbon, on whom I can always count as a sounding board, editor, and one-woman cheering squad.

To Paula Sarson, I offer up heartfelt admiration and appreciation for encouragement, editorial skill, and sensitivity to nuance, and to Heather Sangster, thank you for applying your own discerning eye and dexterity to my words and phrases.

Special thanks to Peter Hicklin of the Canadian Wildlife Service for leading me through the science of the Bay of Fundy shorebirds and for helping me get the facts right. And to the Reverend Roland Hutchinson for sharing his insights into Polish culture, his thick file of newspaper clippings, and his observations during his long friendship with the Majkas.

There were so many people in Mary's life that it was impossible to interview everyone. As I began to work my way through interviews, many seemed to flow in the same direction, with similar sentiments, experiences, and insights. In the end, I tried to select a good cross-section of anecdotes in an attempt to gain different perspectives. I hope that her dear, close friends and neighbours whom I did not interview will understand.

I wish, as well, to gratefully acknowledge ArtsNB for providing financial support as I drafted this manuscript.

Lastly, my unfailing love and gratitude to my husband, Pat, who lifted me, held me, believed in me, then pushed me forward...and who — I might add — slept quite soundly "on the hard old edge" as I tossed and turned like an auger through too many sleepless nights to count.

છ૭

Notes

CHAPTER ONE

1. Polish nomenclature dictates that male gender names are spelled with a *y*, as in Chorinsky, while female names are spelled with an *a*, as in Chorinska.

2. November 9, 1893, is the date originally supplied by Mary Majka. Later, a reference surfaced in the *Almanach de Gotha*, a directory of Europe's nobility and royalty, which stated Maria was born on November 29, 1893, and died May 18, 1975. The date of her death in this record was wrong, so I chose to stick with Mary's own record.

3. Prior to 1918, Olmütz (which today is called Olomouc and is part of the Czech Republic) was within the boundaries of the Austro-Hungarian Empire, but following World War I, Olmütz fell within the bounds of the new independent country of Czechoslovakia. Because of this, Maria has been referred to as either an Austrian or a Czechoslovakian countess in magazine articles and even some of Mary's own writings. However, Mary says her mother's family always thought of themselves as Austrian.

4. The official spelling for Kiev is now Kyiv according to *Columbia Gazetteer of the World* edited by Saul B. Cohen, and the city is situated in modern-day Ukraine.

5. Mary Majka, "Life Before and After Birth," undated essay.

6. www.jasnagora.pl

7. The shrine survived bombardment during the Swedish Deluge of the seventeenth century, when cannonballs and arrows reportedly bounced off the walls, and then further attacks of Tsarist troops under Catherine the Great of Russia. Roman Catholic Poles needed little else to convince them the shrine was protected by the Virgin Mother. The monastery had been a pilgrimage destination prior to these sieges, but afterwards Jasna Góra became the symbol of strength, hope, and perseverance for the Polish people, a holy national shrine holding great emotional significance for a nation continually forced to fight for its freedom. The city of Częstochowa shared the symbolism and reverence, accommodating great masses of pilgrims each year during holy weeks.

8. Mary has no records of her father's death, but the *Almanach de Gotha* records Henryk's death as September 18, 1935.

CHAPTER TWO

9. Kazimiera's ex-husband, Bronisław Kalitowicz , a physician, was serving as an officer in the Polish army. In April 1940, he was executed in the infamous Katyn Massacre.

CHAPTER THREE

10. www.worldwar-2.net/timelines/war-in-europe/eastern-europe/eastern-europe-index-1939. htm

11. In her later years, Mary Majka's age was often erroneously reported in newspaper articles —

and even in her own writings — as if the experience left her with difficulty remembering her true age.

12. In November 1943, Ebensee had officially become one of forty satellite camps associated with the notorious Mauthausen concentration camp, which used slave labour to supply the German armament industry. Early on in the war, while Marysia was incarcerated there, it was a forced labour camp.

13. Mary clearly recalls returning to Ebensee in October/November 1945, and her memories support this; however, her official DP papers indicate she returned on October 19, 1946.

14. Mary Majka, "My Most Memorable Christmas," undated essay.

15. The Almanach de Gotha records the marriage date as June 22, 1946.

16. Mary Majka, "Thanks for the Memories," *Reader's Digest* (November 2007): 28.

17. Mary's DP papers state she left for university on December 1, 1948; however, she is certain she arrived in October.

CHAPTER FOUR

18. A civil wedding took place on November 5, 1949, and a church wedding on November 6, 1949.

CHAPTER FIVE

19. Income Distributions by Size in Canada, 1995 — Prepared by the Centre for International Statistics, using Statistics Canada (www.ccsd.ca/factsheets/fs_avgin.html).

CHAPTER SIX

20. In addition to the Majka family, the first members of the club included Roy Hunter (a photographer with the *Times & Transcript*), Doug Whitman, Fred Bone, Peter Candido, and Alan Madden.

21. Roland Henry Hutchinson, *Sing a Song of Trust: A Biography of Rev. and Mrs. Thomas James Gamble* (Ann Arbour, MI: University of Michigan, 1977).

22. David Christie, "Hawk and Owl Protection," *Saint John Naturalist Club Bulletin* 10 (October 1964).

23. The changes came none too soon. In 1976, the bald eagle was listed in New Brunswick's first Endangered Species Act, joining the eastern panther (eastern cougar), Canada lynx, osprey, and peregrine falcon.

24. Susan Gallant, "Importance of Birds of Prey," *Leisure Living* (1979): 12.

25. Harry Thurston, "Our Lady of the Mudflats," *Harrowsmith Magazine*, January/February 1990.

CHAPTER SEVEN

26. David S. Christie, Brian E. Dalzell, Marcel David, Robert Doiron, Donald G. Gibson, Mike H. Lushington, Peter A. Pearce, Stuart I. Tingley, and James G. Wilson, *Birds of New Brunswick: An Annotated List* (Saint John, NB: New Brunswick Museum, 2004).

CHAPTER EIGHT

27. Letter, Majka/Cameron, October 11, 1967.

28. Mary Majka, "A Sense of Wonder," *N.B. Naturalist* 4 (1973): 6-7.

29. Mary Majka, "My Friends the Trees," *N.B. Naturalist* 14-1 (1985): 3.

30. Email, Majka/Carr, September 28, 2004.

31. Mary Majka, "Parents Are the Best Teachers," undated essay.

32. Correspondence, Heggie/Majka, July 29, 1971, and Majka/Heggie, September 1, 1971.

33. Harrisville School, grades five and six, "Letter to the Editor," *Moncton Transcript*, May 14, 1973.

34. Recommendations of the Moncton Naturalists' Club to the City of Moncton, April 26, 1971.

35. www.cnf.ca/about_history.asp

36. "Canadian Nature Federation," *N.B. Naturalist* 2-3 (May 1971): 22. Mary, as well, served on the CNF board for a number of years, including as provincial director from 1984 to 1986. She occasionally contributed articles to the CNF's magazine, *Nature Canada*, giving her conservation causes national coverage.

37. David Christie, "From the President's Niche," *N.B. Naturalist* 4-1 (February 1973): 1-2.

38. Mary Majka, "New Brunswick Federation of Naturalists—A Brief History," *N.B. Naturalist* 12-3 (1983): 100.

39. David Christie, "From the President's Niche," *N.B. Naturalist* 4-1 (February 1973): 1-2.

40. Author unknown, "About the Federation," *N.B. Naturalist* 4-2 (1973): 17.

41. David Christie, "President's Report to the First Annual Meeting," *N.B. Naturalist* 4-5/6 (1973): 59.

42. B.J. Schneider, "At the F.F.N.C.: Mount Carleton Provincial Park," *N.B. Naturalist* 4-5/6 (1973): 65.

43. David Christie, "N.B.F.N. Brief on the Development of Mount Carleton Provincial Park," *N.B. Naturalist* 4-5/6 (1973): 65.

44. David Christie, "Vanishing Wilderness," *N.B. Naturalist* 7-3/4 (1976): 31.

45. "Atlantic Naturalists' Policy Session," *N.B. Naturalist* 2-3 (1974): 17-18.

46. Department of Natural Resources Letter, *N.B. Naturalist* 4-5/6 (1973): 76.

47. Mary Majka, "Report of Machias Seal Island Committee," *N.B. Naturalist* 4-4 (1973): 61.

48. Mary Majka, "Machias Seal Island," *Nature Canada*, October/December 1974.

49. A proposed moratorium had been presented at the Stockholm Conference in 1972 but was defeated days later due to opposition from Japanese and Russian governments.

50. Letter from Mary Majka on New Brunswick Federation of Naturalists letterhead, January 20, 1974, requesting other organizations make their views known to the Japanese trade delegation.

51. The Crown land of the Phillipstown Blue Heron Nesting Site was set aside as an ecological reserve in 1985.

52. "Formal Start for Nature Trust May 31," *N.B. Naturalist* 16-2 (1988): 26.

53. Conservation Council newsletter, November 8, 1981; letter, J.W. Bird, Minister of Natural Resources, January 20, 1981, acknowledging request and asking the Environmental Council to consider proposing a reserve for the area.

54. The group included Don Vail, Hal Hinds, and Jim Goltz.

CHAPTER NINE

55. Letter, Mary Majka, February, 16, 1976.

56. The founding members were Bertram Hawkes, Borden Steeves, John Bonser, and Tom Barnes (men chosen for their interest in heritage conservation), plus Bill MacFarlane and the two Marys.

57. Letter, Mary Majka, February 16, 1976.

58. Letter, Mary Majka, February 16, 1976.

59. In 1978, excerpts from the book were reprinted in *Conservation Canada*, a magazine published by Parks Canada, and twenty years later in an anthology of women's writings on nature: *Living in Nature: Nature Writing by Women in Canada*, edited and introduced by Andrea Pinto Lebowitz (Victoria, BC: Orca Book Publishers, 1996).

60. This event took place on July 29, 1975.

61. Dale Garland, *Caledonia, Albert County, N.B.: The Last 200 Years* (Moncton, NB: self-published, 2005).

62. Historian, botanist, and cartographer W.F. Ganong wrote about Mary's Point in 1906: "I am [was] in error in stating it is locally said to be properly St. Mary's Point. It is said locally that it was for a squaw of that name (Mary), and one old and well informed resident told me that it was early called La Pointe de Marie Bidoque. I have no doubt this explanation is in essence correct." William Francis Ganong, *Additions and corrections to Monographs on the place-nomenclature cartography historic sites boundaries and settlement-origins of the province of New Brunswick* (Ottawa: J. Hope & Sons, 1906). Additionally, a magazine article mentions this same Marie, so she was clearly part of the local lore: "Impressions of a Stranger," *Chignecto Post*, 1880, Archives of the Albert County Museum.

63. Peter Hicklin, "Nomads of the Air," *Tantramar Magazine*, Summer 1981.

64. Letter to the editor, Chris Majka, undated.

65. David Christie, "Nature News," *N.B. Naturalist* (September 1980): 62.

66. Mary Majka, "Wings Over Fundy," *Nature Canada*, July/September 1978, 46.

CHAPTER TEN

67. Jill Little, "Giving Nature a Helping Hand," *Telegraph Journal*, August 17, 1996.

68. The Western Hemisphere Shorebird Reserve now includes many other critical links in the chain — among them Delaware Bay, James Bay, and Surinam. Each of these locations needs special care and monitoring, as an environmental change in any one of these links could be catastrophic to the survival of the birds.

69. The designation of Ramsar sites throughout the world began after a 1971 conference in Ramsar, Iran, brought together conservationists from around the world to raise awareness of the necessity to protect wetlands of international importance to wildlife. This conference opened an international doorway to allow countries to take an active role in the protection of wetlands.

70. Michael R. LeBlanc, "Historic Building Benefits While Sanctuary Unscathed," *Times & Transcript*, November 24, 1987.

71. Letter, Passfield/Engram, "The CPS Cultural Resource Management Policy," January 4, 1991.

72. Liz MacQuade, "Fundy Park Project Bridges History," *Telegraph Journal*, July 2, 1992.

73. Letter, Passfield/Engram, January 4, 1991.

74. Laura Greer, "Harvey Wharf Rehabilitation Latest Project for Majka," *Times & Transcript*, December 9/10, 1995.

75. Email, Mary Majka, NB Nature Listserv, October 26, 1999.

76. Email, Majka/Christie, January 8, 2001.

77. Rhonda Whittaker, "Prominent New Brunswick Conservationist Honoured," *Times & Transcript*, October 4, 2003.

78. Email, Peter Hicklin, January 13, 2010.

79. Mary Majka, "My Friends the Trees," *N.B. Naturalist* 14-4 (1985): 3.

Index